HUMAN RESOURCE MANAGEMENT

'This book is a great starting place to develop an understanding of the important issues and challenges in the field of HRM. It is a *must* for business students and the busy professional manager alike.'

John Benson, *University of South Australia*

'This collection covers all of the main functions associated with people management. Each essay provides a valuable shorthand to understanding the content of the function covered and the contested debates around it.'

Paul Sparrow, *Lancaster University, UK*

Human Resource Management: The Key Concepts is a concise, current and jargon-free guide that covers the main practices and theories that constitute human resource management (HRM). The entries, defined and discussed by an international range of expert contributors, are drawn from the following areas:

- employee resourcing
- employee rewards
- employee development
- employee relations.

Fully cross-referenced and with suggestions for further reading, this book is a valuable reference for students and professionals seeking to understand more about the what, why and how of HRM across a range of national, industrial and organisational contexts.

Chris Rowley is the inaugural professor of HRM and founding director of the Centre for Research in Asian Management at Cass Business School, City University London, UK. His books for Routledge include *The Changing Face of Management in China* with Fang Lee Cooke (2010).

Keith Jackson is a tutor and researcher at the School of Oriental and African Studies, University of London, UK. He also works as a consultant in international HRM. His books for Routledge include *The Changing Face of Japanese Management* with Miyuki Tomioka (2003) and *Innovation in Japan: Emerging Patterns, Enduring Myths* (2009) with Philippe Debroux.

ALSO AVAILABLE FROM ROUTLEDGE

HUMAN RESOURCE MANAGEMENT

The Key Concepts

Edited by Chris Rowley and Keith Jackson

Routledge
Taylor & Francis Group

LONDON AND NEW YORK

166382756

First published 2011
by Routledge
2 Park Square, Milton Park, Abingdon, Oxon, OX14 4RN

Simultaneously published in the USA and Canada
by Routledge
270 Madison Avenue, New York, NY 10016

Routledge is an imprint of the Taylor & Francis Group

Typeset in Bembo by The Running Head Limited, Cambridge,
www.therunninghead.com
Printed and bound in Great Britain by TJ International Ltd,
Padstow, Cornwall

British Library Cataloguing in Publication Data
A catalogue record for this book is available from the British Library

Library of Congress Cataloging in Publication Data
A catalog record for this book has been requested

ISBN 13: 978–0–415–44042–4 (hbk)
ISBN 13: 978–0–415–44043–1 (pbk)
ISBN 13: 978–0–203–84181–5 (ebk)

To Clive and Jean Rowley,
the most wonderful and caring parents

Keith Jackson thanks the students, apprentices and
trainees he's worked with over the years and hopes this
book will feed their curiosity

CONTENTS

KEY CONCEPTS

induction
information systems
international HRM

job planning

knowledge management

labour markets
leadership development
legal aspects

management styles
models of HRM
motivation and rewards

non-monetary rewards

organisational exit
organisational learning
outsourcing

pensions and other benefits
performance and rewards
performance management
psychological contract

recruitment
resourcing
retention

selection
strategic HRM

talent management
teams
trade unions
training and development

valuing work

CONTRIBUTORS

We are grateful to all those who advised on the selection of concepts, and particularly those who wrote the concept essays. The initials of the author(s) appear after the title of each concept entry. In alphabetical order, the contributors to this book are as follows.

Peter Ackers (PA) is Professor of Industrial Relations and Labour History at Loughborough University Business School, UK. He is co-editor of *Understanding Work and Employment: Industrial Relations in Transition* (Oxford University Press, 2003). His main current research interests are worker participation and post-war industrial relations history. He is currently completing a biography of Hugh Clegg and the Oxford School of Industrial Relations.

Cameron Allan (CA) is an OHS policy officer for Workplace Health and Safety, Queensland. Prior to working in government, he was a senior lecturer in the Department of Employment Relations at the Griffith Business School, Griffith University, Australia. His research interests include non-standard employment, working time, high performance work systems, occupational health and safety, young people at work, management strategy and employment relations in the service industry.

Stacey Conchie (SC) is a lecturer in Psychology at the University of Liverpool, UK. She has published and presented extensively on the role of trust and supervisor-subordinate relations in workplace safety. She is co-author of a special issue of the specialist journal *Risk Analysis* focused on trust in high-risk settings (2006).

Ian Donald (ID) is a Professor of Organizational Psychology and Head of the School of Psychology at the University of Liverpool, UK, currently specialising in risk culture in financial sectors and disease spread in the farming industry. He has held visiting scholar positions at universities in Hong Kong, Brazil and Spain. He is on the editorial board of the *Journal of Environmental Psychology* and is a member of the Scientific Committee of the International Facet Theory Association. He has given invited talks internationally.

Tony Dundon (TD) is Senior Lecturer at the J. E. Cairnes School of Business and Economics at the National University of Ireland, Galway, Ireland. He has published on systems of employment relations in small firms and non-union employee voice. He is co-author of *Employment Relations in Non-union Firms* (Routledge, 2004) and *Understanding Employment Relations* (McGraw Hill, 2007). He is currently editor of the *Human Resource Management Journal*.

Charles H. Fay (CF) is Professor of Human Resource Management at Rutgers University, USA. He is co-author or editor of several books, including *Compensation Theory and Practice*, *The Compensation Sourcebook*, *The Performance Imperative*, *Rewarding Government Employees* and *Executive Handbook on Compensation*. He was a presidential appointee to the Federal Salary Commission and is a certified compensation professional. He served as Chair of the Research Committee of the ACA. He is associate editor of *Human Resource Management*.

Wes Harry (WH) is a highly experienced international HRM professional who has held top management positions in two airlines, two Arab banks and has been Adviser to a Gulf State oil company and Asian Sovereign Wealth Funds. He has published on a wide variety of HRM, cross-cultural and other management topics. He holds a PhD in international HRM from Strathclyde Graduate School of Business, and he is an Honorary Visiting Research Fellow at Cass Business School, City University London, and an adjunct staff member at the School of Management, University of Bradford, UK.

Keith Jackson (KJ) is a consultant and researcher in international HRM, focusing on professional development, talent management, and the design and delivery of executive MBA programmes. He is senior partner of the Institute for Applied Trust Research (www.ifavf.de) and holds visiting positions at universities in China, Germany, Switzerland, Turkey and the UK. He is an Honorary Visiting Research Fellow at Cass Business School, City University London, reviews editor of the *Asia Pacific Business*

Review, and a co-editor and author for the Routledge 'Working in Asia' series.

(Irene) Hon-fun Poon (IP), CCP, CIPD, MBA, PhD is based in Hong Kong and has been a management consultant and HR practitioner for many years in various countries. Her research interests include cross-cultural management and Asia Pacific management and business. Her recent publications are in the *Asia Pacific Business Review, 21st Century Management, Handbook of Technology Management and Management through Collaboration*.

Chris Rowley (CR), BA, MA, DPhil, GradCIPD is the inaugural Professor of HRM and founding Director of the Centre for Research in Asian Management at Cass Business School, City University London, UK and research and publication advisor to the HEAD Foundation, Singapore. He is the editor of *Asia Pacific Business Review* and series editor for 'Asian Studies' and 'Working in Asia'. He is on the editorial boards of leading international journals and a visiting professor at several Asian universities. He has written over 350 articles, books, chapters and entries in the area.

(Jean) Qi Wei (QW), CIPD, MBA, PhD. Her research interests include reward management and IHRM. Her research publications are in *Asia Pacific Business Review* and *The Changing Face of Performance Management in China*.

Adrian Wilkinson (AW) is Professor of Employment Relations and Director of the Centre for Work, Organisation and Well-being at Griffith University, Queensland, Australia. He has written extensively on many aspects of human resource management and employment relations. He is a member of the Australian Research Council College of Experts and currently Editor-in-Chief for the *International Journal of Management Reviews* and an Associate Editor for *Human Resource Management Journal*. He holds Visiting positions at Loughborough University, University of Sheffield and Durham University, UK.

ABBREVIATIONS

ACAS	Advisory, Conciliation and Arbitration Service (UK)
AFHRMA	African Federation of Human Resource Management Associations
APFHRM	Asia Pacific Federation of Human Resource Management
BARS	behaviourally anchored rating scales
BOS	behavioural observation scales
BPO	business process outsourcing
BSC	balanced scorecard
CAC	Central Arbitration Committee (UK)
CCHRA	Canadian Council of HR Associations
CCMT	cross-cultural management training
CCT	cross-cultural training
CEO	chief executive officer
CFO	chief financial officer
CIPD	Chartered Institute of Personnel and Development (UK)
COSHH	control of substances hazardous to health
CQ	cultural intelligence
CV	curriculum vitae
EAPM	European Association for Personnel Management
EBRI	Employee Benefit Research Institute (USA)
ED	employee development
EEO-1	Equal Employment Opportunity form 1 (USA)
e-HRM	electronic (virtual) HRM
EI	employee involvement
ELM	external labour market
EQ	emotional intelligence
ER	employee relations
EU	European Union

FIDAP	Interamerican Foundation of Personnel Administration
FSA	flexible spending account
GLOBE	global leadership and organisational behaviour effectiveness
HASAW	Health and Safety at Work Act (UK)
HCD	human capital development
HMO	health management organisation
HR	human resources
HRD	human resource development
HRIS	human resource information systems
HRM	human resource management
HRP	human resource planning
HSE	health and safety executive (UK)
ICE	information and consultation of employees (UK)
ICT	information and communications technology
IDS	incomes data services (UK)
IHRM	international human resource management
ILM	internal labour market
ILO	International Labour Organization (Geneva, Switzerland)
IPM	Institute of People Management (South Africa)
IR	industrial relations
IT	information technology
JIC	Joint Industrial Council or National Joint Industrial Council (NJIC) (UK)
KM	knowledge management
KSA	knowledge, skills and abilities
LA	local authority (UK)
LD	leadership development
LSE	London School of Economics and Political Science (UK)
MBA	Masters in business administration
MBO	management by objectives
MNC	multi-national corporation
MNE	multi-national enterprise
NAHRMA	North American Human Resource Management Association
NGO	non-governmental organisation
NICs	National Insurance contributions (UK)
NPM	new public management
OHS	occupational health and safety
OL	organisational learning

OSHA	European Association of Occupational Safety and Health (EU)
PA	performance appraisal
PM	performance management
PM	personnel management
PPO	preferred provider organisation
R&D	research and development
SEC	Securities and Exchange Committee (USA)
SHRM	Society for Human Resource Management (USA)
SHRM	strategic human resource management
SI	statutory instruments
SMART	specific, measureable, achievable, relevant, time-based
SME	small and medium-sized enterprise
SQ	social intelligence
T&D	training and development
TUC	Trades Union Congress (UK)
VP	vice president
WFPMA	World Federation of Personnel Management Associations

INTRODUCTION
Human resource management in context

This book is about human resource management (HRM). Each of the 50 essays or 'key concepts' that comprise the core of the book says something significant about what HRM is, has been, and is becoming. This introduction gives context to the concepts discussed in this book by giving a brief definition of HRM as a concept and by highlighting some of the current debates in the combined fields of HRM theory and practice.

HRM: putting people in boxes?

In general language terms, a concept refers to an idea, and especially an abstract idea that in scholarly terms can be classified in pursuit of organising knowledge and human experience. HRM is an experience that most of us undergo; most of us experience some form of employment; most of us experience 'being managed'. In such contexts, not all of us are equally enamoured by being labelled 'human resources'.

In the tradition of studies in management, concepts often appear as discrete 'boxes' in models connected by arrows that seek to trace the relationships between such concepts, for example, in attempting to describe processes of cause and effect. Consequently, reference to 'HRM' as a field of study and professional practice might appear at face value to put people into such a 'box', i.e. a box labelled 'resources' that contains other strategic organisational resources such as capital and equipment, and (less tangibly, perhaps) time, knowledge and organisational brand. Many organisations continue to claim that 'people' represent their 'greatest asset', whereas some senior members of these very same organisations might perceive these same people as the major generator of cost (cf. Mayo, 2001).

In selecting, listing and connecting between key concepts in HRM for this book we have followed scholarly tradition: we use these concepts to organise current HRM knowledge and experience. However, we do this for ease of reference only and not because we believe that people experience HRM in this compartmentalised way. We keep in mind that 'human resources' have been people long before they became 'employees' or 'managers' – human resources both – in any given organisation.

A brief history of people management

It is valid – and perhaps more honest – to refer to HRM as 'people management' (cf. Rowley, 2003). The practice of people management has a long history. Indeed, writing on the area dates back to at least the 1st century, with Columella, a Roman farmer and former soldier whose *De Rustica* featured one of the earliest tracts on people management. The more recent incarnation of the management of people as HRM has earlier guises. This range includes the more obvious ones such as personnel management (PM) as well as those concerned with notions of 'welfarism' and 'paternalism', with many examples around the world from what were often labelled 'enlightened employers' and those trying to ameliorate some of the harshness of industrialisation and provide basic working conditions. While somewhat historical, these management forms are not totally exclusive and modern versions and examples can be seen, to greater or lesser extents, in each of these.

Personnel management

The phrase 'personnel management' (PM) continues to be used in some contexts as synonymous with HRM. These contexts tend to be given in reference to bureaucratic organisations and institutions where objective stability and rational (albeit largely inward-looking) decision-making and steeply vertical hierarchical report lines are emphasised (cf. Weber, 1947). In such organisational contexts, management mindsets that draw on impersonalised tradition and established approaches towards managing people and interacting with other stakeholders tend to dominate and thus support perceptibly rigid interpretations of PM (cf. Flynn, 2007; Torrington et al., 2008). However, the concept of PM lives on in more general contexts for HRM theory and practice, as in the title of the Chartered Institute of Personnel and Development (CIPD), the UK-based community for HRM professionals (available at www.cipd.co.uk). Consequently, readers might wonder whether there are any real, 'hard' differences

Table 1 PM and HRM: key distinctions

	Dimension				
	Implementation	*Stance*	*Practices*	*Timescale*	*Level*	*Importance*
PM	Professional	Reactive	Ad hoc	Short	Oper-ational	Marginal
HRM	Line	Proactive	Integrated	Long	Strategic	Key

between earlier forms of managing people (as illustrated by the Columella example above), PM, and more contemporary, post-1980s HRM. In relabelling activities that formerly distinguished PM now as HRM, some readers might ask whether we are simply putting 'old wine in new bottles' (Armstrong, 1987); readers might ask whether by attempting to rebrand PM as HRM we are merely engaging in a scholarly attempt to apply scholarly 'rhetoric' to the complex 'reality' of managing and working with people in organisations (Legge, 1995).

If pressed, HRM scholars might argue that we can tease out useful distinctions between PM and HRM, not least in the six areas illustrated in Table 1.

During the so-called 'golden age' of Western-style planned economies from the 1950s to the oil and currency crises of the 1970s, PM appeared to offer most answers to 'people management' problems in response to relatively stable or expanding business and employment opportunities (cf. Bratton & Gold, 2007; Tyson & Fell, 1986). Correspondingly, PM also became readily associated with the type of bureaucracy that introspectively assumed a significant degree of stability in the strategic environment for management decision-making and, thus, assuming a relatively smooth flow from stage to stage in what Torrington et al. (2008) identify as the 'personnel/HR process' or cycle from **resourcing** to **development** to rewards and to **employment relations**. This staged division is reflected in the domains underpinning the organisation of, and cross-reference between, concepts discussed in this book.

HRM as a 'paradigm shift'

Against this general background the concept of HRM can be regarded as having emerged from established references to PM (cf. Storey, 1989). In terms beloved of researchers, the move from the aforementioned PM to HRM can be described as a 'paradigm shift', i.e. a shift in emphasis and mindset in respect of what a sufficiently influential cadre of HRM scholars and practitioners appear to interpret generally as 'achieving organisational objectives through people' (cf. Armstrong, 2006; Mullins, 2006). Establishing a mindset that seeks to explore and interpret HRM as a patterned series of activities and interventions that should serve to add business value to the organisation allows for interpreting HRM as a series of activities that can be explained and, if needs be, justified in relation to helping the organisation achieve its business objectives. Interpreted thus, HRM becomes a 'strategic' activity, thus allowing 'strategic HRM' to emerge as an elaboration of the HRM paradigm (cf. Mabey & Salaman, 1995). Retrospectively, therefore, identifying and then attempting to operationalise shifts in emphasis between PM and HRM might serve to develop a more strategically sensitive approach to any over-generalised 'people management' mindset. Thus, HRM decisions should be justifiable with reference to a business strategy that itself is responsive to changes in the organisation's strategic business environment. One common criticism of the PM mindset was that it encouraged retrospective thinking along the lines of 'it's worked well so far so why should we change it?'

HRM as a management concept

As a management concept, HRM came to greater prominence during the mid-1980s with researchers identified collectively as the Harvard School (Beer et al., 1984). This framework usefully outlined several areas and linkages, including the diverse stakeholder interests and the impacts of situational factors that feed into HRM policy choices and HRM outcomes leading to long-term consequences. At about the same time the 'Michigan School' (Fombrun et al., 1984) sought to emphasise the strategic interconnectedness of HRM activities and, above all, of HRM decision-making. This outlined the key areas of HRM and their linkages and feedback loops between them, with 'performance' the outcome – a causal assumption explored in more detail below and discussed subsequently in this book under the concept heading **models of HRM**.

To illustrate such ideas we note the following. Management decisions with regards to job design will have resource implications for staff **selection** procedures: for example, the type of people who are likely to apply for a given job vacancy and are likely to be accepted for it. The consequences of selecting this or that candidate will have implications for the future appraisal of new and existing employees. Differentiated performance appraisals will have resource implications for reward management and, where relevant, provision of further **training and development**. This more integrated approach towards managing people can be interpreted as being more strategic than traditionally associated with PM, where – in the illustration set out above – the emphasis might be on 'fitting' people to an existing job rather than remodelling job design.

Related to HRM here are concepts of human capital development (HCD) and human resource development (HRD), where the emphasis is on managing the development and expression of skills and intelligence that people as employees might bring towards adding value to the organisation and, ultimately, its customers and other key stakeholders. In a contrastive emphasis, HRM tends to emphasise people and **development** as costs (cf. Mayo, 1999, 2001). Related concepts to HRD/HCD include social capital, intellectual capital and organisational capital management and development. Each of these overlapping concepts assumes that those managers assuming the responsibility and opportunity to 'manage people' are also able and willing to recognise, encourage, guide and co-ordinate the intelligence, skills, motivation and effort that employees individually and collectively bring to their work in organisations (Davenport, 1999; Mullins, 2006; Schultz, 1961).

Linking HRM to performance

As highlighted in Table 1, one of the key variables in the practice of HRM is business strategy. Organisations clearly have varied business strategies, each with implications for HRM. We can see these in a range of management and business models. These include so-called 'lifecycle' models (cf. Kochan & Barocci, 1985), where 'start-up', 'growth', 'maturity' and 'decline' phases appear. Porter (1985) has 'cost reduction', 'quality enhancement' and 'innovation' as generic strategies, each of which will seek a distinctive HRM response. Another version is Grubman (1998), which aligns HRM practices to strategic styles labelled 'products', 'operations' and 'customers'. Earlier role-attribution models such as 'defender' and 'prospector' (Miles & Snow, 1978) have been developed into 'internal' and 'market type' employment systems (Delery & Doty, 1996). What these typologies indicate is that there are various organisational-related impacts on how people are managed in terms of both HRM policies and practices, and as illustrated in Table 2.

Table 2 Impacts on types of HRM

Impact on organisation	Impact on HRM	Timescale focus	Option range
Phase Maturity; decline	Resourcing		
		Short	Simple–complex
Strategy Cost; quality; innovation	Rewards		
		Long	Cheap–expensive
Focus Product; operation; customer	Development		

Other writers have been at the forefront of emphasising how HRM as a people-oriented management process needs to justify itself with reference to business performance; and, increasingly now, with some assurance that HRM interventions serve to add value to customers (cf. Huselid, 1995; Huselid et al., 1997; Varma et al., 2008). Several concepts in this current book make explicit connections to individual, team, and organisational performance; others immediately imply such connections, as in the first concept listed in this book: **assessment**. In truth, many HR managers – together with line managers, team leaders, and other managers with some level of HRM responsibility and opportunity – often appear to forget this, focusing too determinedly on the 'here and now' of their contribution to organisational performance and underemphasising (as suggested in Table 2) the complex and long-term 'value added' that HRM might secure.

HRM across business sectors

This shift in emphasis accorded to HRM has impacted on people management activities across a full range of business sectors; not least, in public sector organisations, non-profit/not-for-profit organisations, and non-governmental organisations (NGOs) which, in combination, remain major employers of people worldwide. To illustrate, under the so-called new public management (NPM) paradigm, even public sector organisations began to recognise the relevance of conversion to an HRM rather than a PM framework in order to make their decisions more systematically 'market-oriented'. This can be seen, for example, in ascribing more of a customer/client status to the taxpayer as a 'consumer' of public services (Flynn, 2007).

HRM across national contexts

Another approach towards both broadening and deepening our understanding of HRM is to develop less ethnocentric and more nuanced, context-responsive and hence more suitable models of HRM that reflect not just countries but also regions, such as Europe and also Asia (cf. Rowley & Benson, 2002; Rowley & Warner, 2004, 2007; Rowley et al., 2004; Zhu et al., 2007). Much of what we have discussed thus far has its conceptual origins in what might be termed 'Western' contexts for HRM practice and research, i.e. in those organisations and institutions concentrated in North America and Western Europe. In a parallel though relocated exercise, Zhu et al. (2009) highlight general trends of HRM changes in terms of people management systems and illustrate the underpinning factors, for example, traditional values and culture, historical evolution, political and economic changes, and characteristics of society, industry and firm in each country) that determine the formation and reformation of management thinking as well as HRM policies and practices.

Indeed, it is possible to interpret the so-called 'paradigm shift' from (localised) PM to 'global HRM' as demonstrating primarily efforts among (mainly) Western scholars to impose some sense of order and control on processes that are vital, complex and still loosely defined (e.g. globalisation) and yet remain fundamental to attempts to interpret organised and 'managed' human endeavour, regardless of social, economic, political and cultural context (Harry & Jackson, 2007). For, we are in the end still talking about 'managing people', as expressed in the title of the recently rebranded house journal of the aforementioned CIPD: *People Management*. To reiterate: we are, ultimately and enduringly, talking about managing and working with people, developing them such that the organisations they work in are able to adapt effectively to changes in their local and global business environments (cf. Marchington & Wilkinson, 2008).

HRM: a working definition

Out of this wealth of scholarly activity, and connecting between research and the evolving complexities of real-life management experience, is it possible to glean one stable definition of the HRM concept? The answer is 'no'. For, and as illustrated in this introductory discussion, the precise nature and future of HRM as a concept and as a management activity remains uncertain; the definition of HRM remains a work in progress.

To illustrate, one working practice-oriented definition of HRM interprets the concept as 'a strategic and coherent approach to the management of an organisation's most valued assets – the people who are working there who individually and collectively contribute to the achievement of its objectives' (Armstrong, 2006: 3). A broader and more inclusive view is to see HRM as the management of people. This is in terms of managing people in the broad areas of **resourcing** (varieties of **recruitment** and **selection**), rewarding (forms of pay), developing (forms of training and **assessment**), and the building and sustaining of relationships, primarily here, **employment relations**.

Against the background of our discussion thus far, this definition 'works' in that it is coherent (i.e. it 'makes sense') and it is consistent in that it might be applied usefully across a wide range of management, organisational and strategic business contexts. However, as a working definition it is not perfect: it raises as many questions as it answers. To illustrate:

- This interim definition compounds the assumption (alluded to in the above discussion) that human beings can be usefully described as 'resources': the term used is 'assets'. How reliable – or ethical, even – is this form of labelling?
- Who defines the relative 'value' of the 'assets' as the 'people' working in an organisation? How is this/their 'value' to be measured over time?
- In terms of measuring and rewarding the relative performance of these 'assets', where are the boundaries to be drawn between 'individual' and 'collective' contributions, and why?
- To what extent is a unitary perspective and ethos implied or integral to the lexicon, stance and practices of HRM and can there be a pluralist HRM?

These represent the type of questions relevant to all levels of research into current and emergent practices in HRM, and, indeed, in business and management generally (cf. Saunders et. al, 2007). These also represent the type of questions addressed by subsequent entries in this book.

Finally, no matter what the view or stance we take on PM, HRM and so on, it is useful and instructive to recall the following pithy points. That is: 'People are the only element with the inherent power to generate value. All other variables offer nothing but inert potential. By their nature, they add nothing, and they cannot add anything until some human being leverages that potential by putting it into play' (Fitz-enz, 2000: xiii). There is an ongoing debate about the importance of this or that function and role in organisations that the organisations would not be there or survive with it. People are difficult to manage; however, they are also *primus inter pares* compared to other aspects of organisations. This book is designed to help readers understand why.

HOW TO USE THIS BOOK

Aims and design

The primary aim of this book is to provide a concise, current and jargon-free guide to management and business students whose interests span a range of management disciplines, together with a range of levels of study: for example, from undergraduate to graduate; from in-company learning and development interventions to participation in MBA programmes. As a secondary aim, this book is designed to inform the decision-making of management practitioners whose activities encompass both major and minor degrees of HRM responsibility and (being optimistic) opportunity.

In line with other Routledge 'Key Concepts' titles, this book is designed primarily to serve as a source of reference and support for students whose focus is on understanding more about the what, why and how of HRM across a range of national, industrial and organisational contexts. Assuming that these students of management seek eventually to become effective practitioners of management, our aim is to provide a reference book in support of further study in the field of HRM generally and in relation to selected key concepts in particular. The references and suggested further reading lists attached to each concept essay offer an accessible entry point to this process of more focused self-study and enquiry. Also in line with other titles in the Routledge 'Key Concepts' series, the concepts in this book are arranged alphabetically and thus can be referenced easily. As part of this 'how to use this book' guidance there is (below) a section that usefully reconfigures the list of alphabetically listed concepts into the four main areas of HRM plus a section on emerging issues in HRM, each with its list of alphabetical concepts. This feature allows readers to interpret HRM in terms of its main areas of strategic practice.

Within each concept essay, key concepts (and their derivatives) discussed elsewhere in the book are highlighted in **bold.** As a further source of cross-reference and guidance, each concept entry has a *see also* section designed to encourage readers to cross-refer systematically between individual concepts and thereby develop a holistic picture of current and emerging trends in HRM research and practice. In terms of style, where HRM terminology usage differs – for example, between standard styles of British and American English (e.g. 'compensation' for 'reward') – these differences are discussed in each concept essay and highlighted again in the cross-referencing 'see also' rubric.

Concept selection

In term of why the particular entries are used, this was an iterative exercise. No list can ever be complete nor satisfy everyone's own personal biases, taste or fashion. We are grateful to the many HRM scholars and practitioners, along with students of HRM, who have commented on earlier drafts of this book. Of course, we can all add more concepts and claim that concept 'x' is missing and is critical to the field. Yet, we are restricted to 50 concepts and 'x' would mean removing which concept from the 50 exactly? For those who radically disagree with our content we simply suggest they do their own book. We originally compiled a long list of possible entries and then sent them to colleagues and took advice from authors in the field. In terms of the background of the book, this is mixed, with numerous experts and authors from, and based in, the UK, USA, Australia and China.

Accommodating a variety of learning styles

Regardless of their individual provenance, we assume that readers will use this book according to their own preferred styles of reading and learning. In this introductory discussion we offer some brief and general guidelines about how to use this book as a source of reference for further studies and as a source of guidance towards improved HRM practice.

As implied already in respect to linking HRM to conceptualisations and experiences of people management, HRM is one aspect of management activity that all working people have direct experience of: we are all consumers of HRM. Indeed, negative experiences of HRM commonly act as a spur persuading working people to engage in further study and strive after higher professional qualifications. It also 'colours' people's views and perspectives of HRM.

At various stages in our life most of us undergo some experience of being employed; and at significant stages in our life experience other people's attempts to 'manage' us. If, for example, you are currently enrolled at a university, you are likely to be combining roles of client, student and member of a particular organisation as you experience other people's attempts to 'manage' you, your course of studies and, in relation to the work you produce, your 'performance'.

By cross-referring between concepts, you will notice that the contributors to this book express different styles and differing perspectives on key issues. This is valid, as there is no one 'correct' answer in discussions of HRM – even the concept of **best practice** in HRM is contentious (cf. Rowley & Poon, 2008) as are its individual practices, such as **performance management** (cf. Rowley & Yang, 2008). Furthermore, you will note that each contributor brings to bear perspectives honed by experiences across business and national contexts for HRM. Indeed, our intention has been to bring together contributors whose views and experiences might reflect in aggregate those of the people likely to read and work with this book: in other words, people like you.

HRM research approaches

There are several tried and tested methodological bases for adopting such an approach. For example, some readers might use this book in support of a 'researcher as participant observer' approach, systematically recording how HRM decisions appear to be made in an organisation or context for work that they are contributing to directly. Alternatively, there is the 'observer as participant' approach, where readers might use this book to inform their reflection on how HRM decisions appear to have been made in an organisation of which they have no direct experience – except, perhaps, as members of case study discussion groups. Readers can find detailed guidance in developing these approaches in a wide range of books focusing on business research methods, several of which appear in the various lists of referents presented at various stages in this book. Of particular relevance here is the section of the book where there is a list of HRM-related open-access websites together with selected other resources such as international HRM and business journals. Many of these also appear in the *suggested further reading* sections that appear at the end of each concept entry in the book.

Key HRM areas and concepts

As explained above, underlying the alphabetical listing of concepts in this book is a structure of both established and emerging HRM research. This structure assumes that, across organisations and business sectors, one way to organise thinking around the necessary or preferred series of strategic HRM decisions and interventions is to identify and locate key functions or strategic decision domains. Thus, the interpretation of the HRM concept developed in this book assumes four core domains of HRM activity – domains that commonly appear in textbooks and programmes of professional development and qualification for HRM specialists. These four domains are: *employee resourcing* (e.g. decisions relevant to **recruitment** and **selection**); *employee rewards* (e.g. decisions about pay and promotions); *employee development* (e.g. decisions to upgrade skill and competence levels of individuals and **teams**); and *employee relations*: the perceptions, processes and institutions in the relationship between employee and employer. In order to reinforce the future orientation of this book, we have chosen to work with an additional section that connects across these four domains and reflects the increasing globalisation of business and thereby of HRM theory and practice: *emerging issues in HRM*.

Hence, implicit within the list of 50 concepts that form the core of this book is a pattern of organisational activity that describes four main areas of HRM practice. Readers might choose thus, to focus on one particular core HRM function. To guide and support this approach, the 50 concepts listed in this book might be reordered and read as follows:

Employee resourcing

These concepts explain (among other key issues) how people might come to be employed as members of staff in organisations and how HR managers can resource business strategies efficiently. The following list identifies the concepts in this category:

- assessment
- contracts of employment
- discrimination
- human resource planning
- induction
- job planning
- organisational exit

- recruitment
- resourcing
- retention
- selection
- talent management.

Employee rewards

These concepts explain (among other key issues) how and why people might choose to remain employed in a particular organisation and how managers can attract, retain, motivate and reward employees fairly and effectively. The concepts listed separately in this category are:

- compensation strategies
- executive rewards
- expatriate pay
- information systems
- labour markets
- motivation and rewards
- non-monetary rewards
- pensions and other benefits
- performance and rewards
- valuing work.

Employee development

These concepts explain (among other key issues) how employees might seek to add value to themselves and to their organisations and how managers might obtain, develop and maintain the skills their organisation needs immediately and in the future. The concepts to be read in conjunction in order to understand this set of HRM interventions better are:

- development
- career development
- cross-cultural training
- cultural and emotional intelligence
- knowledge management
- leadership development
- models of HRM
- organisational learning

- performance management
- teams
- training and development.

Employee relations

These concepts explain (among other key issues) perspectives and how both managers and employees might negotiate and otherwise manage the employment relationship which, in many ways, represent the core of how we all experience employment and of being managed as a 'human resource'. The concepts that help us understand this experience are:

- collective bargaining
- conflict management
- dispute settlement
- employment relations
- employee involvement and participation
- frames of reference
- grievance and discipline
- health and safety
- legal aspects
- management styles
- psychological contract
- trade unions.

Emerging issues

These concepts examine and explain some of the emerging issues in HRM. As highlighted in the introductory discussion above, as a concept HRM is itself a work in progress. Concepts in this book that serve to illustrate this work are:

- best practice
- diversity management
- international HRM
- outsourcing
- strategic HRM.

These five concepts in particular illustrate how interpretations of HRM are shifting in response to increasingly turbulent international and global business environments.

HUMAN RESOURCE MANAGEMENT

The Key Concepts

ASSESSMENT

It is as well to begin a series of discussions highlighting key concepts in HRM with one that emphasises performance. Performance becomes vivid and measurable as an aspect of assessment otherwise referred to in terms such as (performance) 'evaluation', 'appraisal', or 'review'. As discussed elsewhere in this book, performance can be measured and improved at various levels of HRM activity: organisational, team-level, and individual. Assessment appears as a specialist and outsource-able activity, e.g. the 'assessment centres' that specialise in recruiting and selecting the staff that organisations need. Thus, assessment is an important part of management including management of perform-ance, discussed elsewhere in this book under specific concept head-ings such as **performance management** and **performance and rewards**. From an HRM perspective, the 'bottom line' remains that performance at any level which becomes manifest and thereby (poten-tially) manageable and improvable in as far as it can be assessed. This holds true regardless of national, organisational or regional context; and regardless of whether we are talking about HRM in 'for profit' or in 'not-for-profit' organisations, in family businesses or venture start-ups, in established small and medium-sized enterprises (SMEs), and in globally influential multi-national enterprises or corporations (MNEs/MNCs).

Assessment as a core HRM intervention

In the experience of many employees, formal performance assess-ment is a once a year activity. However, from an employer perspec-tive assessment is something that all supervisors and senior managers might undertake regularly, and both formally and informally. Clearly, the continuous micro-management of employee perform-ance within the organisation can be disruptive; as one HRM inter-vention too many. Worse, applying systems of assessment might add little to performance if carried out with little regard to employee motivation, capability and productivity. Nonetheless, from a com-bined business and HRM perspective, performance assessment remains an essential part of managing an organisation and the people within it. The crucial parts of the assessment process are to provide accurate feedback of assessment and to link assessment to jobs and organisational objectives. Here we discuss assessment as a core activ-ity in the context of **resourcing** and **retention** – processes given separate and detailed discussion elsewhere in this book.

Assessment of employees has to have clear links back to the business plan and HR plans so that employees have objectives and resources connected to these plans. The assessment process is not an HRM function exercise to have supervisors and supervisees tick boxes in 10 minutes once a year. Assessment is a regular and ongoing activity of the line manager and subordinate and should be undertaken informally whenever there is a performance issue to be attended to (for example if it is noticed that the employee seems distracted or unmotivated or if mistakes are made or if the employee is producing particularly good results which should be commended). More formal reviews are best undertaken each three months (or at appropriate intervals for the job and industry).

Actively assessing performance

The employee's performance is assessed in a structured way based upon the job description, i.e. as one outcome of a process discussed elsewhere in this book under **job planning**. But the job description, while being important, is not the only factor as the employee's potential in terms of succession planning and career path planning is also being assessed. An employee who is being moderately stretched in the job is more likely to be retained than one who is underachieving and bored. But the key is being 'moderately' stretched. If the person feels that they are having a greater workload or more work stress than they can handle or a greater stretch than their colleagues they may feel victimised or taken for granted. This is especially likely to be the feeling of the employee if they are not given resources (in terms of management support, sufficient financial or material resources, enough time during normal working hours or necessary training) to be successful in the undertaking. It is a regular practice of some managers (and co-workers) to put newcomers under pressure and then have them fail. Even those who do not fail will start to look for a new opportunity where their performance is supported with resources and assessed in terms of their contribution to the organisation and not assessed in terms of them being old, or female, or from a different ethnic group or just being a new recruit (cf. CEBC, 2004).

Even when the employee is assessed as not being at the required standard there must be a system of performance recovery to have the employee come up to the required standard before a decision is taken to dispense with their services. The organisation has spent time and money in the recruitment of the employee so to throw them out without trying to improve performance and without trying to understand why the recruit has not performed is a waste of those resources.

The organisation, this means mainly (but not solely) the HRM function, has to understand what factors led to high and low performance and feed this information back into the **human resource planning, recruitment** and **selection** systems, discussed elsewhere in this book under these headings. More of the candidates with the attributes leading to high performance should be targeted, for recruitment and promotion, and fewer of those with the low performance attributes should be selected – while making sure that the attributes do not mean that some groups within the potential workforce are not being discriminated against on the basis of non-work related factors.

Most employees want to perform well and want to stay with the employer's organisation for a while. They want to develop their skills and capabilities while earning a fair reward package (cf. Lewis et. al., 2003), if given clear guidance and appropriate objectives related to the job and future career. To help judge the appropriateness of the objectives it is useful to remember the acronym SMART (specific, measurable, achievable, relevant and time-based). In fast changing organisations it may not be possible to set SMART objectives but at least a deviation from SMART should be thought out and still be appropriate.

Some organisations use peer review and 360-degree assessment to ensure that it is not just the bosses who assess employees but these styles of assessment are not valid in all cultures and as the peers, customers, co-workers and others making the assessment may not be fully aware of the job description or business plan it is not always appropriate to rely on these people's opinion as they are likely to be more subjective and personality based than job based.

No matter what systems are used to assess employees to retain staff, the focus has to be less on the techniques and more on the outcomes. These outcomes are related at a macro-level to the business and HR plans and at a micro-level at the job description and potential for career development of the employee. The aim of the assessment is to keep the employee in service, and performing well, while their abilities and contributions are needed.

WH & KJ

See also: **best practice; employment relations; human resource planning; job planning; information systems; outsourcing; performance management; performance and rewards; strategic HRM; valuing work**

Suggested further reading
Burke & Cooper (2008): HRM assessment made relevant to organisation-level performance.
Fletcher (2007): A systematic assessment differentiated with reference to processes of performance appraisal, feedback, and employee development.
Purcell et al. (2008): A practical and comprehensive guide towards connecting people (employees) and performance.
Varma et al. (2008): A wide-ranging scholarly review of systems for the management of organisational and employee performance across national, international and business contexts.

BEST PRACTICE

Since the 1990s there has been a considerable degree of interest in the notion of *best practice* in HRM. Sometimes this is part of the areas of high-performance work systems (Appplebaum et al., 2000; Berg, 1999), 'high-commitment HRM' (Guest, 2001; Walton, 1985) or 'high-involvement' (Wood, 1999b). Whatever the terminology and lexicon, the idea is that a particular set (or number) of HR practices can have the potential to bring about improved organisational performance for all organisations.

What are best practices?

This idea can be traced back over some time. The dominant schools within classical management thought assume that efficiency imperatives press for a 'one best way' in management, irrespective of cultural or national context (Smith & Meiskins, 1995). Taylor, Barnard and Mayo as well as Mouton and Blake stand as examples of management theorists who sought to develop management principles that could be universally employed as single best practices.

In the 1990s, the notion of best practice in HRM was inspired, at least in part, by the work of Pfeffer via two of his popular books, *Competitive Advantage through People* (1994) and *The Human Equation: Building Profits by Putting People First* (1998). Pfeffer argues that a particular set of HR practices can increase company profits, that the impact is more pronounced when complementary groups (or 'bundles') of HR practices are used together and that this conclusion holds good for all organisations and industries irrespective of their context. A best practice list of HRM outlined by Pfeffer (1998) can be seen in Table 3.

Table 3 Best practices in HRM. *Source:* adapted from Pfeffer (1998)

Components of best practice / high-commitment HRM
Employment security and internal promotion
Selective hiring and sophisticated selection
Extensive training, learning and development
Employee involvement and voice
Self-managed teams/team working
High compensation contingent on organisational performance
Reduction of status differentials/harmonisation

Universal application of best practices

One of the key features of Pfeffer's (1998) argument is that best practice may be used in any organisation, irrespective of product market situation, industry or workforce. This is evidenced by a range of industries and studies which he claims demonstrated the case for 'putting people first'.

This work has been complemented by many other US studies (Arthur, 1994; Delancy & Huselid, 1996; Delery & Doty, 1996; Huselid, 1995; Huselid & Bechker, 1996; Ichniowski et al., 1996; MacDuffie, 1995; Youndt et al., 1996), by some in the UK (Guest & Conway, 1998; Guest et al., 2000a; Guest et al., 2000b; Patterson et al., 1997; Wood, 1995, 1999a; Wood & Albanses, 1995; Wood & de Menezes, 1998) and by some in Asia (Bjorkman & Xiucheng, 2002; Rowley et al., 2004; Takeuchi et al., 2003). However, despite this prolific output, it is still difficult to draw generalised conclusions from these studies for a number of reasons. There are differences in the HR practices examined, in the proxies deployed for each of these practices, in the methods used to collect data and in the respondents from whom information was sought. Guest (1997: 263) argued some time ago that such works had 'little additive value . . ., and while statistically sophisticated, they lack theoretical rigour'.

Critical views of best practices

Despite the fact that there has been some empirical support for the best practice approach, it is not without its critics. For instance, the studies do not always name the same practices as 'best' and at times one particular best practice is associated with high performance while at others it is associated with low performance (e.g. Arthur, 1994; Huselid, 1995). Moreover, as Becker and Gerhart (1996) point out, the term 'best practice' is used as if it referred to the architectural level of a system, where it is possible to generalise their effects; while in reality some studies name specific HR practices (e.g. psychological selection tests) which are more difficult to generalise.

In a similar way Guest (1997) stresses the lack of theory about the nature of HRM practices and the limited consensus as to what these are. Moreover, he adds that best practices do not consist of the presence of **selection** or **training and development**, but rather that it is a distinctive approach to selection or training that counts. In addition, the comments of Boselie et al. (2001: 1116) are interesting as they state that: 'In general, a variety of exogenous influences are seen to restrict management's room for manoeuvre, notably collective bargaining and labour laws'. These authors argued that variables of an institutional nature (e.g. **legal aspects** of employment) or market structures can carry a lot of weight in the choice of the type of HR practices to be applied in an organisation.

At a conceptual level there are a number of reasons to doubt that a best practice is universally applicable (Marchington & Grugulis, 2000). First, it is apparent that the best practice approach is underpinned by an assumption that employers either have the luxury of taking a long-term perspective or, with some foresight, that they could do so. Second, it is rather easier to engage in this list of high-commitment HR practices when labour costs form a low proportion of controllable costs. In capital-intensive operations it probably does not make sense to cut back on essential staff who have highly specific and much needed skills. Third, much depends on the categories of staff which employers are trying to recruit. Fourth, the dramatic growth in 'non-standard' contracts has led many commentators to question if 'flexible' employment is compatible with best practice HRM, and whether or not the latter can be applied to all employees in one organisation.

Rowley and Poon (2008) also provide reasons to question best practices in terms of precisely what they are and what their universal application is. First, there is no consensus on what best practices are in studies. Their conceptualisation, interpretation and measurement remain subjective and variable among people, countries and time. Second, we can question the extent to which all organisations might wish, or be able, to implement best practices due to costs and/or sectors in business strategy and location. Third, we need to ask for whom this best practice is for: organisations, share-holders, senior executives, managers or employees? Much literature fudges this question (Boxall & Purcell, 2003) or blithely assumes 'for all' (Redman & Wilkinson, 2006). Yet, such unitary perspectives are not common throughout the world (Rowley & Warner, 2007b) and organisations are composed of a plural and divergent range of interests. Fourth, to whom are these practices applied, and is a minimum coverage needed of such groups and the organisation's total HR to make it a best practice organisation? Fifth, there has been only limited actual diffusion and take-up, both at individual practice or HRM system level. In short, opaqueness remains about exactly what are best practices, mutual exclusiveness and 'tipping points' (i.e. coverage of people, organisations, etc.) needed as evidence.

Best practice in HRM: the convergence/divergence debate

The search for best practice in HRM at the macro-level is closely related to the debate on cross-national convergence versus divergence of managerial processes. For Kerr et al. (1962) there exists a universal logic of industrialisation which is accompanied by a logic of the development of organisations and management. The direction of this development is determined by the best practice of economically more advanced countries, with latecomers following and adopting similar organisational structures, strategies and processes, resulting in a convergence of management systems. Consequently, authors who perceive management as rather independent from the respective national culture and focus on the importance of learning from best practice in order to increase national competitiveness, are more positive about cross-national convergence as best practice is held to determine the direction of convergence (Child & Kieser, 1979; Heneerz, 1996; Levitt, 1983; Toynbee, 2001; Waters, 1995).

Despite some support for convergence of economic and management systems, a number of international comparative studies report differential characteristics in each nation or region. Cultural theory and institutional theory are often cited as divergent theories. Cultural theory emphasises culture as a factor that makes people's behaviour and economic activity different. While cultural values are considered to be deep-seated and enduring, culture is considered to be immutable. Economic activity between nations with different cultures should on that basis remain divergent. Institutional theory emphasises that a nation's economic activities are influenced by social institutions, key institutions being the state, legal system, financial system and family. It stresses the historical embeddedness of social structure and process. Institutional theorists acknowledge the significance of culture, but allow for the possibility of cultural modification. These theories are usually viewed as being at the opposite pole from universalistic perspectives which support the theory that economic activities around the world are convergent towards best practice (Child, 2000; Lane, 1995; Whitley, 1992, 1999).

QW & CR

See also: **assessment; development; diversity management; employment relations; frames of reference; international HRM; legal aspects; management styles; models of HRM; organisational learning**

Suggested further reading
Boselie (2005): Focuses on how organisations select, adopt and retain best practices in HRM.
Marchington & Wilkinson (2002): Identifies the business benefits that may be gained from adopting best practice HRM.
Purcell (1999): Provides a comparison between best practice and best fit approaches in HRM.

CAREER DEVELOPMENT

Organisations have a significant impact on employees' careers through their efforts in the HRM process. Recruiting, selecting, training, developing, appraising, retaining and separating the employee all affect the person's career. Some organisations institute relatively formal career development programmes, while other organisations do relatively little. Traditionally, career development efforts targeted managerial personnel to assist them to look beyond their current jobs and to prepare them for a variety of future jobs in the organisation. The contemporary view is that development for all employees is crucial for organisations' competitive capabilities for future growth and change.

Definitions

A career is generally defined as a person's movement through a sequence of jobs over his or her life (Stumpf & London, 1981). The word 'career' can be viewed from a number of different perspectives. From one perspective, a career consists of a sense of where a person is going in his or her work life. This is the subjective career, which is a property of an individual and is held by a self-concept that consists of perceived talents and abilities, basic values, and career motives and needs (Schein, 1996). From another perspective, a career is a sequence of positions occupied by a person during the course of a lifetime. This is the objective career, interpreted as a structural property of an organisation (Schein, 1996) and the organisation plays a role in a person's career development.

Both of these perspectives of careers assume that people have some degree of control over their destinies and that they can manipulate opportunities in order to maximise the success and satisfaction derived from their careers. Career development is an organised, planned effort comprising structured activities that will result in a mutual planning effort between employees and their organisation (Gilley & Eggland, 1989). It is an ongoing process by which an individual progresses through a series of stages or movements through career paths, each of which is characterised by a relatively unique set of issues, themes and tasks.

Two concepts related to career development are promotion and succession planning. First, in the management literature, studies of promotion have emphasised internal processes, focusing on factors at the organisational level (organisational attributes) as well as at the individual level (individual characteristics) (cf. Bamberger et al., 1995; Stumpf & London, 1981).

Second, succession planning is a process most often done for upper-level management positions. It requires senior managers to identify employees who should be developed to replace them. Under an ideal succession planning system, individuals are initially identified and nominated by management. Then performance evaluation data are reviewed, potential is assessed, developmental plans formulated and career paths mapped out. One problem with many succession planning efforts is that management considers for advancement only those who have managed to become 'visible' to senior management (McElwain, 1991) and another issue is that so much information must be tracked that it is very difficult to do succession planning and career development programmes manually.

Career development programmes

A formal career development plan typically consists of career planning and career management. Career planning involves HRD activities to recognise career stages, help employees become aware of their

personal skills, interest, knowledge, motivation, acquire information about opportunities and choices, identify career-related goals,
and establish action plans to attain specific goals. Career management is the process through which organisations select, assess, assign
and develop employees to provide a pool of qualified people to meet
future needs.

Career planning and career management reinforce each other.
From the organisation's viewpoint, career development has three
major objectives: to meet the immediate and future HR needs of the
organisation on a timely basis; to better inform the organisation and
the individual about potential career paths within the organisation;
and to integrate with and utilise other HR programmes to the full-
est (Winterscheid, 1980). Many corporations prefer promoting their
staff from within (using their internal labour markets) to hiring 'new
blood' from the open job market (using external labour markets). In
the context of long-term staffing needs, career planning and management are some tools for developing people potential (Wakabayashi & Graen, 1989).

Due to the importance of career development, exactly who has
the primary responsibility for it is an important question. The answer
is that the organisation, the manager and the employee all play roles
and share responsibilities in planning, guiding and developing the
employee's career. Minor (1986) distinguishes the responsibilities of
employees, managers and organisations in career planning and career
management activities (see Table 4, opposite).

Nevertheless, career development programmes may or may not
generate positive outcomes for organisations and their employees. If
programmes raise people's aspirations to unrealistic levels or confirm
that their personal career plans do not match those of their organisation, knowledge of organisational career opportunities may force
them away from an organisation rather than bind them to it (Granrose & Portwood, 1987).

Career paths: traditional versus boundaryless

Traditional career paths define a point-to-point progression that targets a select few for specific managerial or leadership positions; and
most career paths are thought of as leading upward. This generally
worked in static environments, stable jobs and for loyal employees.
These conditions are less common in today's world of work. Job
jumping, career changing, volatile industries and shifting work environments are now more a way of organisational life for many.

Table 4 Responsibilities of employee, manager and organisation in career development. *Source:* adapted from Minor (1986)

Responsibility	Career planning activities	Career management activities
Employee	Self-assess abilities, interests and values Analyse career options and decide on development objectives Communicate development preferences to managers Map out mutually agreeable action plans with managers Pursue agreed-on action plans	Provide accurate information to management as needed regarding skills, work experience, interests and career aspirations
Manager	Act as catalyst, sensitise employees to development planning process Assess realism of employees' expressed objectives and perceived development needs Counsel employees and develop mutually agreeable plans Follow up and update employee plans as appropriate	Provide information about vacant job positions Identify all viable candidates for vacant positions and make a selection Identify career development opportunities for employees and place them accordingly
Organisation	Provide career planning models, resources, counselling and information needed for individualised career planning Provide training and counselling Provide skills training programmes and on-the-job development opportunities	Provide information systems and processes to accommodate decision-making needs Organise and update all information Collect, analyse, interpret and use information and monitor and evaluate effectiveness of the process

Career opportunities can exist in cross-functional, horizontal directions, or even lateral movements. Career paths can also exist on an informal basis in almost all organisations. Mohrman (1998) argues that, as organisations locate operations throughout the world to tap needed resources, to be close to customers and to gain access to world markets, career paths should become unrestrained across geography, time and organisational boundaries.

The 'boundaryless career' is characterised by movements across the boundaries of several employers and the use of supportive external networks and information. It does not characterise any single career form, but rather a range of possible forms that defy traditional employment assumptions (Arthur & Rousseau, 1996). It is independent from traditional organisational career arrangements and breaks hierarchical reporting and advancement principles. Such a career tends to be characterised by features such as:

1 portable knowledge, skills and abilities across multiple organisations
2 personal identification within meaningful work
3 on-the-job action learning
4 development of multiple networks of associates or even 'virtual teams' – a process discussed in more detail under the concept entry **teams**.

Managing global careers

The boundaryless career, virtual teams and international assignments can provide constraints and opportunities for career development. The necessity for organisations to take a global and cross-cultural perspective is being highlighted by the nature of world trade, the rapidity with which political and economic changes can occur and the resulting commercial pressures to adapt. For instance, some contemporary literature perceives the emergence of a new form of 'Euromanager'. Such people transcend the complex cultural legacy of European history and become transnational managers (Polet & Nomden, 1997). Other studies come up with some similar cultural values that seem common across Asia as 'Asian values' (Rowley et al., 2004).

For this reason, effective global career development requires a continual feedback process that can make adaptation possible across different countries, economies and cultures. Nobody can ever possess completely accurate information about themselves or the environment, especially when people and the world are in a state of rapid change. There are two schools of thought regarding how organisations should manage global careers. According to one approach, the world and workplace are becoming increasingly diverse and, therefore, organisations must hire and develop the most talented individuals from all backgrounds in an effective and fair manner. This approach is most consistent with transaction cost and resource-based arguments. The second approach asserts that organisational diversity is healthy and beneficial in its own right and, therefore, organisations must bring in different employees from different cultural groups to enhance their effectiveness. Therefore, global career development should be an ongoing part of planning and management processes.

IP & CR

See also: **collective bargaining; cultural and emotional intelligence; development; diversity management; international HRM; labour markets; talent management; teams; training and development**

Suggested further reading

Duggan & Jurgens (2006): Provides information on career development interventions and covers the historical perspective of career counselling, career development theories, career assessments, employment campaigns, and programmes development.

Jackson & Tomioka (2003): Identifies the essential currents of change in Japanese management and explains how and why these impinge on the experience of managers in Japan.

Reardon et al. (2005): Focuses on cognitive information processing theory with detailed practical examples of the application of theory in career situations, and concrete steps for executing a strategic career plan.

COLLECTIVE BARGAINING

Collective bargaining is a method by which the representatives of workers and employers regulate the terms of **employment relations**, typically through negotiation and consultation. Collective bargaining agreements tend to produce two distinct types of employment relations rules: substantive and procedural. Substantive agreements are the ones most typically associated with collective bargaining in that they set out the main terms and conditions of employment, such as wages and holidays or hours of work. Procedural agreements, on the other hand, determine the mechanisms by which the parties can adjust substantive terms; for example, by agreeing which **trade unions** are recognised for the purposes of collective bargaining and the frequency with which negotiations occur.

Background

Collective bargaining emerged in the 19th century in Britain along with the growth of craft unions. Beatrice Webb coined the term 'collective bargaining' over 100 years ago (Webb & Webb, 1897), commenting that, as an individual, a worker is relatively powerless in comparison to an employing organisation when making a bargain. A logical conclusion of this was that workers band together to act collectively. As they are then represented with one voice, the practice of employee relations is therefore subject to collectivist features, typically the involvement of a trade union in determining (negotiating) employment contracts. This means that the relationship between management and employees is somewhat detached; what Hyman (2003) refers to as 'arms length' or an 'adversarial' employment relationship.

Perhaps surprisingly at the time, employers in some of the main industries such as engineering and shipbuilding realised that this sort of adversarial relationship provided a degree of stability. By regulating the terms of the employment relationship through collective bargaining, both employers and unions were able to control and manage conflict and dissent, often referred to as the 'institutionalisation' of employee relations. With the subsequent growth of craft and general unions along with the pressures of the First World War, the British government increasingly intervened in collective bargaining, culminating in the Whitley Inquiry of 1917. This recommended national collective bargaining through Joint Industrial Councils (JIC). Although many of these JICs (or Whitley Committees, as they became known) dwindled in many of the industries for which they were intended, the Whitley Report 'constituted an official recognition of trade unionism and collective bargaining' in British industrial relations (Clay, 1929). Subsequent government support for collective bargaining was considered crucial again with the 1939–45 war effort. Significantly, government support for collective bargaining during times of crisis had effectively legitimised its role across all industries post-Second World War.

Purpose

In the eyes of most people, collective bargaining serves an *economic function* with trade unions and management negotiating over the price (wages) of labour in an industry or enterprise. However, to view collective bargaining as simply an economic transaction is to diminish its scope in employee relations. For example, over the last two decades trade unions have sought to widen the bargaining agenda to include other employee relations concerns, such as work–life balance and the **training and development** needs of employees (Dundon & Eva, 1998).

Arguably, there is a wider purpose to collective bargaining beyond its economic gain: something Flanders (1968) alluded to when drawing attention to the idea that collective bargaining is also a political process. Clegg (1979) elaborates on this, arguing that since managers (as the agents of employers) and unions (representing workers) become the joint authors of *substantive* and *procedural* rules, collective bargaining is ultimately a process of 'codetermination' (see Ackers, 2007). Thus collective bargaining has a much wider purpose beyond setting wages, which can be traced to the influential work of Chamberlain and Kuhn (1965), who commented on three distinct yet overlapping functions.

First, the main and primary function of collective bargaining is *economic* regulation: that is the fixing of wages and other terms and conditions. A second and often simultaneous function, according to Chamberlain and Kuhn (1966), is *governmental*. In this the parties agree to rules that then provide for a degree of stability in terms of labour productivity. In other words, by agreeing the rules for acceptable behaviour, collective bargaining can ensure there is consistency in how managers and unions adjust the terms of the employment relationship. Finally, collective bargaining supports the notion of *industrial democracy* because workers, through their union representatives, participate with management in the making of rules. Therefore collective bargaining provides for a pattern of mutual accommodation *and* resistance between workers and managers when regulating employee relations. These three functions *economic*, *governmental* and *democratic* are not separate but very much interconnected. For this reason collective bargaining is capable of dealing with a very wide range of topics that could virtually embrace everything in employee relations; at least everything in union-recognised establishments.

Application

In addition to the three broad functions of collective bargaining, there is also considerable diversity in its application. Collective bargaining can occur in very different ways, each of which can serve one or more of the three functions noted above. Traditionally, the practice of collective bargaining has been examined in relation to a fourfold framework; namely, its *level, form, unit* and *scope*.

The *level* of bargaining is quite diverse. 'National' level bargaining can exist for all organisations and workers in a particular sector: for example, the printing industry. In addition, bargaining can simultaneously exist at the 'organisational' or 'workgroup' levels. At each of these levels bargaining can take the *form* of formal or informal negotiation. Indeed, at workgroup level informal customs and practices between line managers and shop stewards have been particularly important in shaping the outcome of collective agreements (Terry, 1977). The *unit* of bargaining is strongly connected to its level and form. For example, a bargaining unit may cover a small group of workers in one section of a company, or the unit may be so large that it covers all employees in an industry. Thus the selection of a bargaining unit is an important strategic issue as it is likely to define which trade unions are recognised. Finally, and perhaps most important of all, is the *scope* of bargaining. This defines the terms of reference for collective negotiations, which can vary between a very 'narrow' to an extremely 'wide' set of issues. For example, negotiations that involve corporate decisions or pay rates would indicate a wide bargaining scope, whereas issues that are minor or non-strategic would signal a narrow bargaining scope.

Complexity: conflict and co-operation

However, presenting collective bargaining in simple structural or hierarchical terms is to gloss over its complexity. While it is more than capable of dealing with a whole range of topics in a professional and co-operative manner at different levels, there are some issues when a more conflictual approach can emerge, such as negotiating over pay rates or job losses. Therefore the claim that collective bargaining is a method for joint decision-making is only a half-truth; for example, the joint authorship of all substantive and procedural rules would require an employer to give up a degree of authority and power in the making of decisions normally regarded as a management right. Furthermore, a complete move to the joint authorship of rules would require a trade union to play a part in implementing management decisions, and this could mean surrendering its role in questioning management authority on behalf of its members.

The co-existence of conflict and co-operation in collective bargaining therefore represents something of a paradox in employee relations, and one of the ways to capture this is through Goodrich's (1975) concept of a frontier of control. Because collective bargaining is capable of determining many of the rules that govern employee relations, the concept of a *frontier of control* illustrates that there are certain boundaries and limits about the scope of bargaining. Frontiers are also multiple, and cover a wide range of issues that change over time. For example, management may seek greater flexibility from employees. Workers might view this move as an attempt by management to increase its frontier of control over the setting of job tasks. Likewise, should a trade union make a claim for a reduction in the working hours of its members, management may regard this as an attempt by workers to advance their frontier of control over the right to determine the length of the working day. Thus the establishment or defence of a frontier ultimately depends on the bargaining power of either party, which changes over time.

International comparisons

As trade union membership has declined in many parts of the world, so too has the coverage and scope of collective bargaining diminished, although there is some variability. In Britain, Australia, Japan and the USA the coverage of collective bargaining has declined quite significantly: in Britain from 70 per cent of the workforce in 1984 to 39 per cent in 2004 (Kersley et al., 2006: 187). In the USA the current figure is around 16 per cent (Ryan et al., 2004: 384). However, in countries such as France, Germany and Sweden the coverage of collective bargaining has remained relatively stable: currently 95 per cent in France; 84 per cent in Germany; and 92 per cent in Sweden (Ryan et al., 2004: 384). One implication is that the decline in collective bargaining coverage is not necessarily attributable to changes in the global economy, but can be explained by managerial preferences for more individualistic and/or decentralised employment relations strategy (Traxler et al., 2001).

Collective bargaining remains an important part of the employment relations landscape, albeit in a modified form in different parts of the world. Contemporary debates have focused attention on the shift from *centralised* to *de-centralised* collective bargaining activity.

In some countries – for example France, Sweden or Germany – it is more common for industry-wide agreements to be made between employer associations and union confederations, even though many individual workers may not actually be union members in some of these countries. This form of *centralised* (or multi-employer) bargaining is argued to have a strong utility for both employers and workers, as it provides considerable cost advantages by establishing predictable labour costs. In other words, there is less chance of a competitor undercutting on salary levels (Sisson & Storey, 2000).

However in other countries such as Great Britain, USA and Australia there has been greater emphasis on *de-centralised* or local bargaining. One of the main reasons for de-centralised bargaining appears to be based on the power advantage this may give employers. For example, the level of collective bargaining can affect a trade union's ability to mobilise its members, and therefore a shift to localised bargaining could well be prompted by tactical reasons on the part of employers (Brown et al., 2003). In this situation a trade union can be excluded from decisions being made at a more senior level. A further implication is that local negotiations can create something of a bargaining 'illusion'.

According to Sisson and Marginson (2003), negotiation at the level of the enterprise may not be full or genuine collective bargaining. They argue that, even when local managers sit at the negotiating table, ultimate control remains with senior managers at a centralised corporate headquarters. Similar evidence has also been reported in parts of the public sector, where local managers are unable to exercise the required authority to make independent collective agreements without recourse to senior executives (Kirkpatrick & Hoque, 2005). Further evidence based on studies of 20 OECD countries shows that collective bargaining coverage declines with the shift to decentralisation and, moreover, this extends the managerial prerogative to make decisions independently of union influence (Traxler, 2003).

Diminishing significance?

In summary, collective bargaining is an important mechanism that is used to determine the rules that govern employee relations. Its prominence has waxed and waned in different countries and over time. What is important is that collective bargaining signals that there are both co-operative and conflictual aspects to employment relations – what the Webbs (1897) recognised as a 'trial of strength' between employer and employee. Collective bargaining exists at multiple levels and serves quite distinct purposes: *economic, governmental* and *democratic* functions. While the coverage and scope of bargaining has declined in many countries, in others it has remained relatively stable. Where bargaining has witnessed a shift from centralised to decentralised levels, there appears to have been a corresponding decline in its coverage.

TD

See also: **conflict management; contracts of employment; employment relations; executive rewards; frames of reference; labour markets; legal aspects; pensions and other benefits; trade unions; valuing work**

Suggested further reading
Chamberlain & Kuhn (1965): A dated but nonetheless classic text on the theory and developments of collective bargaining.
Dundon & Eva (1998): Considers the wider scope of bargaining, including bargaining for training and workplace skills.
Goodrich (1975): A classic text that illustrates eloquently the interplay of power and bargaining.
Kersley et al. (2006): Extensive workplace survey reporting changes in collective bargaining in the UK.
Terry (1977): Demonstrates the importance of informal bargaining.
Traxler et al. (2001): Reports international changes in bargaining.
Webb & Webb (1897): The Webbs are the founding scholars on collective bargaining, providing insightful analyses on the antecedents and purpose of collective bargaining.

COMPENSATION STRATEGIES

A number of compensation scholars have developed compensation strategies, and a few have brought benefits into the fold. However, there have been few attempts to develop a total compensation strategy. Such a strategy would have to cover base pay, merit pay, short- and long-term incentive compensation, attraction and retention awards, perquisites ('perks'), recognition awards, the full range of benefits, and speak to work–life balance programmes as well. This strategy would have to be applicable to the whole range of employees, from hourly non-exempt workers to senior executives, and be relevant to sales workers, expatriates and unionised employees. Finally, the total compensation strategy should speak to the wide range of contingent workers, contract employees, and even the employees of other organisations who might be permanently assigned to – or poached by – the receiving organisation.

Every organisation has a compensation strategy, although it is frequently implicit rather than explicit. The difficulty with this approach is that implicit strategies are ambiguous and are unlikely to be a function of organisational strategy or the HR strategy. This lack of vertical alignment means the compensation programmes may not be working in tandem with programmes that are driven by organisational strategies. For example, if the organisation's overall business strategy is based on product or service differentiation, a low-cost compensation strategy will work in opposition to achieving the business strategy.

It is also important that a compensation strategy be horizontally aligned with other HR strategies. An organisation with an internal staffing strategy should pay less attention to benchmarking against **labour markets** than to developing an accurate internal hierarchy of value that mirrors typical **career development** paths. Similarly, an organisation that values an egalitarian culture would do well to avoid perquisites.

Thus, the organisation's compensation strategy is a derived strategy, depending both on the organisation's business strategy and the overall HR strategy. It needs to take into account the organisation's culture together with key environmental constraints. Finally, the compensation strategy must be internally coherent. Developing a compensation strategy relies on understanding the options open to the organisation with respect to rewards and choosing that set of rewards packages perceived as being internally consistent and supportive of other organisational strategies.

Key questions in compensation strategy

The key compensation options are summarised below in a series of questions. The organisation that answers these 12 questions has in place the basis of a coherent compensation strategy.

1 What is the purpose of the compensation strategy? Compensation programmes are said to attract, retain and motivate staff that the organisation wants. Should each do all three? Are there other goals? What are the constraints? Should compensation systems be expected to promote government social policy?

2 What compensation will be included in the strategy? Ostensibly, most organisations would choose to include all compensation in the strategy, but others might not. An organisation might omit one type of reward – such as work–life balance programmes – from the strategy, or might have a separate strategy for sales or executive rewards.

3 How consistent will the compensation treatment be? Will everyone holding the same job title have equivalent rewards? In global organisations this is usually not the case across countries. It may not be appropriate even within a single country. To illustrate: if a company's differentiation strategy relies on research and development (R&D) it can be argued that all employees in R&D should receive higher compensation than their counterparts in less strategically important units. R&D administrators under this approach would receive higher and possibly different compensation than their counterparts in human resource units. This seems unreasonable until one realises that such differentiation already goes on between administrators serving different levels of executives. It has been said that administrative staff salaries are a function of the salaries of the managers they report to, even though the secretarial tasks they perform may be identical. The difference lies in the criticality of the work they support. By the same argument, the work of the administrator in R&D is more critical to the success of the organisation than that of their counterparts in human resources. Benefits treatment varies similarly across employees, although not necessarily in an organisationally productive way. Only employees with children use day-care benefits, only the sick use employer-supported health care, and so on. A strategic approach to benefits would include making sure that the design of benefits packages would focus on the needs and wants of the most critical employees.

4 What characteristics make an employee valuable, and how will value be determined? Organisations have many choices here. Traditionally it is jobs that have had value and employees were selected according to who best fits the job specifications. Jobs themselves were valued through job evaluation, and the resulting hierarchy was priced in the marketplace. More recently some employers have used market value as the primary means of valuing jobs and valuing work, with some adjustments based on job relations within the organisation. Even more recently some organisations have begun person-based value systems, measuring employee skills, credentials, or even competencies to determine value.

5 What competitive stance will be taken for each individual component of the compensation programmes, and for the total compensation package? This question really raises two main issues. The first is a choice of whom the organisation is going to benchmark against. The benchmark may be labour market competitors for each labour category, with some competitors being local, others being regional, still others being national. In some cases even global labour market competitors could be chosen for benchmarking. The alternative benchmark may be product market competitors, regardless of location. The second choice to make is whether to compensate below market, at market, or above market levels. These two choices must be considered for each component of the compensation mix and for the entire compensation package. These choices must be reconsidered frequently, since different rates of market increase change the competitiveness of organisational offerings.

6 How will risk be divided between the employee and the employer? Base pay and merit pay increases involve little or no risk to the employee: all the risk is borne by the employer. The same is true of defined benefit pensions, health care, and other benefits components. In contrast, most incentive pay schemes and defined contribution benefit schemes assume that all risk is borne by the employee.

7 What will drive changes in compensation systems? This question focuses on the offering of new rewards or increases/decreases in already received compensation. Changes in compensation can be driven by employee performance, employee seniority, employee power, changes in labour markets, organisation profitability, organisational culture, and many other factors. The choice that organisations face focuses on whichever factors are likely to trigger a change in the compensation offered or a change in the level of rewards already given. While most organisations claim that performance drives changes in reward systems, this rarely represents the whole story.

8 What choice does the employee have in the rewards components received? Some rewards segments, such as pensions and other benefits or work–life programmes, routinely allow some employee choice between rewards components. Employers could allow limited choice between fixed and variable pay, with payout amounts of pay components adjusted to provide the same expected value outcome. Risk is already a sorting mechanism between organisations,

with risk-averse employees tending to choose firms with mostly base pay, and employees who are less risk averse and who have high personal performance expectations choosing firms with large variable pay components.

9 What is the role of employees in the design and administration of compensation systems? Traditionally, pay systems have been designed exclusively and administered by compensation professionals. Benefits and work–life balance programmes more routinely include employees in their design and administration. It is worth investigating whether greater inclusion of employees in the design and administration of all rewards systems produces more efficient and more effective programmes.

10 How will compensation systems be co-ordinated such that they avoid working at cross-purposes? It makes little sense to have one compensation system that promotes organisational loyalty and another that reduces it. Many organisations, for example, increase vacation allowances as seniority increases. Some of these organisations require that an employee produce a written offer of employment from another organisation to be eligible for an out-of-cycle salary increase. If the organisation wants to promote loyalty then at best all compensation systems will be influenced to some extent by seniority; certainly no system should put employees into situations that might increase undesired turnover.

11 How will compensation systems be integrated with other human capital strategies? Who will be responsible for assuring that compensation strategies work in concert with staffing (resourcing) and training and development strategies? Does completion of training programmes have any impact on compensation received? Organisations frequently promote further education for employees, and even subsidise it with tuition remission programmes. But what happens when an employee receives the degree or other further qualification? Few organisations will increase compensation in recognition of degree attainment, even though new hires with the same degree from outside the organisation with no experience and no performance record might earn much more.

12 Who is responsible for compensation decisions? The choices here include shareholders and boards of directors, senior executives, managers, compensation professionals, consulting firms and employees

themselves. The critical point to consider focuses on who should contribute to specific compensation systems decisions and on who sees to it that the choice is consistent with organisational culture and good governance.

Finally, developing a compensation strategy is a time-consuming and difficult task. Without the investment, the likely outcome is a jumble of unrelated programmes that are inefficient at best. At worst, they might well operate counter to the strategic plans of the organisation.

CF

Editors' note: In discussions of HRM, references to 'compensation' and 'rewards' are synonymous. Contexts most influenced by North American style HRM tend to prefer the term 'compensation'. Both terms are used in this book.

See also: **collective bargaining; executive rewards; expatriate pay; labour markets; pensions and other benefits; performance and rewards; resourcing; strategic HRM; valuing work**

Suggested further reading

Armstrong & Brown (2006): Offers a practice-oriented perspective on compensation strategies.

Armstrong & Murlis (2004): Develops a British perspective on rewards strategy from two leading compensation experts.

Gerhart & Rynes (2003): The perspective of two leading US scholars on compensation and compensation strategy.

Heneman (2002): Written by a rewards scholar, this book focuses on the practical aspects of strategic compensation.

Manas & Graham (2003): Offers a practitioner perspective of strategic rewards.

White & Druker (2000): Offers a further British perspective on strategic rewards.

Zingheim & Schuster (2000): How to 'create great companies' by 'paying people right'.

CONFLICT MANAGEMENT

In the real world, conflict is quite normal and the management of conflict is embedded in organisational life (Alderfer & Smith, 1982). In almost all companies workers and managers can have very divergent interests. This means they often have competing priorities as to what are the most important objectives at any moment in time. For example, managers may require increased flexibility from among their employees in order to carry out a whole range of job tasks. In contrast, workers may be concerned that flexible work practices may dilute their skill and weaken their position in **labour markets**. Thus workers and managers will deploy different tactics in order to protect their concerns and priorities at a given moment in time (Pfeffer, 1992).

Because the employment relationship is an indeterminate relationship, with the potential co-existence of antagonism and co-operation, conflict is often hidden and tends to develop beneath the surface. It is therefore both a complex and emotional issue in **employment relations**. For many employers the idea that conflict is something that is normal in their organisation is often misunderstood. Managers tend to view all forms of conflict as *dysfunctional*; something which diverts attention away from productive relationships and company efficiency. This is often because many managers adopt a unitarist perspective to employment relations and assume that employees are all working towards the achievement of a common goal (Rollinson & Dundon, 2007). In contrast, a pluralist view would regard some forms of industrial action as *dysfunctional* while other conflictual episodes can be quite normal and may even lead to *functional* or productive outcomes. Because workers, managers and **trade unions** have different objectives, conflict is something that ought to be managed through efficient employment relations policies. These include **grievance and disciplinary procedures** or **dispute settlement** agreements. In this view it is recognised that conflict is inevitable some of the time. Thus conflict may be good or bad but it cannot be eliminated completely.

The claim that conflictual episodes may result in *functional* outcomes rests on the idea that a degree of diversity in employment relations means policies and procedures become more robust and relevant to each of the stakeholders. For example, by incorporating divergent interests into the decision-making process, more creative ideas can emerge than under the unitarist assumption that all organisational members are supporting the same objective. A pluralist viewpoint would argue that disagreements can lead to stronger solutions which in turn support and improve managerial systems for employment relations (Pfeffer, 1992). These diverse perspectives and viewpoints are discussed elsewhere in this book under the heading **frames of reference**.

The nature of conflict

Conflict in **employment relations** is often *vertical* in nature (Rollinson & Dundon, 2007). That is, when workers question or resist employer decisions, this is symbolic of a very visible challenge to managerial authority and power. In vertical conflicts workers are lower down the hierarchy, and are therefore questioning the legitimacy and power base of managers above them. As individual employees tend to be powerless in contrast to the power of resources available to an employer, conflicts are commonly pursued as collective forms of action. This makes for a very emotional and highly visible conflictual episode. But these can and often are quite rational. Consider the mechanisms for **employee involvement and participation** and for **collective bargaining**, each discussed separately elsewhere in this book. These are power-centred employment relations processes that send a strong message that conflict may be present. For example, trade unions with a history of militant action can use this as a form of persuasion or a bargaining tactic against an employer (Cohn, 1993). At the same time, management seeks to counterbalance a union's source of collective power by dividing workers or threatening to discipline those who pursue industrial action. Above all else, forms of industrial action are a means to try to achieve a specific objective: that is, conflict is not an end in itself (Rollinson & Dundon, 2007).

Comparing types of industrial action

Given this complexity, it is no surprise that industrial action can take a variety of forms. While strike action is often associated with conflicts in **employment relations**, there are several other forms of action, some of which can be pursued by workers and unions for very tactical and strategic reasons. For all the types described in Table 5, the manner in which the action is pursued can be of a *constitutional* and/or *unconstitutional* nature. *Constitutional* action is a form of conflict that is recognised as official and legitimate, more often than not pursued when agreed procedures to try to resolve the issue have been exhausted. *Unconstitutional* action may occur without the sanction or approval of a **trade union** and may be used to disrupt negotiations that could still be progress. However, this simple distinction between *constitutional* (e.g. official) and *unconstitutional* (e.g. unofficial) action can be much more complicated in reality. It has been reported that employers might continue to bargain with a union in the full

Table 5 The type and character of different forms of conflict in employee relations. *Source:* adapted from Rollinson & Dundon (2007: chapter 11)

Type	Definition and characteristics
Strike	A temporary stoppage of work by employees. Strikes vary from indefinite stoppages that can be of a long undefined duration, to demonstration strikes, which are much shorter.
Work to rule	Workers refuse to comply with instructions that are not specified in their contract or job description.
Overtime ban	The refusal by employees to work additional or extra hours over and above those defined in their contract or job description.
Go-slow	Employees perform their work duties at a purposely slower pace than normal.
Withdrawal of co-operation	Employees work only to formally agreed procedures or object to certain flexibilities necessary to meet production schedules or service delivery targets.
Sit-in	A form of action in which employees occupy their place of work. This form of action typically occurs as a response to management plans to close a workplace.
Lock-out	A situation when management lock-out workers and prevent them from attending work or entering their workplace.

knowledge they are not going to agree to certain demands made by workers, but give the impression that negotiations are making progress. Thus while unconstitutional (unofficial) action may appear more dysfunctional, it may in reality be a union's (workers) only tactic to advance its interests and objectives while negotiations are taking place. It is for these reasons Roy (1980) comments that the very idea of 'bargaining in good faith' is a very tricky concept to define in practice.

Industrial action: international comparisons

The level of industrial action has declined across most Westernised economies. Of the different types of conflict, strikes are the only consistent method used to record industrial action. The most typical measures include the *number of workers involved*; the *number of days lost*; the *total number of stoppages*; and/or the *duration of a strike*. Table 6 (overleaf) gives a summary of the trends measured by working days

Table 6 Working days lost per 1,000 workers, selected dates, selected countries. *Source*: adapted from Ryan et al. (2004: 387)

	1992	1995	1998	2001	Average 1992–2001
Australia	148	79	72	50	87
Canada	184	133	196	164	183
France	37	304	52	83	84
Germany	47	8	1	1	9
Italy	180	65	40	66	116
Japan	5	1	2	1	2
Sweden	7	177	0	3	30
UK	24	18	12	20	21
USA	37	51	42	9	48

lost (Wallace & O'Sullivan, 2006). As can be seen here, there is considerable diversity across countries with Canada, Italy, Australia and France topping the league for the number of days lost through strike action. With the exception of Canada, all countries have witnessed a marked decline in the number of days lost through strike action, reflecting in part the decline in unionisation reported earlier in this section of the book, as well as global and economic changes that have fundamentally altered the nature of work and the labour market (Bach & Winchester, 2003; Nolan & O'Donnell, 2003).

Calculating strike data

However there are some significant limitations with the quality of strike data, especially when comparing trends across different countries (cf. Wallace & O'Sullivan, 2006). For example, in Britain only those strikes that are deemed *official* (constitutional) and cover more than 10 employees are recorded. Unless they involve the loss of at least 100 working days, strikes that last less than one day are not included. As a result, some highly significant and prolonged disputes have simply been ignored, such as the strike involving Liverpool dock workers which was supported by like-minded dock employees in America and Australia. Dockers in Liverpool were on strike for almost three years, from 1995 to 1997. Because the dispute started as an *unofficial* strike, it was never recorded. However these sorts of *indefinite* strikes are rare these days and most disputes last for less than one day.

One consequence of short duration strikes is that many disputes are not recorded in official data (Brown, 1981). In the USA recorded strikes must involve at least 1,000 workers. Yet in Australia there is no minimum size threshold as long as a total of 10 days is lost by aggregating the number of all the workers involved in the strike. In other words, strikes that last only a few hours involving a few hundred workers are included in Australia, but not in some other countries. There are further differences in France, Belgium, Greece and Portugal where public sector strikes are omitted from the official records (Gall, 1999). The case of France is particularly interesting. Strike action is often associated with unionisation, yet in France union density is comparatively low compared to other countries – around 10 per cent of the working population. Yet France has one of the highest strike rates measured by the total number of stoppages (Monger, 2004). This reflects a very particular strike culture: strikes are relatively short and include non-union workers who protest in sympathy in the form of a *demonstration* strike, often with a political purpose (Wallace & O'Sullivan, 2006).

While strike action has diminished in many countries, it is often a mistake to assume that a decline in official strike records is the same as saying there is less conflict or greater co-operation: it might indicate a fear of management or that fewer strikes show employers have a greater degree of power at a given moment in time (Edwards, 1995). It is plausible that conflict can take other forms, often demonstrated as 'flight' rather than that of 'fight' (Rollinson & Dundon, 2007). In other words, workers may engage in *unofficial, unorganised* and even individualised forms of conflictual behaviours. In this regard, Bryman (2004) distinguishes between *passive* and *active* forms of conflict, which may have a greater relevance among many of the smaller and non-unionised service sector companies (Dundon & Rollinson, 2004). Passive protesting occurs when employees mentally 'switch-off' from their job. This may take the form of being polite to a customer or agreeing to management requests without any sincerity or recognition. In contrast, *active* conflict behaviours take other forms: consciously objecting to new work rules in some way or being rude to a customer to 'get-back' at management for some reason. As with other forms of industrial action, passive/active conflict responses can be quite rational for workers depending on the situation and the context in which they occur.

A little understood phenomenon

In summary, conflict in employee relations is often misunderstood. It can be *functional*, but also *dysfunctional*, depending on the scope and form it takes. For this reason it is also quite complicated and emotional; its potential to surface ever present. The most visible and dramatic form of conflict, the strike, has declined significantly across most countries. However, it should be noted that the way strikes are recorded is problematic for international comparisons. Less visible forms of protest behaviour remain an important but often neglected dimension of **employment relations** conflict.

TD

See also: **dispute settlement; employee involvement and participation; employment relations; frames of reference; grievance and disciplinary procedures; legal aspects; management styles**

Suggested further reading
Ackroyd & Thompson (2003): A highly analytical text that discusses the sociological aspect of conflict and resistance. Includes humorous examples of different forms of conflict and misbehaviour.
Mumby (2005): Theoretical analysis of resistance and conflict.

CONTRACTS OF EMPLOYMENT

It is in the interest of organisations to know how many employees they have available at any one time in both internal and external labour. Organisations also need to have an idea about the extent to which they can both attract and acquire these employees and, having employed them, require these employees to make a value-adding contribution to the organisation's activities. In other words, organisations need to balance their attention to **labour markets** with their internal processes for **valuing work**. Consequently, having predicted the number and types of jobs required and taken steps to acquire or hire the staff needed to achieve the organisational objectives, employers generally seek to establish and define the type of relationship that should obtain between the people they recruit and hire (the employees) and the organisation itself. Assuming the organisation has a legal identity, the nature of this relationship becomes defined in the form of a contract of employment.

International comparisons

Not all formal contracts need to be written down, although it is common to do so in case, subsequently, one or other party retrospectively disputes the nature of the terms and conditions assumed to define the initiation of the relationship (cf. Torrington et al., 2008: 124–5). In the UK all employees have the right to demand a written contract of employment, and even where no written document (yet) is available, the contract as a legal entity is assumed to begin as soon as the term of employment begins (cf. www.direct.gov.uk/n/Employment). In some countries such as the USA, detailed contracts of employment are seldom; traditionally in East Asian contexts for employment, a brief yet deeply (in psychological intent) binding statement of mutual commitment to each other's welfare might suffice (cf. Jackson & Tomioka, 2003). This issue is discussed elsewhere in this book as a **psychological contract**. Codified legal traditions in Western Europe, including the UK, give context to employer and employee expectations of a more detailed document, the purpose being to regulate the employment relationship from beginning to end. In short, the employment contract makes explicit what both parties in the employment relationship can expect from each other. In response to business pressures understood generally – and often loosely – as 'globalisation', HRM generally and employment practices in particular appear to be embracing increased flexibility in the terms and conditions that employees in Europe might expect or claim from employers (cf. Holt Larsen & Mayrhofer, 2006). Unsurprisingly, these trends towards contract flexibility describe a worldwide phenomenon.

However, and as with deep elements of national, regional and industrial cultures, such trends remain anchored in the traditions of employer/employee expectation. In the UK, for example, **legal aspects** of employment stretching back to the 1960s set out what must be included within the contract (cf. www.acas.org.uk). Case law adds to the recommendations on what could be included in the contract. Sometimes the contract even includes a job description based on the **job planning** analysis discussed above – however employers in the commercial sector usually prefer not to include this as they wish to have flexibility from the workforce so just give a job title. Too much flexibility can lead to misunderstandings and courts or employment tribunals discourage lack of clarity in the contract documents. Lack of clarity often becomes a source of dispute.

Key elements in contract design

Applying a UK model (cf. Armstrong, 2006; Torrington et al., 2008) the key terms of a contract of employment typically include:

- Job title
- Duties, preferably making explicit the extent to which these might need to be flexible, e.g. in terms of work time and place
- Date when continuous employment commences and (where relevant) when it is due to end
- Rate of pay, including allowances and so on, together with method of payment
- Hours of work, including allowable break times
- Holiday arrangements (paid and unpaid allowances)
- Sickness, e.g. days allowable (paid and unpaid); deduction of National Insurance (UK) and other benefit contributions
- Length of notice available to both employer and employee
- Grievance procedures
- Work rules and regulations specific to the particular employment, e.g. trade union membership
- Regulations for confidentiality, intellectual property rights.

Beyond the UK context, local, national and (perhaps) universal rights of employer and employee influence the design and content of employment contracts and/or the expectations that one or other party brings to them. One influence is the *core labour standards* benchmark set out by the International Labour Organisation (cf. www.ilo.org) and discussed from an international HRM perspective in Briscoe et al. (2009). However, and as with all 'benchmarks', these might soon be perceived as superseded or 'inappropriate' and in reality maintain their significance more as a consequence of breach than of compliance.

Despite the emphasis given above to 'key' design elements, actual contracts in the UK and elsewhere will vary. As a minimum requirement, however, a contract of employment in the UK must be a written agreement, although verbal agreements will be recognised for the first month of employment. The contract must refer to any agreement, for example, with a specified trade union (cf. www.tuc.org.uk): a 'closed shop' of compulsory **trade union** membership and subscription levy for employees might obtain. The contract might invoke a set of regulations, such as an employee handbook within which it operates. The similarity here is that the contract of employment stands as a formally prepared, signed and dated document; it is and can be taken to hand should misunderstandings or disputes over conditions of employment arise. This insight distinguishes the employment contract to what is elsewhere discussed in this book as the **psychological contract.** As outlined above, the contract must specify matters such as the parties involved (employer and employee), rate of pay, holiday entitlement and (where relevant) entitlement to breaks during the work time. The work location and various other matters are included in the contract. The CIPD website (www.cipd.co.uk) gives more details about best practice in terms of employment contract design.

Legal status

It is important that specialist employment lawyers prepare or examine the proposed contract, although many employers save costs by using contract templates or using their own contract design. For international assignments, legal specialists commonly check what is or is not considered legal or customary – or, indeed, ethical – in local employment contexts (cf. Briscoe et al., 2008). As employment law is complex and regularly changing in every national context, a decision to avoid using lawyers can result in substantial costs if the employment relationship is terminated in difficult circumstances. It is also important that both parties adhere to the contract despite the temptation to introduce flexibility and apparently mutual benefits from making adjustments. One example is increasing work hours beyond the maximum allowed by legislation in return for higher pay. Adjustments that may look beneficial are anything but when, for example, a **health and safety** issue arises.

The contract as process

The UK sociologist Anthony Giddens (2006) reminds us that institutions once seen as adding stability to people's experience of social life (including employment) are becoming perceived as more fluid and processual in modern times. This is true also of contracts of employment that are 'settled', i.e. designed, dated and signed. This process perception of contracts actually begins at the initial stage and supports the claim made by some HRM scholars that, in routine and practical terms, the **psychological contract** is more important to employees and employers than the more formalised or written version. It is often only in moments of perceived dispute or crisis that employees check again the specific terms of the employment contract they once signed. For, when employers have identified suitable candidates, both parties negotiate and seek agreement on the employment contract: it is the process of negotiating and re-negotiating the terms of agreement that make 'the employment contract' relevant and vivid. Usually the scope for negotiations is limited by employment law or by existing trade union agreements. Even when external regulation or other parties are not directly involved in negotiations the impact of an agreement on other employees both current and potential – has to be considered. Examples of adverse impacts of negotiated agreements are when the negotiator has a contract, which is of greater or lesser benefit than those negotiated by other employees differentiated in terms of gender, ethnicity or age – a process discussed elsewhere in this book under **discrimination**. If this is the case, other employees (including new recruits), have tangible evidence in support of claims for unfair HRM practices – a process described elsewhere as **grievance and disciplinary procedures**.

Thus, key features of the contract of employment tend to include indication of how and when issues relating to discipline, grievance and termination become operative. The first two matters are often detailed in the other agreements such as a staff handbook. This is because the employer does not usually choose to highlight problems in an initial negotiated document of employment. However, it is necessary to include conditions relating to termination of employment within the contract: minimum terms of notice, and so on. In fact, all employment contracts come to an end sometime as an employee, for example, opts for a better offer elsewhere, is made redundant, retires, or dies.

Markets for employment

As indicated above in our discussion, the content and design of employment contracts evolve over time in response, for example, to emerging notions of **best practice** and as **labour markets** or markets for employment evolve generally and specifically to particular business sectors. **Legal aspects** of employment and contract negotiation also change over time. Anecdotally, people might talk about an employer's or an employee's market depending on which contract party appears to be the stronger at any one time.

As discussed elsewhere in this book under **human resource planning**, it is accepted by both parties to the contract that some employees will decide to move on due to changes in their own circumstances or the changes in the external labour market (ELM). Sometimes the changes will occur within the internal labour market (ILM) when the employer no longer needs particular types of jobs at the current number in the present locations. Here a process often euphemistically termed 'restructuring' might be initiated under which targeted employees might be required to 'reapply' for an existing job and thereby declare themselves ready to enter negotiation of a new contract of employment. In such situations some employees might discover that their contracts have been terminated irrevocably. Employers might do this in contradiction of the conditions specified in the contract, and thereby risk a legal challenge. Given the two-way nature of the contract and its negotiation, employees might quit and thus choose to take a similar risk. Generally speaking, the clearer the conditions within the contract for termination by one or other party, the lesser are the problems arising during the ending of the employment relationship – a balance of interest discussed elsewhere in this book under the heading **organisational exit**.

WH & KJ

See also: **employment relations; grievance and disciplinary procedures; health and safety; human resource planning; labour markets; legal aspects; organisational exit; pensions and other benefits; psychological contract; trade unions**

Suggested further reading

Aikin (2001): A practical approach towards designing employment contracts.

Brodie (2005): As above, but with more detail on the legal aspects of contract design.

CIPD (2002): A rich and reliable resource outlining a UK perspective on best practice in the field regularly updated.

Fox (1974): A seminal work outlining how contracts give structure to societies and relationships between people.

Lewis & Sargeant (2004): Another publication from the CIPD stable; this one outlines essential legal aspects of contract design.

Rollinson & Dundon (2007): Puts employment contracts into the context of employment relations.

CROSS-CULTURAL TRAINING

Global capabilities as well as local cultural sensitivity to employees, customers, and patterns will be increasingly critical to the success of organisations. The challenge for HRD is to find, develop and retain people who can work in cross-cultural environments and assist organisations in adapting to changing business, social, economic and political conditions. In this aspect, cross-cultural training (CCT) is very important. Cultural astuteness enables managers to comprehend the diversity of market needs and to improve strategies with minority and ethnic groups at home, or foreign markets abroad, while having a good cultural understanding can improve acculturation to different environments. CCT can also enhance managers' cultural capabilities and proficiency and facilitate their ability to cope with changes.

Some researchers suggest that organisations need a network of managers who are specialists in global issues, and that organisations do not need to globalise all managers (Bartlett & Ghoshal, 1992) in order to succeed in a global environment. Several scholars identify different transnational skills that they believe are necessary for global competent managers to be effective in cross-cultural situations, for instance global perspectives, local responsiveness, synergistic learning, transition and adaptation, cross-cultural integration, collaboration and foreign experience (Adler & Bartholomew, 1992). Still, some others highlight the importance of focusing on future challenges that may require different competencies than those required today (Spreitzer et al., 1997). These approaches illustrate how the global environment can impact on the HRD approach taken to develop global managers.

Cross-cultural management training (CCMT)

While general management training programmes are concerned with encouraging managers to improve their skills (such as leadership, decision-making, communication, and innovation), there are unique cross-cultural competencies and transnational skills needed to deal with people of different cultures, languages, and other diversity factors. Black and Mendenhall (1990) use social learning theory to illustrate cross-cultural learning and training. They argue that there are essentially three key aspects (that is, the self, the motivational, and the perceptual) relevant to an individual's learning within the theoretical framework of social learning theory. These are:

1   The 'self' dimension focuses on increasing managers' self-confidence and their ability to act effectively in a cross-cultural setting. This is in line with the argument that self-efficacy is an important aspect of the motivational facet of cultural intelligence.

2   The 'relationship' dimension deals with managers' relational skills and behaviours when interacting with members of other cultures. Behavioural training moves beyond mere language training or the proper way to shake hands and includes drama-based training as well as mimicry techniques.
3   Finally, the 'perception' dimension serves to provide managers with information on the worldview and cognitive tendencies of members of other cultures.

Cognitive training may include specific information concerning practices and rituals in a given culture. This can build individual greater tolerance towards ambiguity or reserve judgements about the actions or behaviours of members of other cultures (Black & Mendenhall, 1990).

Brislin and Hovarth (1997) expand Black and Mendenhall's work and include three other aspects: attributional, experiential, and self-awareness. For training purposes these are:

1   Attributional training, where the emphasis is on cultural relativity. This method of training is based on different interpretations of critical incidents, such as a set of social situations that can lead to misunderstanding among people from different cultural backgrounds.
2   Experiential training focuses on 'hands-on' training so that managers can emotionally engage in this kind of training as they get to experience the real culture.
3   Self-awareness training deals with managers' awareness of their own culture and the typical reactions people have when their self-esteem is challenged in other cultures.

There are different applications for CCMT. Some companies have formal training programmes aiming at the delivery of skills to enable managers to quickly become professionally productive and interpersonally effective when working on assignments abroad, or when working anywhere with others from an unfamiliar culture. Examples here include global management training, virtual team facilitation, international mergers and acquisition integration, cross-cultural project management training, executive coaching, and so on. Other companies use international assignments for training purposes. These assignments include relocation, assistance, tax planning, language training, family adaptation, and so on. To some researchers (e.g. Chen & Starosta, 1996), CCMT should include training of intercultural communication competency so that people can become more competent when dealing with the complexities of new and different environments. Furthermore, CCMT enables the individual to anticipate necessary emotional adjustments and increase cultural intelligence (CQ). Such CQ includes:

1 the ability to understand and make sense of cultural cues as well as to develop new cultural schemas (cognitive component)
2 the drive and the motivational force to adapt to the new cultural environment (motivational component)
3 the ability to enact culturally appropriate behaviours (behavioural component) is discussed in more detail under the concept entry **cultural and emotional intelligence**.

CCMT programme design, methodology and effectiveness

Several extensive studies have been conducted on workplace values around the world. The most widely known of these is the Hofstede (2003) model of cultural dimensions that describes and compares five dimensions of value perspectives between national cultures. These five dimensions are:

1 *power distance* (the degree of acceptance of unequal power distribution)
2 *collectivism* (the extent to which individuals are integrated into groups)
3 *masculinity* (the distribution of roles between the genders)
4 *uncertainty avoidance* (the degree of tolerance for uncertainty and ambiguity)
5 *long-term orientation* (values oriented towards the future).

From this framework, it is noted that hardly any country has the same cultural dimensions or values. Even within the same country, variations in culture can be found.

Inasmuch as national cultures remain different, cross-cultural differences in HRM practices will continue to exist. Besides, language is another strong factor in cross-cultural contexts. Hence, in designing CCMT programmes, one should be aware of the local cultures, values and languages because they impact on the participating managers' learning styles, and in turn affect the programme's structure and curriculum, as well as the delivery methodologies. For example,

North Americans have a culture system, learning style and reasoning preference that tends towards an inductive task or problem-centred approach. Some other parts of the world, however, have a strong preference for deductive, topic-centred reasoning (Marquardt & Kearsley, 1999).

Another factor affecting programme design is the interaction with members of other cultures. This can be measured by intensity, duration and nature of interaction. Intensity of interaction is characterised by the frequency of contact with members of other cultures. For high intensity, a manager may need to socialise and practise with more foreign individuals more frequently. Duration of interaction refers to the length of time a manager is in contact with a foreign culture. If the contact time is short, CCMT tends to be of a less serious nature. Lastly, nature of interaction refers to the type of interaction, formal or causal. If formal interaction is required (e.g. business negotiation, hiring interviews), more training will be required.

Depending on the culture, specific training methods may be effective or ineffective. Participants from Asian cultures prefer to observe the instructor demonstrating a skill rather than face the possibility by being seen as foolish through risk-taking and learning-by-doing methodologies. The Japanese are accustomed to lectures, note-taking and very respectfully asking questions of teachers. The use of case studies and analysis in Arab countries may be ineffective because Arab culture encourages verbal comments by only the leader or manager of the group and not the individual participants. The preferred methodology for learning is group discussions.

The effectiveness of a CCMT programme is usually evaluated on a manager's successful adjustment in overseas assignments. The success of overseas assignees can be conceptualised at three levels (Zakaria, 2000): *intercultural competency* (effectiveness in the work role); *organisational success* (the impact of the training programmes); and *training effectiveness* (from the point of view of the host country). A number of factors can affect CCMT effectiveness. For example, cultural difference or cultural distance between the host country and home country, or the degree of adaptation required for learning materials and training curriculum.

IP & CR

See also: **career development; cultural and emotional intelligence; development; diversity management; international HRM; leadership development; management styles; organisational learning; teams; training and development**

Suggested further reading

Cutler (2005): Outlines useful information on CCMT content, design and delivery, as well as a series of action planning activities on assessment and evaluation of cross-cultural training events.

Tjosvold & Leung (2003): Explains the fundamental theories and frameworks of cross-cultural management and how they can be applied to management knowledge.

Rowley & Warner (2007a): Focuses on relevant current and future developments in areas such as business culture, enterprises and HR, covering a range of industries, size of firms and Asian countries.

CULTURAL AND EMOTIONAL INTELLIGENCE

Globalisation, internationalisation and shifting political environments make intercultural work the norm for most large companies. Today's managers are usually required to work in multi-cultural, multi-racial and multi-lingual environments. Inter-cultural differences have long been a challenge confronting multi-national organisations (Hofstede, 1991). In face of new global challenges and cultural adaptation issues, Earley and Ang (2003) propose a model of cultural adaptation called *cultural intelligence* (CQ).

Definition

According to Earley (2003), CQ refers to a person's capability to adapt effectively to new cultural contexts. This adaptation requires skills and capabilities quite different from those used by people within their own cultural context. Three general components capture these skills and capabilities: metacognitive/cognitive, motivational, and behavioural.

Metacognitive/cognitive CQ

Metacognitive/cognitive CQ refers to a person's cognitive processing to recognise and understand expectations appropriate for cultural situations. It can be further broken down into two complementary elements: metacognitive knowledge and metacognitive experience. Metacognitive knowledge refers to what and how to 'deal with knowledge' gained under a variety of circumstances, and it reflects three general categories of knowledge (Flavell, 1987). First, it reflects the personal aspects of knowledge. Second, it reflects task variables, or the nature of the information acquired by an individual. The final aspect refers to the strategy variable, or the procedures used to achieve some desired goals (Earley, 2003). In addition, metacognitive experiences are conscious experience about what and how to 'incorporate relevant experiences' as a general guide for future interactions. People from certain cultures possess metacognitive characteristics that differ from people elsewhere. Many studies confirm differences in the pattern and style of decision-making of Western and non-Western cultures related to metacognitive experience. For example, deep-rooted differences in experiences of culture and values in Asian economies may imply different management practices than those in the West (Rowley & Poon, 2008) and hence require different CQ.

Motivational CQ

The second component, *motivational CQ*, is a self-concept which directs and motivates oneself to adapt to new cultural surroundings. Knowing oneself is not sufficient for high CQ because awareness does not guarantee flexibility. A certain level of cognitive flexibility is critical to CQ since new cultural situations require a constant reshaping and people must be motivated to use this knowledge and produce a culturally appropriate response. According to Erez and Earley's (1993) cultural self-representation theory, the self can be thought of as embedded within a general system of cultural context, management practices, self-concept, and work outcomes. Early (2003) conceptualises motivational CQ as intrinsic motivation (drivers of performance that originate from within an individual) and self-efficacy (people's belief that they can be effective on a given task).

Behavioural CQ

The last component, *behavioural CQ*, reflects the ability to utilise culturally sensitive communication and behaviour when interacting with people from cultures different from one's own. This CQ reflects a person's ability to acquire or adapt behaviours appropriate for a new culture.

Cross-cultural competencies, skills and abilities

Global economic interactions and highly competitive marketplaces require sophisticated competencies necessary to work with people with different values, assumptions, beliefs and traditions. A competency refers to areas of personal capability that enable employees to successfully perform their jobs and achieve outcomes. Over the last decade numerous authors have sought to describe competencies. Some portray competencies as motives, traits, self-concepts, attributes, values, content knowledge, and cognitive or behavioural skills. Some others describe them as any individual characteristics that can be measured or counted reliably and that can be shown to differentiate significantly between superior and average performers or between effective and ineffective performers (Spencer et al., 1994). As such, there are perennial issues of whether the competencies of successful managers are universal or organisation-specific, and whether the absence of one can be compensated for by the presence of another. These are related to the **training and development** of competencies.

Competency models are useful for training and development in several ways. First, they identify behaviours needed for effective job performance and provide a tool for determining what skills are needed to meet today's needs as well as the company's future skill needs. Second, they can provide a framework for ongoing coaching and feedback to develop employees for current and future roles. By comparing their current personal competencies to those required for a job, employees can identify competencies that need **development** and choose actions to develop those competencies.

While the general competencies are important, there are unique cross-cultural competencies, skills and abilities required to respond effectively to people of various cultures, languages, classes, races, ethnic backgrounds, religions and other diversity factors. Operationally defined, cultural competence is the integration and transformation of knowledge about individuals and groups of people into specific standards, policies, practices, and attitudes used in appropriate cultural settings to increase the quality of service, thereby producing better outcomes. Cultural competence is not static nor does it come naturally, but it requires relearning and unlearning about cultural diversity. An inventory of cross-cultural competencies identified by researchers and practitioners (e.g. O'Sullivan, 1999; Taylor, 1994) includes communications skills, tolerance for ambiguity, emotional stability, flexibility, ability to adopt to dual focus, focus on both task and relationship, positive attitude to learning, cultural knowledge, and ability to succeed in multiple and diverse environments, among others.

Borrowing from Chen and Starosta (1996), cross-cultural competency can be presented as a three-part process that leads to cultural awareness, cultural sensitivity and cultural adroitness.

1   *Cultural awareness:* once people become more self-aware, they tend to be better at predicting the effects of their behaviour on others. After they learn something about other cultures, they know how to adjust their behaviour to meet the expectations of the new situation.
2   *Cultural sensitivity:* includes values and attitudes such as open-mindedness, high self-concept, non-judgemental attitudes and social relaxation, in order to understand the value of different cultures and become sensitive to the verbal and non-verbal cues of people from other cultures.
3   *Cultural adroitness:* when people know what to do and what not to do, they will be able to communicate effectively without offending any parties.

Types of intelligence?

There are two concepts related to CQ, *emotional intelligence* (EQ) and *social intelligence* (SQ). EQ refers to an ability to recognise the meanings of emotions and their relationship, and to reason and solve the problem basis of them. It involves the capacity to perceive emotions, assimilate emotion-related feelings, understand the information of those emotions and manage them (Mayer & Salovey, 1997). According to Goleman (1995), there are two processes to demonstrate EQ. First, a person must be able to respond to the arousal from an external stimulus; and second, this person within a short period of 'reflection' time must assess the meaning and quality of his or her emotional response, and act on that understanding in an adaptive fashion. As for Bar-On (2000), EQ is conceptualised as a set of non-cognitive capabilities, competencies and skills that influence one's ability to succeed in coping with environmental demands and pressures. These capabilities and competencies include:

1   intrapersonal skills such as emotional self-awareness
2   interpersonal skills such as empathy, adaptability and flexibility
3   stress management such as stress tolerance and impulse control
4   general mood such as happiness and optimism.

Another related concept is SQ. Earlier theorists, such as Thorndike (1920), conceptualise SQ as the ability to understand and manage people and act wisely in human relations. Walker and Foley (1973) further elaborate SQ in three approaches. First, SQ is the ability to react cognitively to an interpersonal stimulus. Second, SQ is defined in terms of behavioural outcomes and is conceived as the effectiveness or adaptiveness of one's social performance. Third, SQ includes both the cognitive and behavioural orientations.

However, an emotionally intelligent or socially intelligent person is not necessarily culturally intelligent. The emotionally intelligent person is able effectively to separate out two features of a person's behaviour: those that are universally human and those that are personal and idiosyncratic. The culturally intelligent person, in contrast, is able to separate out three features of a person's behaviour: those that are universally human; those that are idiosyncratically personal; and those that are rooted in culture. In other cases, some managers can be highly socially intelligent within their own cultural setting but rather culturally unintelligent and, therefore, ineffective in novel cultural settings. In sum, CQ focuses specifically on individual differences in the ability to discern and effectively respond to dissimilar cultures and is vital for global managers to acculturate to multi-racial and multi-lingual institutional environments.

IP & CR

See also: **career development; cross-cultural training; diversity management; employee involvement and participation; international HRM; knowledge management; leadership development; management styles; models of HRM; organisational learning; training and development**

Suggested further reading
Ciarrochi et al. (2006): Summarises the current state of emotional intelligence theory and research.
Hooker (2003): Illustrates how to survive in unfamiliar cultures by understanding and tapping into the stress management mechanisms used by the people who live there.
Peterson (2004): Examines cultural style in six areas: management, strategy, planning, personnel, communication and reasoning.
Tan et al. (2006): Details the various components of CQ; provides realistic practices, and culture-sensitive stories from intercultural work settings.

DEVELOPMENT

In a growing number of organisations, human resources are viewed as a source of competitive advantage. There is greater recognition that distinctive competencies are obtained through highly developed employee skills and employee development (ED). HR development (HRD) is a process for developing employee knowledge, skills and abilities (KSAs), as well as competencies through training and development (T&D), organisational learning (OL), leadership development (LD) and knowledge management (KM) for the purpose of improving performance.

Purpose of development needs assessment

Needs assessment is a process by which an organisation's HRD needs are identified and articulated. It is the starting point of various T&D initiatives. Werner and DeSimone (2006) suggest that an HRD needs assessment can identify:

1 an organisation's goals and its effectiveness in reaching the company's goals
2 discrepancies or gaps between employees' skills and the skills required for effective current job performance
3 discrepancies or gaps between current skills and the skills needed to perform the job successfully in the future
4 the conditions under which the HRD initiatives will occur.

As needs assessment is the first step in the instructional design process, if it is poorly conducted, regardless of the training method or learning environment, ED will not be able to achieve the outcomes or benefits the company expects. There are, however, some misperceptions that a needs assessment can be a difficult and time-consuming process – for instance, that frequently conducted needs assessment is likely to lead to manager fatigue and resistance.

Needs assessment phases

A complete needs assessment involves reviewing a variety of factors at multiple levels of the organisation. The processes of analysing, measuring and evaluating HRD needs can be viewed as a cycle, starting with the assessment phase, then moving through the development phase and finally the evaluation phase.

Phase 1: assessment phase

This phase includes three sets of analyses: organisational analysis, job and task training analysis, and person analysis.

Organisational analysis

This begins with an **assessment** of the short- and long-term strategy and business objectives of the organisation. The intent of such analysis is to better understand the characteristics of the organisation to determine whether HRD efforts are needed and the conditions within which T&D, OL and LD will be conducted. This type of analysis is sometimes referred to as strategic analysis (Gupta, 1999). Goldstein et al. (2001) suggest that a thorough needs assessment should also look at organisational maintenance (support of KSAs), organisational efficiency (degree of goal achievement), organisational culture (philosophy and system architecture of the organisation) and environment constraints (such as legal, social, political, and economic issues faced by the organisation). The important question then becomes, 'will training produce changes in employee behaviour that will contribute to the achievement of the organisation's goals?' Typically, organisational analysis will result in the development of a clear statement of the goals to be achieved by the organisation's HRD activities, the appropriateness of training, its resources available for training, and support by managers and peers for training activities. Therefore, organisational analysis requires a broad or 'whole system' view of the organisation and what it is trying to accomplish.

Job and task training analysis

This is the process of identifying the purpose of a job and its component parts, as well as specifying what must be learned in order for an employee to be effective. There are many approaches to job and task training analysis. The most common approaches are:

1   problem-centred analysis, which focuses on defining problems which require a training solution
2   competency-based approaches, which involve identifying what is needed to produce effective performance in a role, job or function
3   role analysis, which emphasises how important the role is if an employee is to be effective, to build up a shared perception of the role between different members of the employee's role set (McGregor, 2005).

Regardless of the approaches, job and task training analysis generally involves:

1   a systematic collection of information that describes how work can be determined
2   descriptions of how tasks are to be performed to meet the standards
3   kinds and levels of KSAs, competencies, knowledge and attitudes necessary for effective task performance
4   identifying and prioritising areas that can benefit from training
5   standards that will operate in the job and criteria for measuring the achievement of standards.

There are several ways to collect such information, including task assessment, work sampling, critical incident assessment, and task inventories in which employees indicate how frequently they carry out a particular activity.

Person analysis

This can be either narrow or broad in scope. The broader approach compares actual performance with the minimum acceptable standards of performance and can be used to determine training needs for the current job. The narrower approach compares an evaluation of one employee proficiency on each required skill dimension with the proficiency level required for each skill. Broad and narrow approaches to person analysis exist. These:

1   determine whether performance deficiencies result from a lack of KSAs (a training issue), or from a motivational issue, or from a work-design problem
2   identify who needs training
3   find out employees' readiness for training.

The outcome of person analysis shows:

1   whether the employees are ready and suitable for **training and development**
2   whether employees have the personal characteristics (abilities, attitudes, beliefs, and motivation) necessary to learn programme content and apply it on the job
3   whether the work environment can facilitate learning and enhance performance.

Phase 2: measurement phase

Once an organisation has gathered needs assessment data, the next step is to analyse information to identify HRD training and non-training needs common to the organisation, several departments or groups of employees. Typical triggers for training include performance problems, poor communication skills, technological advances, or strategic initiatives (such as a move towards cross-country operations or diversification). HRD professionals then begin to develop learning objectives for the various performance discrepancies. The learning objectives are important because they identify criteria for measuring HRD initiatives and direct the training programmes to specific issues and content to focus on. Besides learning objectives, this phase also includes considering the following questions.

- Where should training take place? This can be on-site on-the-job, on-site off-the-job or in separate locations.
- What type of programme is needed? LD, coaching, mentoring, management training, etc.
- Who provides such programmes? This can be provided by in-house or by external consultants.
- What type of media? Classroom lecturing, e-learning, etc.
- What is the amount of direction? Self-directed and participative versus trainer driven and less participative.

Phase 3: evaluation phase

The evaluation phase involves two processes: (1) to establish measures of success (criteria) and (2) to design and determine what changes have occurred during T&D initiatives. Criteria describe the behaviours required to demonstrate the trainee's skills, the conditions under which the trainee is to perform, and the lower limit of acceptable performance. Criteria must be established for both the evaluation of trainees at the conclusion of the training programme and the evaluation of on-the-job performance. Besides criterion development, the evaluation phase focuses on the necessary design to assess if changes have occurred. Common tests used to evaluate the veracity of design are as follows.

- *Training validity:* did trainees learn during training programmes?
- *Transfer validity:* is what has been learned in training transferred to the job and hence enhanced performance in the work organisation?

- *Intra-organisational validity:* is the performance of new trainees in the same organisation that attended the training programme consistent with the performance of previous trainees?
- *Inter-organisational validity:* can a training programme validated in one organisation be used successfully in another organisation?

Other evaluation methods include Hamblin's (1974) multi-level method. This is composed of different levels of objectives and effects, such as reactions, learning, job behaviour and organisation.

In sum, the analysis, measurement and evaluation of a company's HRD needs can provide a good foundation for its subsequent implementation of T&D initiatives, LD programmes and KM activities, and foster an organisation learning culture.

IP & CR

See also: **assessment; career development; cross-cultural training; cultural and emotional intelligence; employee involvement and participation; human resource planning; leadership development; organisational learning; outsourcing; training and development**

Suggested further reading
Barbazette (2006): Covers the essentials of needs analysis from the emerging trainer's perspective and includes when and how to do training needs analysis, using informal and formal analysis techniques and tips on how to develop a training plan.
Noes (2008): Provides examples of the developments in training research, the strategic role of training and the use of technologies in training.
Sims (2006): Provides a practical guide to how HRD functions or areas can be strategic partners in helping the organisation achieve its success.

DISCRIMINATION

It is not long ago that employers routinely discriminated against groups of potential employees on the basis of non-job related criteria. Although UK legislation has been in place for up to three decades forbidding discrimination on the grounds of sex (1975) or race (1976), and later the grounds of disability (1995), religion (2003), age (2006) and sexual orientation (2007) it is apparent from surveys and statistics that such discrimination still takes place – particularly in the case of pay and bonuses (especially for females), recruitment and promotion.

Whither discrimination?

Discrimination between candidates is allowed on the basis of capability to perform the work tasks (with some exceptions for disabled candidates who may be favoured even if they cannot fully undertake all the tasks – see www.ehrc.gov.uk) and the whole process of selection is to appoint the 'best' candidate – that is the candidates who best fit or exceed the standard requirements of the work. But the selection must be made using work related criteria – hence the need for a suitable and objective candidate specification, discussed elsewhere under **recruitment**. Recruiters (whether HRM, agency or line managers) often introduce subjective or discriminatory factors to support their own or the organisation's biases. If these subjective and discriminatory factors are allowed not only does the employer risk legal sanctions including fines, hefty damages (a London-based employee of Schroder received £1.6 million and a US employee of Union Bank of Switzerland received US$27 million for sex discrimination – guardian.co.uk, 2006) but they also lose the chance to employ more capable staff than they could have recruited and risk alienating customers, suppliers (in the 2010 Equality Bill it is proposed that local authorities will take into account diversity policies and practices when awarding contracts) and other employees.

The UK public sector and not-for-profit organisations try particularly hard, in general, to encourage applications from disadvantaged groups. Some organisations, however, often seem to want clones of existing staff so, for historical reasons, will tend to favour fit young men for some positions and attractive young females for others although older/younger, male/female or disabled workers might be at least as capable. Prejudice rather than job requirements and lack of imagination or innovation sometimes prevent the most suitable candidates being appointed.

A retail organisation may believe that selling pork and alcohol is a necessary part of a shop manager's job so not consider Muslims for such jobs. But a Muslim candidate may understand that this is a job requirement and be willing to undertake these tasks while not willing to consume the products. A sports organisation may have all its matches on a Saturday so not consider Jewish applicants even although the Jewish person may be willing to work on their Sabbath day.

Even if disabled workers seem to not possess the capability of a job, with some imagination and willingness the work can often be redesigned to enable someone with different abilities to produce similar outcomes to an employee with typical levels of fitness. For the disabled the law allows what is in effect positive discrimination (Department for Business Enterprise and Regulatory Reform 2008, see www.berr.gov.uk) while for other under-represented groups positive discrimination is forbidden (Equality and Human Rights Commission 2008, available at www.ehrc.gov.uk). In this context positive discrimination includes favouring candidates from groups which are underrepresented in the organisation, for example the police service in Bristol was found to have been in breach of race discrimination legislation by excluding white male applicants from consideration (*Personnel Today*, 2006), Positive action, however, is not forbidden.

The need for positive action

There is no need for positive discrimination if organisations and recruiters take positive action to relate recruitment criteria to the actual job requirements and to seek out disadvantaged groups who may be fully capable of undertaking the required work at fully acceptable standards. Positive action includes the UK Armed Forces placing recruitment adverts in gay magazines (Proud2Serve), employers allowing flexitime or adjusting work patterns to suit parents with young families (not just working mothers) better, making clear that older candidates will be welcomed (for example B&Q, a DiY retail company (BBC, 2006).

Practices which have led to indirect discrimination, such as relying on existing employees to recommend suitable applicants, have been discouraged or stopped as this type of recruitment leads to self-perpetuating groups as only the existing pool of workers are told about vacancies. Members of a dominant group may at first resent the recruitment of those from non-dominant groups (this could be argued to be part of a human being's fear of competition or of the unknown) but it does not usually take long for the newcomers to become part of the organisation's community of employees rather than be seen as outsiders. If management makes efforts to build that community feeling, then a more capable workforce is likely to be created. If the capable candidates are not recruited by the organisation, other employers will offer jobs to the long-term benefit of those organisations.

In cases of alleged discrimination it is up to the employer, or potential employer, to demonstrate that there has been no discrimination, and not up to the candidate to prove that they have been overlooked – so it is worthwhile making sure that not only are recruitment systems objective and job related but also that they are clear and can be understood by all those involved in recruitment as well as by potential candidates.

An organisation which is willing to put substantial efforts into selecting the best candidates is likely to be one which will continue to make efforts to have staff perform at their best in employment. An organisation that is discriminatory and disdainful of candidates is likely to continue the same attitudes with those who join it. Fair and reliable systems of recruiting will lead to better candidates being selected and higher productivity will result.

Ensuring objectivity

Some organisations (especially in the public sector) make great efforts to create diverse work groups and **teams** and have, at times, favoured applicants (see, for example, the Bristol police case mentioned above) and promotees from groups considered to be under-represented. This outcome risks a backlash (poorer work performance, low morale and even claims for damages) from those individuals in the groups deemed *over* represented. If employers use objective methods of selection for recruitment, promotion, redundancy, etc., they reduce the risk of upset, damages claims and increase the chance of making much more suitable selections.

The type of **selection** methods discussed in more detail elsewhere in this book are likely to increase objectivity. It is recommended (for example by the Commission for Equality and Human Rights) that those making selection decisions undertake training to ensure that they apply methods and techniques in a proper manner and avoid allowing prejudice to interfere with their judgement. Many employers in the UK use a system of monitoring the profile of the existing workforce and candidates using forms (with information on age, sex, sexual orientation, race, marital status, etc.) which are not available to those making recruitment decisions but which enable trends to be checked and specific instances of discrimination to be scrutinised. The cost of prejudice in HRM is high not only in terms of financial damages and fines (mentioned above) but also in the adverse impact on employee (and customer) morale and in the organisation operating at lower levels of productivity than would be the case if the most suitable (in objective terms) employees are in the relevant jobs.

WH

See also: **assessment; career development; cross-cultural training; cultural and emotional intelligence; employee involvement and participation; human resource planning; leadership development; organisational learning; outsourcing; training and development**

Suggested further reading
Cassel (1999): Makes a strategic HRM case for women's progression at work.
CIPD (www.cipd.co.uk): Offers a series of updated reports such as Tackling Age Discrimination in the Workplace (2005) and *Managing Diversity* (2006).
Daniels & Macdonald (2005): An accessible student textbook connecting between concepts of equality, diversity and discrimination.
Wolff (2007): A case study on discrimination in the UK passenger transportation industry prepared for the *Equal Opportunities Review* journal.

DISPUTE SETTLEMENT

In the HRM area the concept of dispute settlement and its processes can be seen as assisted continuation of negotiation and related to conflict – they are an intervention process (Rowley, 2002a, 2002b) and an 'adjunct to the collective bargaining process' (Salamon, 2000: 457). From a unitary perspective dispute settlement may be viewed as irrelevant (Rowley, 2001a, 2001b). However, one inherent outcome of managing people from a pluralist (or radical) perspective, is conflict (Rowley, 2002c). Of course, there can be a range of conflict types, but here we are more concerned with the more formal and visible forms. Once this type of conflict leading to a dispute occurs, some sort of settlement and resolution will be needed.

Some people may believe that, with enough time and goodwill, all disagreements and disputes can be settled and resolved. This may not always be the case. If neither side can then walk away, as is often the case in the employment area with the high costs that would be involved, the disagreement or dispute needs to be resolved. If informal and internal ways to settle and resolve disputes fail or there is stalemate or an impasse is reached, resort to forms of more formal processes may be considered. Again, such processes can be internally or externally facilitated and range from ad hoc to more permanent systems and from voluntary to prescribed and compulsory, even as parts of procedural agreements. While some disputes can be handled by law or labour courts, others require assistance from intervention by a neutral third party in processes such as conciliation, mediation and arbitration.

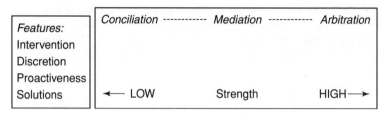

Figure 1 A spectrum of processes and features in dispute resolution

There can be publicly supported and funded systems of dispute settlement. These supports have a long history in some countries and with varied preference for, and use, over time of each type. For example, in the UK there was an early 19th-century system of compulsory and binding arbitration. Then came the 1896 Conciliation Act allowing government appointed arbitration (voluntary, except during wartime) to settle disputes. From 1919 the Industrial Relations Court was used by government to refer disputes to if both sides agreed. Renamed the Industrial Advisory Board in 1971, this body was replaced by the Central Arbitration Committee (CAC) in 1976. The independent, albeit government-funded, Advisory, Conciliation and Arbitration Service (ACAS) can appoint arbitrators or refer matters to the CAC. ACAS remains the UK's main provider of dispute settlement assistance of the types in its title. Similar ideas of state-encouraged dispute resolution systems can be found in other parts of the world.

The main types of dispute settlement process can, in some respects, be seen on a spectrum, ranging from, at one end, conciliation, to mediation in the middle and arbitration at the other end. These can be seen in Figure 1. While each of these types involves neutral, mutually accepted third parties, who these are, what they do and the type and 'strength' of intervention and discretion, and so on, all vary, as is shown in Figure 1.

Conciliation

Conciliation involves an independent, neutral third party acting as interpreter and messenger in identifying the causes of differences and relative significance of issues and positions of the parties in order to help develop mutually acceptable solutions. Agreement to these ideas and possible solutions remains the parties' own, joint decisions as conciliators do not impose or recommend solutions. Conciliation may be provided by private or public facilities. In the UK the best known provider is ACAS, with conciliation provided by its full-time staff, almost all civil servants. This UK system is voluntary and arises via the parties' requests, procedural agreements or ACAS volunteering its services in disputes.

Mediation

Mediation is defined as the process whereby a third party 'works jointly . . . to overcome problems' (Lewis et al., 2003: 416). Mediation involves an independent, neutral third party helping parties to resolve differences and come to some agreement and end the dispute. The mediation process is more proactive than conciliation as mediators may suggest their own ideas and proposals for a settlement. However, possible solutions are still non-binding on the parties. The parties may accept, reject or alter the ideas and proposals. In the UK, such mediators are drawn from an ACAS list, whose members are often academics.

Arbitration

Arbitration is defined as involving the parties 'jointly asking a third party to make an award that they undertake to accept in settlement of the dispute' (Lewis et al., 2003: 409). Arbitration is a method of settling disputes by referring them to an independent, neutral third party but now with both parties having agreed beforehand to abide by the decision. The arbitrator hears the arguments of both sides and decides on them.

The process of arbitration is often criticised because of some resultant tendencies it engenders and encourages. One is a 'flip-flop' effect, with decisions being awarded to one side then the other each time a dispute is referred. This alternate switching is irrespective of the merits of the particular case in an attempt to maintain the image of arbitrator neutrality and impartiality. Another tendency is to 'split the difference' in decisions, encouraging more intransigence and extreme positions in offers and demands from both parties. There will be the lowest offers and highest demands from each side tabled as they know that while these 'extremes' will not be agreed, it will maximise the median and 'real' result if split.

One possible solution to these issues of 'splitting' decisions is seen in the concept of so-called 'pendulum arbitration'. This system allows arbitrators to choose only between final offers and demands in their entirety. The argument is that this process encourages less extreme positions in final offers and demands as neither side can risk being seen as 'unreasonable' and thus not attract the arbitrator's decision (i.e. the 'pendulum') their way. Also, a by-product of this moderating influence is that, in turn, this can encourage voluntary dispute settlement as parties will be closer together in offers and demands before going to arbitration.

Yet, there are issues and problems with pendulum arbitration, not least that the decision implies that one side is totally 'right' and the other side is totally 'wrong' in a dispute and offers and demands. Also, the system does not allow for 'classic' negotiating, with its trade-offs and compromises over issues between parties. Indeed, in disputes there is rarely a simple choice between offers and demands, but complex packages with conflicting views and evaluations of data (Kennerly, 1994). In sum, 'The "winner takes all" concept underlying pendulum arbitration is incompatible with the principles of compromise and flexibility underlying the negotiation process' (Salamon, 2000: 485).

We have distinguished and outlined the three main types of dispute resolution process. However, in practice the dividing line between dispute resolution processes is thin and can blur. The process of mediation may be similar to conciliation, or it may be more formal and similar to arbitration, except with no final binding award.

Key issues

There are several key, often conflicting, issues and considerations around the concept of dispute settlement and its processes. These include the following. On the one hand:

- Conciliation and mediation, unlike arbitration, avoid giving third parties power to resolve disputes on what might be uncongenial terms.
- Resolution processes do force both sides to re-examine cases which can as a result make some movement, and hence settlement, possible.
- Independent third parties – conciliators, mediators and arbitrators – approach issues with fresh minds and can also bring their own suggestions and proposals for resolutions.
- Resolution processes provide 'public relations' aspects, being used to shift some blame and responsibility for final decisions and settlements onto others and outsiders, rather than being presented as the 'failures' of the parties themselves.

However, on the other hand:

1   The actual calling for processes of dispute resolution can be seen as a sign of weakness and can undermine the authority of the parties.
2   Reliance on resolution processes can become addictive, 'chilling' other important processes such as negotiation, making earlier settlement less likely as parties simply wait to go to dispute resolution.
3   Third parties do not have to live with the consequences of their actions or decisions in the processes.

Nevertheless, despite these issues, there can be benefits in using dispute settlement process. After all, disagreements will need to be resolved as amicably and agreeably as possible in some fashion or future disputes will erupt. Given this, dispute resolution and similar areas will remain important ones for HRM.

CR

See also: **conflict management; employee involvement and participation; employment relations; frames of reference; grievance and disciplinary procedures; legal aspects; management styles**

Suggested further reading
Bruce & Cerby-Hall (1991): Offers a useful development on this concept discussion.
Elkouri & Elkouri (1997): Details various aspects of dispute settlement.
Goodman (1995): Discusses skills relevant to dispute settlement.
ILO (1980): Offers international perspectives on the field.
Kheet & Lurie (1999): Offers a useful development on this concept discussion.
Lowry (1990): Develops a practitioner view.
Margerison & Leary (1975): Stands as a classic discussion of dispute settlement.

DIVERSITY MANAGEMENT

Diversity has, in the USA particularly, become a popular term to describe the changing mix of the workforce which is becoming more heterogeneous. A plethora of academic and journalistic articles that have appeared on the subject since the late 1980s point to diversity as a critical human resource issue due to two major reasons (Jackson &

Schuler, 1995). First, changing demographic trends indicate that populations and workforces in developed countries are aging and birth rates are low. So, organisations in North America and in Europe are making efforts to ensure more attractive working environments for older people, women, and minorities. Diversity is an increasingly important factor in organisational life as organisations worldwide become more diverse in terms of the gender, race, ethnicity, age, national origin and other personal characteristics of their members (Gupta & Shaw, 1998). Second, another reason is that business today is increasingly global. Operations and customers are based across borders and cultures. The workforce comprises people who are varied and share different attitudes, needs, desires, values and work behaviours (Birkinshaw & Morrison, 1995; Delua & McDowell, 1992; Rosenzweig & Nohria, 1994). Therefore, managing diversity is considered to have been one of the most popular HRM strategies of the post-1990s and has become more widely accepted as an important and powerful management tool (Litvin, 1997).

What is 'diversity management'?

Thomas (2000) argues that, with growing numbers of mergers and acquisitions, workforce diversity will become more of a priority for organisations and, therefore, in the future, people will become clearer on what diversity is and how to manage it. As with the debates surrounding definitions of human resource management and human resource development, managing diversity as a concept means different things to different people. The Department of Education in America (1999) described managing diversity as a key component of effective people management, arguing that it focuses on improving the performance of the organisation and promotes practices that enhance the productivity of all staff. Their dimensions of diversity include gender, race, culture, age, family/carer status, religion and disability. The definition provided also embraces a range of individual skills, educational qualifications, work experience and background, languages and other relevant attributes and experiences which differentiate individuals.

Managing diversity and equal opportunities

Existing literature relating to managing diversity can be broadly categorised into two groups, the first of which can be seen as doing little more than reiterating the traditional arena of equal opportunities

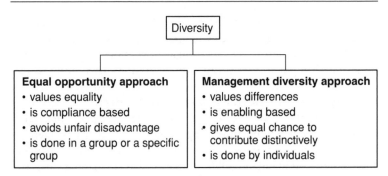

Figure 2 Conceptualisations of diversity. *Source:* adapted from Millmore et al. (2007)

(Cooper & White, 1995; Copeland, 1988; Ellis & Sonnerfield, 1995). The second literature group views managing diversity as going far beyond the conventional approach to equal opportunities, such as compliance to legislation and targeted group initiatives, and views it rather as an explicitly strategic approach to valuing individual differences (Dickens, 1994a; Miller, 1996; Stringer, 1995; Thomas, 1990).

In the strategic HRM (SHRM) literature, there are distinct differences between equal opportunities and managing diversity. Hicks-Clarke and Iles (2000) and Millmore et al. (2007) noted that the equal opportunities approach, which has a legislative and compliance focus, is concerned with equality of status, opportunities and rights. This, it can be argued, is deeply rooted in traditional approaches to HRM: the managing diversity approach focuses upon an explicit holistic strategy of valuing differences, such as age, gender, social background, ethnicity and disability. This, it can be argued, is like SHRM, driven by organisational needs (see Figure 2).

Equal opportunity approaches stress the importance of treating people equally irrespective of their sex or ethnic origin. Its objective is that individuals should be appointed, rewarded, or whatever, on the basis of job-related criteria. Their sex or ethnic origin should not be considered to be relevant, either to their favour or to their disadvantage (Dickens, 1994b). The limitations of this approach, which suggests that individuals can be stripped of their gender and ethnicity for the purposes of organisational decision-making, have been widely recognised.

In contrast to equal opportunities approaches, managing diversity approaches aim for workplaces where an individual's sex and race is of no greater significance than the colour of their eyes in determining the treatment they receive. The core idea behind managing diversity seems to be to encourage organisations to recognise differences. The approach shifts from a conventional legislative focus upon equal opportunities to an explicit strategy of valuing differences, such as gender, age, social background, disability, personality, ethnicity and work style (Kandola & Fullerton, 1994).

So far in the literature a clear distinction between managing diversity and equal opportunity approaches to diversity management has been maintained. However, are they separate or inter-dependent approaches? McDougall (1996) suggests that managing diversity should not be 'instead' of equal opportunities, otherwise the equal opportunities issue may be lost in the general search for valuing all aspects of differences. It is important to note that SHRM needs to adopt either an equal opportunity or a managing diversity approach. In reality they are often considered as inter-dependent, managing diversity seeking to value individual differences, and equal opportunities seeking to ensure that specific groups and sub-groups are not discriminated against (Millmore et al., 2007).

Connecting with HRM?

What evidence is there that managing diversity is a distinct approach to managing people? Liff (1993) argues that conventional equal opportunities approaches are deeply rooted in the old approaches to managing labour which tend to see the workforce as a collective, and she views equal opportunity approaches as bureaucratic in style, relying on setting rules for managers to follow and policing whether they do so. However, managing diversity, like HRM and HRD, is driven by business needs, with a holistic strategy involving culture change and 'individual nurturing' in order to improve the workplace environment, and becomes the concern of all in the organisation. Bennis (1991) states that, to manage the changing workforce, you must be flexible, individualise your approach, include and empower others in your organisation, reward performance, and support the personal and professional needs of others, which is a general replication of the philosophy of HRM and HRD.

What happens in practice?

The rhetoric claims that there are differences between equal opportunities and managing diversity, but have organisations embraced these differences in their approach to ensuring equality in the workplace, while managing diversity? Kandola and Fullerton (1998) surveyed 445 organisations from 30 different industrial sectors to discover what diversity initiatives had been implemented to date in organisations. This perspective indicates that for organisations managing diversity is a 'good thing' and therefore they should have done so. However, their research concludes that managing diversity is not being fully embraced; the majority of organisations were still focusing on those initiatives traditionally categorised as equal opportunities, such as the emphasis on fair recruitment and selection. Collett and Cook (2000) completed a study based on a self-completion questionnaire, mailed to the top companies in the UK and selected from the *Financial Times* 500. This study showed that one-third of the top British organisations were actively involved in the management of diversity, while 12 per cent of the remaining organisations were planning to do something in this area over the next 12 months.

Williams and O'Reilly (1998) conducted a large literature review and found that most of the research that supports the claim that diversity is beneficial for **teams** had been conducted in classroom or laboratory environments. They argue that such studies neglect some important variables, such as time, and the research carried out in groups with a short lifespan cannot be a good foundation for assessing the effects of diversity in real organisational environments. The literature review of Williams and O'Reilly identifies a smaller number of studies conducted in real organisational contexts. The findings of those studies evidenced an increased numbers of conflicts and stereotyping within groups as a result of workforce diversification. Wise and Tschirhart (2000) critically examined 106 empirical findings from 33 studies of the outcomes of diversity. They found that the general applicability of many of the findings was limited due to the use of students as research subjects. Generalisability was also limited by the fact that, in most cases, the interpersonal interaction that was studied was artificially constructed.

Millmore et al. (2007) summarise that managing diversity remains a theoretical concept rather than a strategic reality, combining equal opportunity and managing diversity approaches. The business case claimed for a managing diversity approach includes a better public image for the organisation, a satisfying working environment for employees, improved **employment relations**, increased job satisfaction and higher employee morale, increased productivity and, for the organisation, improved competitive edge. It is argued that organisations will only survive and prosper in an increasingly competitive and dynamic global environment if they respond to the heterogeneity of their markets. However, there is limited empirical evidence to support these claims in either the UK or USA. Despite a lack of evidence, it seems probable that the benefits of managing diversity will only be realised within the context of the re-alignment of an organisation's culture to one where diversity is valued. For this to happen, it will be necessary to persuade those in power that this will impact positively on organisational effectiveness.

QW & CR

See also: **best practice; collective bargaining; cross-cultural training; cultural and emotional intelligence; discrimination; frames of reference; international HRM; labour markets; management styles; psychological contract; talent management; teams; training and development**

Suggested further reading
Audretsch & Thurik (2000): Includes case studies useful for understanding cultural diversity.
Brief (2008): Provides a solid conceptual foundation for studying diversity in organisations.
Kirton & Greene (2005): Presents a picture of managing diversity in the UK and European context.
Rowley et al. (2010): This chapter usefully covers the area.
Wrench (2002): This paper demonstrates various critics of managing diversity.

EMPLOYEE INVOLVEMENT AND PARTICIPATION

Employee involvement and participation are rather elastic terms with considerable width in the range of definitions available. As Heller et al. (1998: 15) note: definitions of participation abound. Some authors insist that participation must be a group process, involving groups of employees and their boss; others stress delegation, the process by which the individual employee is given greater freedom to make decisions on his or her own. Some restrict the term 'participation' to formal institutions, such as works councils; other definitions embrace 'informal participation', the day-to-day relations between supervisors and subordinates in which subordinates are allowed substantial input into work decisions. Finally, there are those who stress participation as a process and those who are concerned with participation as a result (Dundon & Gollan, 2007).

It is therefore necessary to deconstruct employee participation on a number of dimensions, such as its *degree, level, range* and *form* (Marchington & Wilkinson, 2005). Degree indicates the extent or depth to which employees are able to influence decisions – whether they are simply informed of changes or are consulted – or actually become a part of the decision-making process. Level refers to where participation takes place; task, departmental, establishment, or corporate. The range of subject matter incorporates the trivial (e.g. such as canteen food) to more strategic issues (e.g. investment strategies). Finally, there is the form that participation takes. Indirect form is where employees are involved through their representatives, usually elected from the wider group and often couched in a language of 'participation' as something distinct from 'involvement' (Batt, 1999). Financial participation relates to schemes such as profit sharing whereby employees participate directly in the commercial success or failure of the organisation. Direct employee involvement (as distinct from participation) involves face-to-face or written communications between managers and subordinates that involves individuals rather than representatives (Dundon & Wilkinson, 2009).

It is also useful to recognise that there are two separate underlying ideologies behind the idea of employee involvement and participation. First, the concept of industrial democracy (which draws from notions of industrial citizenship) sees participation as a fundamental democratic right for workers to have an input into managerial decision-making in an organisation (Poole et al., 2001). Second, there is a business case for participation and involvement: it may make sense for employers to encourage greater participation from employees as it could help create more understanding and commitment but also allow employees to contribute to business goals. This perspective is also useful in helping us chart the changing fashions with participation over time. One might also add an individual case in that participation can help dignity within the workplace, with employees treated as having views to be respected (Budd, 2004).

Background

The topic of employee participation and involvement has been a recurring theme in **employment relations**. The wider political and economic environment has had a key influence in facilitating this particular agenda. The 1960s was often preoccupied with a search for job enrichment and enhanced worker **motivation**, rather than the mechanisms that allowed workers to have a say about organisational decisions. The 1970s witnessed a shift in focus towards industrial democracy where worker rights to participate and power sharing via **trade unions** are emphasised. In Britain such initiatives were abandoned with the new neo-liberal agenda of the Thatcher Government in 1979, although the potential impact of the 2004 Information and Consultation of Employees Regulations (ICE) in the UK has led to renewed debate.

Currently, the employment relations environment is in a period of significant change. Pressures of globalisation have intensified competition in product and **labour markets**, emphasising the need for greater efficiency and productivity, and leading to a greater focus on the link between employment practices and organisational strategy, a process discussed elsewhere under **strategic HRM**. In the area of participation this has led to a renewed focus on employer-sponsored employee involvement arrangements with direct engagement with workers and co-workers in autonomous or semi-autonomous **teams**. From this perspective, prescriptions are less concerned with issues of social justice and organisational democracy, and are more focused on the alleged business benefits (Sako, 1998).

This agenda has been subsumed most recently within the debate surrounding the implementation of high performance work systems. Leading advocates have described such approaches in terms of high involvement management, high commitment management or high performance work systems under a mutual gains approach (Wood & Wall, 2007). Some research would suggest that these direct methods of communication between senior management and the workforce have replaced more indirect forms conducted through employee representatives (Millward et al., 2000), while other studies have emphasised the mutual reinforcement of direct and representative forms of participation (Markey et al., 2001).

Supporting organisational objectives

A range of studies suggests that employee involvement and participation, often under the rubric of high performance work systems, can support organisational goals in three ways (Wilkinson et al., 2004; Wood & Wall, 2007). First, valuing employee contributions might lead to improved employee attitudes, and such attitudes are then translated into greater employee loyalty, commitment and more co-operative employee relations. Second, it could lead to improved performance including increases in general productivity and individual performance due to lower absenteeism and greater teamwork. Third, it could improve managerial systems by tapping into employees' ideas, knowledge and experience, thereby promoting greater diffusion of information and facilitating improved relations with trade unions. However, the evidence on the precise business impact from employee involvement and participation is mixed, and it seems that if there is a clear impact, then this is often skewed in managements' favour (Wilkinson & Dundon, 2010).

The current management rhetoric is for organisations to be flexible and innovative rather than seeking economies of scale through mass production (Piore & Sabel, 1984). The age of Taylorism is dead and workers are not just to be controlled but empowered (Wilkinson, 1998, 2002). As Walton (1985: 76) put it, managers have now 'begun to see that workers respond best – and most creatively – not when they are tightly controlled by management, placed in narrowly defined jobs, and treated like an unwelcome necessity, but instead when they are given broader responsibilities, encouraged to contribute, and helped to take satisfaction from their work'. Whether this happens in practice is of course another issue, and one that has been the subject of considerable debate for some time.

Implications for HRM practice

In summary, it is important to examine what the terms 'involvement' and 'participation' mean, and to uncover the different dimensions in practice: *degree*, *level*, *range* and *form*. The public policy context has also affected the nature and dynamics of participation in recent years, through the development of social partnerships between employers and employees' representative bodies, such as trade unions and works councils. Furthermore, the European policy context has led to the introduction of the 2004 Information and Consultation of Employees (ICE) Regulations, providing employees with new rights to be informed about the economic situation of their company and consulted about decisions that are likely to change their working and contractual conditions (Gollan & Wilkinson, 2007). This would create a universal right to representation, which in turn creates opportunities for unions. Because of such initiatives and changes, employee involvement and participation is high on the management agenda. More research is now being undertaken on multiple channels of information and consultation and many organisations are exploring different participative structures.

Looking to the future, one crucial issue is how multiple channels operate together or whether they generate structural tensions or organisational conflicts. However, and despite the range of different structures, it seems that few organisations have an involvement strategy that can be defined as *deep*, wide in *scope* and covering an extensive *range* of matters that are the subject of participation. The emerging evidence is that multiple channels are here to stay, that employees prefer this and that they are perceived as most effective from an employee viewpoint.

AW & TD

See also: **diversity management; employment relations; frames of reference; knowledge management; management styles; organisational learning; psychological contract; teams; training and development**

Suggested further reading
Budd (2004): A scholarly book that argues voice is important for key employee and organisational outcomes: efficiency, equality and fairness.
Dundon & Gollan (2007): A conceptual paper that debates the diversity in the purpose and utility of voice, both as a source of organisational effectiveness and as a managerial control strategy.
Wilkinson (2002): Provides a deeper and more theoretical treatment of empowerment.
Wilkinson & Dundon (2010): Additional explanation about the types of direct employee involvement practices.

EMPLOYMENT RELATIONS

There are three overlapping usages of the term, 'employment relations' or 'employee relations' (ER), itself a modernisation of industrial relations (IR). One centres on the 'employment relationship' (Edwards, 2003) between employers and employees. A second refers to a specialism within personnel management (PM) that addresses this relationship. Finally, there is an academic field or discipline within the social sciences that studies the employment relationship and the various actors and institutions that regulate it (see Ackers & Wilkinson, 2003). The fact that all companies who employ labour have an employment relationship; but that many small businesses have no specialist management function to deal with this, while many countries with advanced management policies, such as Sweden, have no dedicated ER field, all demonstrates the value of distinguishing these three faces.

In a broad sense, the *employment relationship* has always been a central feature of human society, wherever and whenever one person has worked for another and been rewarded for this. Medieval feudalism was a system of work relationships and payment, but the employment relationship properly understood is a child of capitalist modernity, wherein free individuals sell their labour to employers, who buy this human resource in a **labour market**. Schemes such as indentured labour in colonies or the annual bond of early 19th-century British miners were not employment relationships in the modern sense, since workers did not retain the right to leave their employers, renegotiate terms with them or take up alternative work elsewhere – all hallmarks of a liberal capitalist society. In the same terms, work in Communist societies, often saw a reversion to pre-liberal capitalist **work relations**, with monopoly state employers leaving workers not free to sell their labour to whomsoever they wished (Nozick, 1974).

Some contemporary workers are not in an employment relationship because they are self-employed (though there are many grey areas). You may counter 'I hired the man who cut the trees in my garden, so that we were engaged in an economic relationship'. However, such labour contracts are short term and have very specific characteristics: the precise work to be done and the price to be paid for it are very clear from the outset. An employment relationship, by contrast, is both open ended and (relatively) long term, two features that are intimately linked. If, for example, we employ a new lecturer in HRM, we have a broad initial idea of what that person's job description is. We may want him or her to teach the second-year module on HRM, do some research in the broad HRM field and maybe take some initial administrative responsibility. But even after the best assessment, we don't know what the full potential of that person is or what new challenges the Business School will face in the future. In years to come, we may develop new specialist degrees, while our employee may develop novel areas of expertise, which we want to harness in new directions. Even in relatively low-skill, low-discretion jobs we expect employees to be flexible and adaptable. As time moves on and the product market of the business changes, these characteristics are essential to business survival and continuity of employment. A secretary first employed in the 1970s with manual typewriter skills, would, by the 1980s, have to have learned word-processing skills to continue doing the same job.

For these reasons, the neo-classical economic way of describing the employment relationship as the buying and selling of labour in a market has its limitations. On the positive side, it does illuminate features sociologists may neglect; notably that the employment relationship is conducted within a capitalist labour market; and that only under these conditions are workers free, in any sense, to choose who they work for and what work they do. This said, employing someone is not like buying a piece of fruit on the market and there is an entire sociological 'black box' left by the economic language of capital, labour and market exchange. Terms such as the '**psychological contract**' (Rousseau, 1995) or 'effort bargain' (Baldamus, 1961) suggest the type of management work that needs to be done to convert the potential of the new employee into an effective worker. At the same time, the image of a balanced, individual free market exchange does not adequately capture the relationship between a huge corporation such as McDonald's and the unskilled youth that work for it. Employment law recognises this special nature of the employment relationship, which also carries with it ethical notions of trust and social responsibility (Ackers, 2005).

Management

Management quickly evolved as a response to the problem of how to turn labour potential or what Marx called 'labour power' into real productive labour (Nolan, 1983). Early in the industrial revolution, individual capitalists devised ways of controlling and driving labour to increase productivity. They introduced strict time measurement into the labour process, through the factory clock, and constructed crude piecework systems to reward high output and penalise slow work. By the early 20th century, F. W. Taylor had synthesised and theorised these various ad hoc labour control techniques as Scientific Management, a systematic approach to maximising effort and output using 'time and motion' study to measure every point of the process (Braverman, 1974). Henry Ford added to this the factory conveyor belt, which facilitated an even greater division of labour. While Fordism became associated with pressure and stress, it also benefited working people by increasing wages and providing cheap mass-produced consumer goods; a combination that made post-war American workers more prosperous than ever before in human history.

Budd (1998) has depicted the employment relationship as a threefold tension between efficiency, equity and voice. If efficiency was well catered for in early management theory and practice, predictably equity and voice were not. A few paternalist companies tried to combine all three (Ackers & Black, 1991; Ackers, 1999; Jacoby, 1997). The Quaker chocolate manufacturer, Cadbury, was among the first British firms to introduce scientific management, but it also pioneered good wages and conditions, high quality company welfare facilities, including housing and playing fields, and forms of consultation that allowed employees to voice their opinions. It was no coincidence that the roots of British personnel management lay in the welfare officers of the Quaker chocolate manufacturing companies. Such employer-led reforms were generally too little too late, for working people had developed their own response to what they saw as the lack of equity and voice in the employment relationship: trade unions. As these self-help organisations spread from the skilled to the unskilled and as employers began to negotiate wages and conditions with them, supported by the state, a new management specialism of IR emerged, exclusively associated with **trade unions**, **collective bargaining** and the surrounding institutions of joint regulation.

Academic industrial relations

Academic industrial relations has long held that the employment relationship is:

1 asymmetrical with a power imbalance towards management
2 collective because wages and conditions are decided for groups of employees and not atomised individuals
3 central to workers' lives and life chances, in a way that other day-to-day market transactions are not.

This approach began with Sydney and Beatrice Webb's *Industrial Democracy* (1897), which anticipated Budd's goals of efficiency, equity and voice. In parallel to employers' recognition of trade unions, the Webbs pioneered a new public policy and academic response to the 'problem of labour' centred on a combination of joint regulation and state regulation to rebalance the employment relationship in favour of ordinary employees and the good employer. As Kaufman (2004) has documented, American employers and academic institutions were much more proactive than those in the Webbs' British homeland. Businessmen funded new departments of IR at American universities and a body of research and theory began to emerge on how to build a new industrial civilisation centred on joint regulation.

After the Second World War, the Oxford School of Industrial Relations, led by Hugh Clegg and Allan Flanders, became a major influence on post-war public policy, including the 1968 Donovan Royal Commission on Trade Unions and Employers Associations (Ackers, 2007). Academic departments were established at many British Universities, most notably Warwick and the LSE. In policy terms, equity and voice were to be assured through joint regulation, whereby on an ever-increasing range of subjects, from wages and conditions to technology, working practices and redundancy, employees' representatives jointly agreed the terms and conditions of employment. By one measure, British academic IR had largely achieved its goal by 1979, when union membership peaked at 55 per cent of the workforce, and more than 75 per cent of employees were covered by collective bargaining agreements negotiated with trade unions. Yet the macro and micro economic efficiency benefits of this new regime for regulating the employment relationship were called into question by very high levels of strike activity, spiralling inflation and low productivity. Since 1979, a combination of New Right policies restricting the power of trade unions, globalisation and increased competition, and the rapid transition from an industrial to a post-industrial service economy have destroyed this old model of IR.

For almost a century the employment relationship was conflated in management, public policy and academic thinking with trade unions and collective bargaining. These institutions are now marginal to the working conditions of most British employees outside the public sector and even there such influence is diminishing. As a result, ER academics have tried to clear a path through the rusting remains of old industrial relations institutions to return to the original sociological conception of the employment relationship. At the same time, with contemporary Britain's more fragmented, service and white-collar workforce, general notions of a subordinated working class need to be revisited. As the IR conflict of the 1960s and 1970s showed, workers en masse are only powerless when there is high unemployment. Many union members today are white-collar professionals; and for some highly sought-after employees, the employment relationship may be better understood as a balanced individual transaction between two parties with equal power resources. In the case of Premier League footballers or TV celebrities, it is quite apparent that the employer has far less power in setting wages and conditions than does the individual employee selling their labour. On the other hand, at the bottom of the labour market are millions of low paid employees with no effective bargaining power. While the employment relationship remains a central issue for efficiency, equity and voice, the public policy task is no longer to rebalance society in favour of one relatively homogeneous majority class of manual workers, but to build workplace cohesion and protect the excluded in an increasingly affluent and individualist society.

PA

See also: **collective bargaining; employee involvement and participation; frames of reference; grievance and disciplinary procedures; labour markets; legal aspects; management styles; psychological contract; trade unions; valuing work**

Suggested further reading

Ackers & Wilkinson (eds) (2003): Explores all the different academic disciplines and approaches that feed into the inter-disciplinary field of employment relations.

Ackers & Wilkinson (2008): Links employment relations to wider developments in institutional theory and is part of the comprehensive *Sage Handbook of Industrial Relations*.

Blyton & Turnbull (2004): A leading British academic textbook on employment relations.

Budd (2004): An American restatement of the pluralist case for balancing the needs of employees and business efficiency.

Edwards (2003): One of the leading research texts on contemporary British employment relations. A third edition was published in 2010.

Kaufman (2004): An academic history of the spread of industrial relations around the world from its origins in Britain and the USA.

EXECUTIVE REWARDS

As F. Scott Fitzgerald noted in *The Rich Boy*, 'Let me tell you about the very rich. They are different from you and me.' The same is true of senior executives in large firms. Their pay systems are very different from those of the typical employee. Although some of the differences in pay vehicles have lessened, the relative and absolute differences in rewards levels have continued to increase.

Executive rewards have been based for many years on a combination of agency theory and market comparability (external equity). Agency theory notes that executives and owners of the organisation (shareholders) may have different objectives. In order to have executives serve the interests of owners (i.e. have them be effective agents) it is important to make executives owners as well. The drive to make executives effective agents is the rationale for the use of stock vehicles (options, restricted stock, etc.) as a major component of executive rewards. As stock markets have surged during the late 20th and early 21st centuries, executive **compensation** has grown much faster than the pay of other employees.

In order to ensure that executives maintain their ownership status, many organisations have ownership requirements. It is not unusual for a CEO to be required to have five times his/her base salary worth of shares, a president to have three times salary, a divisional vice president to have twice their salary and a senior vice president to have share holdings equal to their annual salary. Some time is usually given for a new executive to attain compliance, and incentive awards may be received primarily in stock options until compliance is achieved.

Characteristics of executive rewards packages differ significantly from packages of other kinds of employees. In most cases the package is negotiated rather than being set following guidelines. Job evaluation is more rarely done for executive jobs, and even then negotiations are still likely to take place. This is because senior executives – and particularly the CEO – are hired based on individual strengths, and jobs are to some extent built around the individual rather than finding the 'best' individual to fit a set of job specifications. Ongoing **contracts of employment** typically have some 'change of control' protections. So if there is a merger or acquisition, the executive has some protection against losing his or her job – indeed, critics argue that they have far too much. Presumably, this allows executives to operate in the best interest of shareholders even though it may mean they lose their jobs.

Maintaining market comparability – or being competitive against a market for executive talent – has been a second main driver of high rewards levels for executives. Every year, consultants together with the executives themselves have been eager to point out that competitive rewards have increased, thus necessitating a large increase for executives in the client organisation. This ratcheting effect has been exacerbated by having the consultant working for the organisation and its executives on terms of executive compensation and of other rewards and management consulting assignments. Finally, weak governance schemes – primarily weak boards of directors – have had little constraining impact on executive power; rich rewards systems for directors are likely to have influenced directors as well.

Government regulations and tax law have had substantial effects on executive rewards levels and the components of the rewards package. In the United States, for example, tax statutes limit base compensation, i.e. in terms of tax deductibility by the organisation. Tax statutes also favour options. Regulatory agencies have required that publicly traded organisations publish information of rewards packages of senior executives. Furthermore, information requirements seem to be growing in terms of the number of executives for which such information must be made public and the level of detail that must be published. There are currently efforts by the US Securities and Exchange Commission (SEC) to force publicly traded organisations to make public details of performance-based bonus plans, including specification of the executive **performance** goals and achievements used to calculate performance related bonuses.

Problems with stock options

Although grounded in agency theory and promoted (in terms of tax regulations) by governments, the role of stock options in executive remuneration has created problems in two ways. A primary criticism of options in a period of rising markets is that even executives, who are generally acknowledged to be ineffective and whose organisations have not increased in market value nearly as much as other organisations in the same industry, still end up making large gains. This situation appears to arise more as a result of general market increases rather than any value they have added to the organisation. Critics have suggested that all option grants be indexed, meaning that instead of receiving any gain in share price when the options are exercised, options holders would only receive gains above the average gains for shares in the industry.

Changes in accounting rules account for the other problem. It is now required that organisations account for option grants when they are made. The only generally agreed upon options valuation system is the Black-Scholes model, which was developed to estimate the value of options purchased in the open market. Valuing options has become a major concern for organisations granting them. Critics argue that the Black-Scholes model overvalues options, and thus discourages corporations from issuing the optimal number of options for attracting, retaining and motivating executive talent. While several approaches each have their proponents, none has been recognised as the 'best' choice for wide usage.

Social perceptions of executive rewards

The more information that becomes available, the more lobbying pressure has been exerted towards making even more information public and limiting either the flat amount that can be rewarded to any executive or to limit executive pay to some fixed multiple of average organisational pay or, in some cases, the lowest paid employee in the organisation. Unions holding shares, individual shareholders, pension fund shareholders, and activist organisations holding shares routinely offer shareholder resolutions limiting or otherwise control-ling executive pay at annual shareholders' meetings.

Social critics in general argue that executive pay is too high, and that the divide between rich and poor is becoming too great. These critics argue that excessive executive pay is tearing the social fabric, and urge higher marginal income tax rates for large salaries and leg-islative curtailment of rewards amounts. In the economic downturn of 2008–9, governments and the public have become enraged over continued high levels of executive pay. Several European countries have imposed additional taxes on bonuses of financial industry exec-utives, arguing that these executives are responsible for the economic collapse and should not be getting large bonuses under the circum-stances. In the United States, President Obama appointed a 'pay czar' to oversee executive pay in companies that took (and have not paid back) federal bailouts. Government officials have also blasted Wall Street bonuses at firms that are not subject to the 'pay czar's' author-ity arguing that organisations responsible for the recession deserve no such rewards, especially when unemployment is in excess of 10 per cent.

Wage differentials between executive levels in an organisation are typically much greater in terms of percentages than is the case between job levels lower down; that is, the executive pay policy line typically has a much steeper slope than does the rest of the organi-sation. Labour economists have advanced tournament theory as an explanation. This theory outlines how executives are willing to forgo remuneration in exchange for the opportunity to compete for the top 'winner take all' job. This is seen as equivalent to a tourna-ment with cash prizes, with the top prize being particularly large, the next prize much smaller, and the third prize being much smaller again than the second prize.

Boards of directors have begun to be more independent under the pressures they face. It is typical now that an executive compensation consultant is hired and instructed to report to the board of direc-tors rather than to the HR department or the senior executive team. Frequently this consultant (or consulting firm) has no other business with the organisation, thus reducing even the appearance of conflict of interest or collusion.

While the components of the rewards package are similar to those of other employees (e.g. in terms of base pay, short- and long-term incentives, benefits and supplemental benefits, deferred compen-sation, and perquisites or 'perks'), the mix distribution is very dif-ferent. Base pay is likely to be much smaller than either short- or long-term incentive payouts. Basic benefits form a much smaller part of the mix for senior executives than for other employees, and senior executives typically get supplemental benefits that are not offered to other employees and may cost the organisation much more than the base benefits package. Senior executives also routinely get perquisites, although some of the more visibly ostentatious of these have been reduced in the last decade – a theme developed elsewhere in this book under the heading **compensation strategies**. The significance of perquisites is discussed in more detail under the concept entry **non-monetary rewards.**

Executive rewards: an ongoing controversy

The current controversy that swirls about executive pay is not new. In the United States at least, there seems to have been major controversy focusing on executive pay every 10 to 15 years since the 1950s. Even after intermittent periods of reform, things calm down and executive pay continues to rise. This iteration of the executive remuneration controversy appears to have more staying power. Most of the executive remuneration controversy has focused on trends in the United States. However, with increasing global corporations, listings of corporations on exchanges in multiple countries, and investments in corporations of one country by investors from many countries, together with the problems associated with setting executive reward levels for managers receiving **expatriate pay** packages, there has been increased attention to executive remuneration in Europe and Asia.

CF

Editors' note: The Black-Scholes model can be used to calculate a minimum risk value for someone holding or having been awarded share options. Black & Scholes (1973) offer a detailed discussion of the original model. Less technical explanations are available elsewhere on-line and in some (albeit few) HRM textbooks.

See also: **collective bargaining; compensation strategies; diversity management; expatriate pay; international HRM; labour markets; leadership development; motivation and rewards; non-monetary rewards; pensions and other benefits; performance and rewards; valuing work**

Suggested further reading

Balsam (2007): A guide to the theory and practice of executive compensation from the influential WorldatWork organisation.

Bebchuk & Fried (2004): Examines most new approaches towards executive pay, arguing that CEO power is a better explanation of executive pay levels than agency or other theories.

Ellig (2007): Ellig is a retired VP at Pfizer who provides great detail on the mechanism of executive pay and does so in the framework of organisational strategy.

Graham et al. (2008): Integrating executive rewards into a total rewards strategy.

Jensen & Murphy (2007): Provides a good analysis of excesses in executive pay and insights on public policy approaches to changing executive pay systems.

Lipman & Hall (2008): A guide to best practice in executive compensation.

Reda et al. (2008): Leading executive compensation consultants describe how the Board of Directors' Compensation Committee can control executive pay while meeting the revised requirements of the Securities and Exchange Commission and other regulatory agencies of the United States Government.

EXPATRIATE PAY

This discussion focuses on two different but closely related areas: *expatriate compensation* (reward) and *global compensation/reward systems*. Most organisations used to rely heavily on expatriate employees to fill management and other key positions in their overseas operations. As organisations have globalised and overseas operations thus become much larger, and as foreign populations have become more viable as alternatives to expatriate employees from the home country, a new emphasis on developing global **compensation strategies** has occurred.

This discussion begins with a section on traditional approaches to expatriate pay and then highlights some of the major problems with widespread use of expatriates. The final section focuses on the developing field of global compensation systems, and the problems organisations are having in implementing such systems.

Expatriate compensation systems

There have been multiple approaches towards managing expatriate compensation systems. In some cases the reward package has been the result of negotiations. Some organisations have tried localisation, where expatriates receive the same reward package as local nationals.

Other organisations have developed special pay structures for international employees or have had regional plans. Still others have tried multiple programmes.

The difficulty with all of these approaches is that **labour market** rates, costs of goods and services, tax rates and government services together with customary rewards packages vary from country to country. The United States, for example, is one of a handful of countries taxing citizens' salaries earned overseas. Housing is much more expensive in Tokyo than in Singapore. Cars (and drivers) are assigned to much lower level managers in China than in London.

For an organisation trying to persuade an employee to take an expatriate assignment – and for the employee to feel persuaded, too – a reasonable outcome would be for the employee to net about as much discretionary income in the expatriate assignment as he/she might expect in the current home country assignment – and probably a bit more for taking on the foreign assignment. In practice, the outcome has been to assure that the expatriate does at least as well in every compensation category as he/she would at home, but to get the customary perquisites or perks associated with the host country, e.g. a car plus driver.

Balance sheet approach

The approach towards achieving this desired effect is called the balance sheet approach. The goal is to keep the expatriate 'whole' by adding the costs of giving up home, moving to and living in a foreign country, plus a premium for taking on the expatriate assignment. A formula for this balance sheet approach is:

home country costs
+ additional home and host country costs
− host country costs paid by company and from salary
= home country equivalent purchasing power

Balance sheet calculations are generally divided into four broad areas: income taxes, housing and related costs, goods and services, and savings, benefits and related areas. The income tax category is most prevalent in balance sheet calculations relevant to US-based expatriates: under tax equalisation principles a hypothetical US income tax is determined for a similar US employee and funding is provided to make sure the expatriate employee does not receive a higher rate or lower net income after paying both US and foreign income taxes.

Balance sheet calculations for housing are based on the distribution of income and housing expenses for a typical family of a given income level. Included in the calculations are extra costs due to selling or renting a house in the home country – some organisations even calculate the opportunity costs of forgone capital gains if the house is sold. Typically, costs associated with getting rid of appliances, curtains, carpets and other furnishings that are not easily stored or moved are also included.

Goods and services calculations such as those for housing are based on income level and expenses for a typical family at a given income in the home country. Adjustments would be made for cost of living and expected customary standards of living in the host country, adjusted for foreign exchange rates.

Expatriates usually get the best of both worlds when it comes to benefits: they get what they would get at home or what locals get, whichever is better. In addition, they are likely to get home leave and travel, rest and recreation allowances, dependent education, special health care and other perquisites.

Finally, expatriates usually get an additional premium, which may be labelled as a 'foreign service premium', a 'mobility premium', or a 'hardship premium'.

Expatriate profiles

Needless to say, expatriates tend to become very expensive employees. From the perspective of local employees, these expats might appear to be treated inequitably and so become referred to as the 'spoiled princes'. The traditional expat has a long-term overseas assignment with the initial purpose to maintain control of a host country operation by having home country management.

The traditional employee is typically a mid-career manager, requiring family relocation and accommodation for the spouse's career. There is a need for extensive acculturation, not only for the expatriate but also for his or her family. Most expat failure has been attributed to family member lack of acculturation. There is also some question of the effectiveness of traditional expatriates. Most countries have a growing cadre of well-educated managers who can do the same job for much less.

Global compensation strategies

The expense of maintaining an expatriate workforce and growing questions about their effectiveness when compared to local nationals has led some organisations to consider developing a global compensation system. This is in line with the globalisation of business and HR strategies. The true global organisation seeks competitive advantage through a uniform global culture, common technologies, and common terms and conditions for its human capital in the context of different legal systems, socio-cultural expectations, economies and labour markets, and opportunities. It is important here to recognise that globalisation is not standardisation, and local differences in compensation systems will continue until the world is much more homogeneous than it is now.

Global organisations have headquarters' domestic employees, expatriates, foreign (local) nationals, and third country nationals in various locations. Any site may have a mix of employees, even in the same job and adding the same value. This creates a problem for compensation systems because equity will be interpreted against different and conflicting benchmarks. In terms of internal benchmarks, employees doing the same job should be paid the same (i.e. assuming similar performance, seniority, etc.). Against geographic benchmarks, these employees may get very different compensation.

A global compensation system would seek common terms and conditions. At the very least, the processes used to determine compensation are likely to be the same, even if compensation levels differ. Compensation practices will include approaches to cash compensation, incentive approaches, ownership opportunities, and benefits. These should be similar. Performance standards and measures and performance management techniques should also be the same. Corporate culture requirements should be the same. As far as possible, work settings should be equivalent.

At the same time, legal constraints (e.g. mandated benefits, rewards limitations, tax and labour relations laws), social customs (e.g. the enduring roles of family, employer and government), and economic realities (e.g. competitiveness levels, standards of living, foreign exchange rates, labour market rates and demographics) must be recognised and accommodated in the global HR strategy for expatriate compensation. It should also be recognised that there are frequently major differences in terms and conditions across organisations within a country that are as great as the differences across countries.

When developing the global compensation system the following 10-stage process is frequently followed.

1 The organisation's global business strategy is formulated. This will form the basis of all global and **international HRM** and all global compensation systems.
2 Analysis of the need to transfer employees across boundaries must be made. The greater the number of transfers, the more important the global commonality of the rewards system.
3 Decision must be made about which employees the global compensation policies will apply to. Executive and professionals are likely to be part of the global system; production workers may not be.
4 The desired organisational culture must be specified. Compensation practices are both shaped by and shape organisation culture.
5 Guiding principles for the compensation system must be established.
6 The compensation mix must be determined in light of the organisational rewards strategy and local requirements.
7 Control and administration procedures must be determined. Is control at headquarters, or regional or local? For which processes?
8 The systems must be checked globally and locally to assure alignment with other human resource strategies.
9 The basis for changes to the system should be determined.
10 Unique situation policies (e.g. shut-downs and expansions, mergers and acquisitions) must be developed.

The catchphrase 'Think global but act local' is often meaningless when applied to global business policies. A better way to think about global compensation systems is in terms of 'global compensation policies and processes, with local outcomes tempered by law, customs and markets'. This perspective is developed in more detail elsewhere in this book under the heading 'reward strategies'.

CF

Editors' note: In discussions of HRM, references to 'compensation' and 'rewards' are synonymous. Contexts most influenced by North American-style HRM tend to prefer the term 'compensation'. Both terms are used in this current text.

See also: **collective bargaining; compensation strategies; international HRM; labour markets; motivation and rewards; non-monetary rewards; pensions and other benefits; performance and rewards; valuing work**

Suggested further reading

Craggs (2002): Develops the perspective of the leading professional association for compensation experts on how to do global HRM, including rewards.

Gomez-Mejia & Werner (eds) (2008): A global perspective on compensation systems.

Herod (2009a): Exploring alternative approaches to expatriate compensation.

Herod, R. (2009b): As above, and focusing on a balance sheet approach.

Perkins (2006): Offers a British perspective on global rewards.

Reynolds (1999): Written by the leading global rewards expert in the United States, this book contains details on global compensation approaches that are not easily found elsewhere.

Reynolds (2006a): Outlines WorldatWork's perspective on global compensation for organisations that are becoming transnational and move employees from many countries, i.e. not just home country nationals.

Reynolds (2006b): Develops WorldatWork's perspective on expatriate pay. Most useful for people who deal with US American expatriates, since US tax law and benefits practices are relatively unique.

FRAMES OF REFERENCE

Alan Fox (1966) introduced this employment relations (ER) approach to describe differing perspectives on the management of employees. He was concerned to challenge an uncritical, managerial view that problems at work could easily be solved by common sense, pointing out that this usually disguised one particular, biased 'frame of reference'. Fox's frames have proved useful in three main ways. First, they define three different ideologies or sociological theories about the nature of the employment relationship, the problems that arise from it and the best ways of solving them. Second, they can also characterise different management styles in organisations. And, third, they can portray employment relations regimes or periods of time, such as 'the pluralist 1970s', according to the dominant public policy mood.

Three frames of reference: unitarism, radicalism, pluralism

Unitarism

Unitarism sees the business organisation as a team united by shared interests and values, with senior management as the sole source of authority and focus of loyalty. Such an approach struggles to comprehend structural conflict at work, such as strikes or opposition to change. Expecting harmony between management and workers, it sees conflict as irrational and unnecessary and unitarists tend to cast 'trouble' of this sort in one of two guises. One is to see it as the work of agitators or ringleaders who – to use a biological metaphor – have infected a healthy organism with an outside virus. Thus, Australians have often blamed strikes on the malign influence of British immigrants or 'winging poms', while in Britain during the 1970s, Communist union leaders were often seen as the cause of bad industrial relations. The logic of this position is a tough 'macho management' to weed out troublemakers. A second, more self-critical approach sees conflict as a product of misunderstanding and bad management communications. This thinking has been the impetus behind many employee involvement (EI) initiatives over the past 20 years (Marchington et al., 1993, 2001). These are discussed elsewhere in this book under the heading **employee involvement and participation**.

Fox argues that '**frames of reference**' are of great practical import, because they influence practical management policy. In the case of unitarism, one consequence is hostility to trade unions, as independent representative organisations for employees. Unions are regarded as opposition groups or factions, cutting across authority lines and as outside bodies interfering in the family relationship between management and their employees, and throwing up rival leaders to challenge management authority. For Fox and other IR writers, unitarism was a 'straw man' to stand for an unrealistic, managerial view of the business organisation, but in the 1980s, the scarecrow came to life, through the influence of US popular management thinking on Excellence and HRM. This more sophisticated neo-unitarism cast managers as charismatic leaders who used EI to win employee commitment (Guest, 1992).

Pluralism

Pluralism is widely used in studies of politics to describe the sociological diversity of advanced capitalist societies, composed of many different interest and belief groups (Ackers, 2002, 2007). In employment relations, the term is used with similar meaning to describe relationships within the business organisation. In direct opposition to unitarism, pluralism rejects the model of the company as a unified order, following management leadership. Equally, it resists the radical view of the organisation as riven by a 'class war' between management and labour. Instead it discerns a plural society, composed of many interest groups, like a microcosm of contemporary Britain or America. These groups are often in conflict with each other, so that there is no single focus of loyalty and authority, but rival sources of attachment. Within a large complex organisation, such as the National Health Service, these interest groups will include professions, such as doctors, nurses and physiotherapists, each with their own associations.

The pluralist approach to ER focuses on the division between the goals, interests and values of management, which revolve around the need to improve profits or performance, and those of employees, which centre on wages and conditions. In this respect, pluralism expects a measure of conflict at the heart of the employment relationship, notwithstanding a degree of shared concern in the long-term success of the organisation. Trade unions play a central role here – not in causing conflict, but as a means of expressing conflicts of interest, bringing them to the surface, channelling and resolving them. For, in this view, conflict is a fact of organisational life, which cannot be wished away. The solution instead, is to manage conflict by institutionalising it, rather as fire-breaks prevent a forest fire engulfing an entire forest. This is done by management recognising **trade unions**, and forming committees for negotiation and consultation and procedures for disputes, discipline, grievances and redundancy. These create order and predictability where otherwise conflict might break out in hidden, explosive forms, such as sabotage, wildcat strikes, absenteeism, low productivity and high labour turnover. Ironically, pluralism lost credibility due to the rash of union-led strikes in the UK during the 1970s, followed by the anti-union backlash of Thatcherism.

Radicalism

Radicals hold a highly critical view of Western liberal capitalist society and regard the business enterprise as divided by class conflict between two main sides: employers and workers (Fox, 1974; Hyman, 1975). Accordingly, the 'bosses' exploit their employees, both in terms of the amount of work they expect from them and the wages they are prepared to pay them for it. This zero-sum power conflict is inevitable, continuous and potentially explosive and, in contrast to pluralists, radicals do not believe that it can be easily contained, managed or institutionalised. Where overt **conflict** is palpably absent, radicals tend to either search for it 'under the floorboards', in instances of shop floor misbehaviour, or to explain workers' 'false consciousness' as the product of management ideological manipulation (Ackers, 2001). The role of trade unions for radicals is to challenge management power and defend workers' interests. Sometimes, this battle is described in terms of a 'frontier control', like the trench warfare of the First World War. In this strife, union leaders are expected to remain unrelentingly and uncompromisingly militant, in contrast to the more moderate partnership approach advocated by pluralists. Ultimately, radicals hope that capitalism will be replaced by a new Socialist order in which industrial conflict is no longer necessary. Radicalism highlights the many injustices of contemporary employment, including overwork and low pay, and the obsession with conflict comes fairly close to the real situation in certain industries at certain times, such as the British coal industry in the 1920s.

Challenges to the 'three frames' approach to ER

The entire frames of reference approach has been destabilised by the dramatic global decline of trade union organisation, strike action and Socialist ideas in recent decades. Since the collapse of Communism, radicals have lost any clear sense of how work or society could be organised differently. Traditional pluralists have largely disappeared from the British HRM profession, while the old institutional toolkit of trade unions and collective bargaining appears increasingly irrelevant outside the shrinking unionised sector where pluralists and radicals still debate partnership in traditional terms (Ackers & Payne, 1998; Kelly, 1996). As pluralism has recognised the need for more active partnership to ensure efficiency and turned more to the state, employer best practice, and non-union forms of employee representation to regulate equity and voice, the gap between neo-pluralism and neo-unitarism has narrowed (Provis, 1996).

PA

See also: **best practice; dispute settlement; diversity management; employment relations; employee involvement and participation; international HRM; knowledge management; management styles; models of HRM; psychological contract; trade unions; valuing work**

Suggested further reading
Bacon (2009): This reading charts the decline of traditional pluralist employment relations practice.
Kelly (1998): A major restatement of the radical position, stressing mobilisation theory.
Provis (1996): An updating of Fox's pluralist/unitarist distinction.

GRIEVANCE AND DISCIPLINARY PROCEDURES

Grievance and disciplinary procedures seldom make headlines in standard HRM texts. They are what happen when things go wrong. Either the organisation or the employee has failed. The modern high-performing organisation with highly committed workers might expect to have little concern with discipline or grievance issues. HRM texts, for example, make scant reference to either issue. However, this appears to be a mythical world. In the real world – and regardless of whether it is a high-performing organisation or not – HR professionals are likely to be dealing with such issues on a regular basis.

Defining key terms

Let us define some terms. Policies and procedures are 'formal, conscious statements' that support organisational goals. However, there is a difference between a 'policy' and a 'procedure', as Dundon (2002: 196–7) notes: policies are written documents that outline defined rules, obligations and expectations for managers and employees. Typically, policy statements cover areas such as discipline, grievance redundancy, reward, recruitment or promotion. Procedures outline the details of how to enact a policy. For example, having a policy of 'rewarding high achievers' or **'talent'** would require some guidance on how managers implement the policy, such as the criteria for promotion or how much they can reward an individual. Similarly, a discipline procedure would outline possible sanctions, areas of conduct, and so on.

An interest in this area stems from industries which were prone to industrial problems and hence a lack of proper procedures was identified as a major cause of industrial disputes (Dundon & Wilkinson, 2003; Marlow, 2002). But while the modern organisation may regard an emphasis on rules and procedures as outdated as workers work beyond contract, it is not apparent that a belief in consistency and fairness is irrelevant to gaining the commitment of employees (Bott, 2003). Indeed, what may appear as flexibility to managers may seem unfair and arbitrary treatment to an employee. Pluralism suggests we need rules of engagement – a perspective discussed in more detail under the concept entry **employment relations**.

Managing problem behaviour

Despite the rhetoric of high commitment management and people being an important resource such that organisations would like to think they are only dealing with the motivated who are expending discretionary effort, organisations still spend time on these issues. Managers from different sectors report having to deal with an extensive list of problem behaviour (Klaas, 2009). This list includes such issues as chemical dependency, employees with weak ethical standards, managers that are personally abusive, employees whose performance is spiralling downward for no obvious reason, and employees who are unwilling to change their behaviour in response to changing conditions (Wheeler et al., 2004). As Klaas (2009) notes, problem behaviour is a feature of organisational life that rarely lends itself to easy solutions. Managers frequently struggle with questions about whether they should just look the other way, whether they need to give a problem employee a chance to improve, and whether treating a problem employee fairly puts the organisation at undue risk (Butterfield et al., 1996).

Thus regardless of the approach employers undertake in adopting HRM, there is a case for using procedures to ensure consistency, equity and fairness. These take different forms:

- Those which are jointly entered into by management and employee representatives, often called 'procedural agreements'.
- Those created and imposed by management unilaterally.
- Those prescribed by legislation or guidance contained in Codes of Practice, and case law (Bott, 2003: 309).

There is no doubt that procedural reform has taken place. In the last 30 years the increasing involvement of employment law and other **legal aspects** of HRM have caused part of this growth. Specifically, the notion of unfair dismissal has emerged as the main objective of any procedure in establishing an agreed set of rules, so as designed to channel any discussion or discontent through the appropriate mechanisms for its resolution. However, procedures cannot solve the underlying causes of conflict. For further detailed discussion on this theme, see the concept entry **conflict management**.

Why have grievance and disciplinary procedures?

There are a number of reasons why employers implement **employment relations** procedures (Bott, 2003). These are:

- They help to clarify the relationship between the two parties and recognise explicitly the right of employees to raise grievances. In short, it can create a framework for good employment relations.
- They provide a mechanism for resolution by identifying the post-holders to whom the issue should be taken initially, and by specifying the route to be followed should there be a failure to agree at that level.
- They act as a safety valve and provide time within which to assess the issue that has been raised.
- They help to ensure greater consistency within the organisation. They can reduce reliance on word of mouth or custom and practice, and minimise arbitrary treatment.
- They lead to more systematic record keeping, and consequently to improved management control and **information systems**.
- If written down, applied appropriately, and meeting the criteria of natural justice, they are important in employment tribunal cases.
- The process of drawing up procedures involves both parties working together to decide on the agreed mechanisms. Thus, joint ownership of the procedure may indicate a willingness to make the agreed procedure work.

It is likely that different levels of management have conflicting perspectives about the utility of such procedures. Many line managers regard procedures as little more than interference in their primary role of production or service and feel that the disciplinary process is long-winded, for example by taking too much time to get rid of unsatisfactory employees. This attitude might translate into distinct **management styles**. Senior managers and HR professionals need to train and develop line managers both in how to use such procedures and in how to explain their value. For example, it can be stressed that arbitrary or hasty action can lead to unfair dismissal claims and damage existing notions of the **psychological contract** in the organisation (Marchington & Wilkinson, 2008).

Examples of disciplinary procedures: unfair dismissal

The concept of unfair dismissal was first introduced into the UK with the Industrial Relations Act of 1971. The basic principle is for disciplinary procedures not to be viewed mainly as a means of imposing sanctions, but more as a mechanism to helping and encouraging improvement among those whose conduct or standard of work is unsatisfactory. Managers should not look simply to punish employees but to counsel them, especially over inadequate performance. If performance is not up to standard, then management should investigate the reasons behind the problem rather than just deal with the 'offence'. Employee performance may vary for reasons other than employee laziness or ineptitude. Lack of training, or problems at home need to be considered, as should the perceived link between **motivation and reward**. Such traditional models of procedures are designed to provide managers with the tools necessary to address problem behaviour, to help employees see the consequences of failing to comply with organisational expectations, and to help employees see managerial actions as being driven by standards of justice (Klaas, 2009; Wheeler et al., 2004). But this is premised on long-term relationships whereas other models are based on more fluid **labour markets** that stress efficiency and managerial prerogative (Colvin, 2004). Tribunals expend a lot of time not just on the substantive case, but fairness. Fairness depends on whether in the circumstances the employer acted reasonably. The most common offences resulting in disciplinary action are absenteeism, poor performance, timekeeping problems, theft and fraud.

Examples of grievance procedures

Grievance is a complaint made by an employee about management behaviour (Gennard & Judge, 2005). The term 'grievances' tend to be used widely and cover both collective and individual issues reflecting the idea that the line between grievance (individual) and dispute (collective) can be blurred. In general, grievance procedures are used for handling individual issues, while collective issues are usually dealt with by disputes procedures. In practice some organisations have a combined procedure that reflects the fact that grievances are often likely to affect more than one employee, and others allow for grievances that can be referred to the collective disputes procedure. Thus, a grievance procedure is a parallel mechanism to the disciplinary procedure (Rollinson, 2002: 98–9). Here we focus on individual grievances.

The aim of a grievance procedure is to prevent issues and disagreements leading to major conflict. This can include employee-to-employee grievances as in cases of racial or sexual harassment with the grievance taken against management for failing to provide protection. As with discipline, the spirit with which the grievance procedure is approached is significant. It may be easy for management simply to follow the letter of the procedure, making it a hollow sham, but once this is known employees will not bother to refer issues to the procedure. Consequently, it is important that HR professionals encourage the proper use of procedures to uncover any problems particularly where line managers wish to hide them because of fear that it portrays them in a bad light. Open-door systems operate in some organisations that allow workers to take up grievances with managers directly rather than follow a lengthy procedure. However, this relies on managers taking the system seriously and being prepared to devote time and effort to keep it going (Marchington & Wilkinson, 2008).

In the US, grievance processes are to be influenced by a union-avoidance motive. As Klaas (2008) notes, by providing employees with an effective voice mechanism, employers are able to reduce the appeal of unionisation. Use of procedures such as peer review has been found to be more likely in firms thought to be facing a greater threat of unionisation (Colvin, 2004). In addition to these external pressures, firms are also likely to be motivated by internal factors. Providing employees with a voice to challenge management decisions regarding discipline and other matters is generally viewed as consistent with high involvement work practices. Providing employees with the right to challenge management decisions is thought to enhance procedural justice perceptions among employees which, in turn, is likely to positively affect other practices designed to affect employee motivation and commitment (Dundon et al., 2004; Folger & Cropanzano, 1998; Greenberg, 2006). For further discussion about employee 'voice' and participation in managing grievance procedures, see the concept entry **employee involvement and participation**.

Generally, grievances should be dealt with quickly and fairly at the lowest possible level in the organisation. Research has found conflict between the perspectives held by HR specialists and line managers. Thus, an HRM policy that appears well formulated, and ensures uniformity and consistency may appear very differently when viewed from the position of the line manager under operational pressures. Here, HRM specialists need to be able to persuade line managers that procedures are valuable tools not nuisances and that the disciplinary procedure represents a useful and necessary guide for managers, encouraging them to follow actions they should be taking. Moreover, by not following procedure they potentially lay themselves and their employer open to the likelihood of appeals, time spent at an employment tribunal, and ultimately financial penalties as well as low workplace morale if members of the workforce perceive unfairness in management's actions.

Implications

Renwick and Gennard (2001: 170) argue that all managers need to be trained properly to handle grievance and discipline cases so that they can draw a distinction between unjustified employee complaints and those that are justified under the organisation's procedure, collective agreement or works rule. Where a dismissal has occurred, in investigating whether or not the employee has a grievance against their employer, tribunals test the issues of fairness and reasonableness by asking whether procedures are those applied to 'conform to the concepts of natural justice'.

Procedures can be seen as an essential element of good employment relations and HR practice. They provide a clear framework for those issues that invariably arise in all organisations, a mechanism in which they can be resolved. Without procedures, every new problem has to be tackled from first principles. This means that both managers and employee representatives will be spending considerable amounts of time trying to establish common ground rules before being able to resolve issues (Renwick & Gennard, 2001). Procedures help create a positive psychological contract by emphasising the importance of fairness. Additionally, they are bound up in issues of workplace justice. Equally there are issues concerning the effect on work unit outcomes, so there are performance and equity dimensions also involved within the process (Klaas, 2009).

AW

See also: **conflict management; contracts of employment; discrimination; dispute settlement; employee involvement and participation; employment relations; frames of reference; legal aspects; management styles; psychological contract; trade unions**

Suggested further reading
Klaas (2009): Provides a review of the theories related to grievance and discipline.

Rollinson & Dundon (2007): Examines grievance and discipline from a more practical perspective.

HEALTH AND SAFETY

Health and safety or, more precisely, *occupational health and safety* (OHS) – is concerned with the management of workplace risk that may lead to accidents, injury or ill health. Focusing on safety, the origins of the modern HRM concept emerged during the industrial revolution when the simple belief that workplace accidents were inevitable was replaced with a demand for them to be controlled. The need to manage OHS was – and continues to be – emphasised with major incidents such as the Bhopal toxic gas leak in India; the Chernobyl nuclear disaster in the former USSR; the Piper Alpha gas explosion in the UK; and both the Space Shuttle Challenger disaster and the Texas City oil refinery explosion in the USA, and the BP oil spill disaster in the Gulf of Mexico. These major accidents show the potential scale of workplace risk and that incidents are not industry or country specific. It was with these observations that the emphasis on managing OHS strengthened at a global level.

Formal OHS legislation

Occupational health and safety is formally governed by legislation. Within the UK, the Health and Safety at Work Act (HASAW, 1974) is the primary piece of legislation that places a duty on employers to ensure the health and safety of employees as far as reasonably practical. HASAW is enforced at a local, regional and national level by government bodies: the Health and Safety Executive (HSE) and local authorities (LAs). Secondary legislation also exists, which are called statutory instruments (SI). SI outline regulations for specific sectors or specific types of work. An example of secondary legislation is the Control of Substances Hazardous to Health (COSHH), which requires employers to control substances that can be hazardous to health. Similar bodies to the HSE at a European and International level are the European Agency for Safety and Health at Work (EU-OSHA), and the Occupational Safety and Health Administration (OSHA).

Both employers and employees have a legal responsibility to ensure occupational health and safety is upheld. Employers have a duty of care to look after the health, safety and welfare of employees and members of the public that visit their workplace. This requires employers to undertake a number of actions, such as training employees and undertaking risk assessments to identify possible health and safety hazards (see www.direct.gov.uk for a list of specific actions that correspond to employers' duty of care). In addition, employers are required to appoint a competent person to take responsibility for health and safety issues at the workplace. This role is often occupied by a senior member of staff or by a safety officer (appointed especially to fulfil this role). Many organisations also have safety representatives who operate at a shop-floor level and represent employees' safety concerns. Depending upon the employees, safety representatives are either self-nominated or nominated by the employees they represent.

Employees also have OHS responsibilities that emphasise the avoidance of actions that threaten their own or another's safety. This requires employees to follow safety procedures, wear personal protective equipment, and report injuries or illness as a result of work. Employees may refuse, under law, to carry out a task that they consider to be unsafe without being disciplined or dismissed for their refusal.

Although legislation and legal responsibilities exist, accidents continue to happen. This is often attributed to a number of organisational and individual factors.

Accidents at work

The immediate cause of an accident is unsafe behaviour. This is defined as 'an active failure that results in an accident if there is a local trigger, and if local circumstances have inadequate defences that provide an opportunity for an accident to take place' (Donald, 1995: 632). Traditional theories of unsafe behaviour have moved through different stages, focusing on poor machinery design, then accident-prone personality, and more recently on cognitive errors – unintentional mental slips or lapses that may occur when carrying out routine tasks. Although addressing these issues resulted in improvements, accidents continued to happen. This prompted a search for new ways to address unsafe behaviour. One approach that emerged from this search was a focus on organisational processes; in particular, an organisation's safety climate and the associated construct of safety attitudes (Canter & Donald, 1990; Cox & Cox, 1991; Donald & Canter, 1993; Zohar, 1980).

Safety climate refers to employees' shared perceptions of safety-related policies, practices and procedures. These perceptions are based on the specific events, conditions and experiences that employees have with safety, which influence their safety behaviour. While early writings emphasised the relationship between safety climate and safety behaviour (Zohar, 1980), it was not until the study of safety attitudes that this relationship was demonstrated empirically.

Attitudes to safety

Initial studies of safety attitudes were driven by the premise that rather than being a result of cognitive slips or lapses, the behaviour which leads to an accident is often intentional and under the direct control of the individual (Donald & Canter, 1993). To understand why employees engage in intentional behaviour that has the potential to lead to an unintended accident, studies focused on employees' safety attitudes. In doing this, safety research was in accordance with mainstream social psychological theory and the widely accepted view that behaviour is governed by attitudes mediated by intentions. Applied to safety, the attitude – intention – behaviour framework suggests that employees' intention to engage in unsafe behaviour, which may lead to personal harm or harm to others, is driven by their attitudes towards safety. Although attitudes are held by an individual, they develop and change in accordance with the local environment: their social and organisational context, including the safety attitudes, behaviours and beliefs of significant others. Therefore, in a working environment where taking short-cuts is common practice, an employee might develop an attitude that reflects a belief that managers and colleagues consider safety to be less important than production. Their behaviour will then reflect this view.

Of the many influences that impact on employees' safety attitudes and consequently their safety behaviour, management support is the most important. Donald and Canter (1993, 1994) were among the first to show this using data from the steel industry. They demonstrated not only that employees' safety attitudes were related to safety performance but also that perceived management support for safety was the factor most indicative of employee accident propensity. The importance of management support for safety in shaping safety climate has since been shown in work settings as diverse as nuclear (Lee & Harrison, 2000), offshore oil and gas (Mearns et al., 1998), construction (Siu, 2001), and health care (Flin et al., 2006). In contemporary research, the importance of management is shown through supervisors' safety leadership and perceived organisational support for safety. As the nature of leadership and **leadership development** changes to become more or less positive, so does the nature of safety climate and safety performance.

It is common practice now for researchers to measure safety attitudes in order to determine the quality of an organisation's safety climate and understand how it influences safety behaviour. However, the insights gained from this research are sometimes discussed in terms of an organisation's 'safety culture'. A safety culture reflects the combination of individual and organisational factors that shape the proficiency of an organisation's OHS programmes. At the core of a safety culture are workers' safety attitudes, and for this reason it is possible to see safety culture as a change in label rather than as a change in the processes being considered. Culture exists at an abstract level, which is often measured through safety climate perceptions and attitudes (see Guldenmund, 2000).

Current developments

In recent years, safety research has been extended in two main ways. The first extension has seen attention paid to the specific processes underlying the relationship between safety climate and safety behaviour. The goal of this research is to explain *how* management have their effect. This research has shown that management influence employees' behaviour through **psychological contract** expectations, trust, and by motivating them to engage in good safety (e.g. Burns & Conchie, 2007; Conchie et al., 2006; Neal & Griffin, 2006).

The second extension has seen a move away from exclusively focusing on unsafe behaviour and towards a more positive consideration of 'proactive' safety behaviours (Hofmann et al., 2003; Turner et al., 2005). Proactive safety behaviours are employees' discretionary behaviours that are not stipulated by their formal **contracts of employment** (cf. compliance to safety procedure), but are carried out voluntarily. Proactive safety behaviours are important for reducing accidents through the development of a supportive safety environment. These behaviours are analogous to 'citizenship', 'extra-role' or 'contextual' behaviours that apply at a general organisational level, and include acts such as helping others, keeping abreast of changes to safety and reporting safety events such as mistakes and violations. Behaviours of this sort allow organisations to take steps to prevent workplace accidents before they occur, and thus allow for the proper control of OHS.

SC & ID

See also: **best practice; contracts of employment; employment relations; grievance and disciplinary procedures; induction; legal aspects; motivation and rewards; organisational learning; psychological contract; training and development**

Suggested further reading
Boyd (2003): Provides information on HRM and OHS. Regulatory factors, social processes and risk factors are discussed, in addition to practical examples at an international level.
Clarke & Cooper (2004): Provides information on the management of occupational stress, one of the main occupational health issues. It provides information on its environmental and psychological contributions, and methods of assessment.
Forsaith & Townsend (2000): Offers information for those responsible for, or affected by, health or employment issues. It offers practical advice and information on where to seek further information.
Glendon et al. (2006): Offers the reader an insight into current thinking concerning occupational safety and risk management. It provides information on safety culture and how this links to safety performance. These links are illustrated by practical examples and case studies.

For further information on the legal responsibilities of employers and employees in UK contexts for occupational health and safety visit www.direct.gov.uk/en/Employment/HealthAndSafetyAtWork.

HUMAN RESOURCE PLANNING

Most business organisations start with *ad hoc* approaches to human resource planning (HRP). Indeed, many have little or no planning at all, as with family businesses or recent dot.com garage start-ups. Over time, however, an organisation grows in size and maturity, rendering less useful a reliance on relationships or chance when selecting people to work with. As HRM practitioners have shifted from being concerned with applying rules and dealing with industrial relations problems and become more concerned to be linked to strategy and business plans, the importance of HRP has become more apparent.

Purpose

The purpose of HRP is to transform strategy and business plans into the HR needs of the organisation, i.e. identifying and highlighting the *right jobs* (see the concept entry on **job planning**), the *right types,* as well as the *right numbers* of employees. The emphasis in HRP tends to be on job types and numbers; the people aspects tend to be the province of the **recruitment** and **selection** processes, discussed in more detail elsewhere in this book. HRP can also involve succession planning as part of the understanding of the internal labour market (ILM) along with data on attrition and retention rates, individual **career development** planning, learning and **development** plans, and likely retirement or redundancy programmes and other forms of **organisational exit**.

Core aspects

The core of HRP is to forecast the number of jobs required by the organisation. This is often done in shorthand and referred to as the number of employees required. However, for most organisations exceptions are discussed, for example, by Collins and Porras (2002) – human resources are only employed to fill jobs; jobs are not created to suit the employee. Along with the forecast of job numbers there is a definition of the types of job required, when the jobs are to be filled, and for how long, processes that combine as **job planning**. For some organisations HRP may forecast for decades ahead. This is particularly the case for organisations involved in capital intensive or large-scale extractive industries, which will operate a plant or facility for many years; this is also true for many government institutions such as the military. For example, an oil production company may predict a need for field maintenance engineers over the decades during which it will be operating. Similarly, a national air force may need to predict the number of fast jet pilots it will need to operate aircraft that are still in the design stage and may not be delivered for another 10 years or so. Authors such as Bartholomew et al. (1991) use sophisticated statistical techniques to attempt to help HRM professionals predict future (i.e. complex and long-term) planning of HR needs. In fast-changing commercial environments or in recently created industries, the practicality and usefulness of detailed HRP is diminished. However, in all cases HRP can make a significant contribution to organisational success.

Links to business planning

HRP can supply predictions of the likely numbers and types of jobs and the timing of recruitment or release from service of current incumbents or jobholders at different stages of the organisation's business plan. For most organisations (i.e. other than governments and those, as mentioned above, with long-term capital commitments) HRP can supply accurate and detailed predictions of HR needs for the current and following years, though with less detailed and less accurate predictions for periods beyond three years. These predictions will be based on the organisation's business plan and the likely economic outlook. Oil companies, among others, use scenario planning in order to guide the combination of business plans and HRP because it is not possible to make accurate views of economic and political outlook (cf. van der Heijden et al., 2002). Scenarios of likely outlooks are produced to give an understanding of the likely external labour market (ELM) and of **labour markets** generally. The HRP will typically offer predictions of jobs based on an optimistic scenario, a pessimistic scenario and a neutral scenario of the economic and political outlook. HRP processes will elicit regular feedback to compare actual and predicted HR needs.

HRP and 'soft' interpretations of HRM

HR needs depend on more than the current and predicted number and types of jobs. Needs are also determined by the number of employees who leave, gain additional skills, or are promoted. These 'softer' HRP issues are well explained in Bowey (1974), who discusses the causes of people staying in or moving from a job and/or seeking opportunities for advancement. The impact of these softer issues is more difficult for HRP processes to predict. However, knowledge of previous rates of employees leaving, average length of service, together with age profiles of existing employees are useful and help highlight how younger employees tend to leave more readily than older employees, while those approaching pensionable age are more likely to retire. It is worth emphasising here that age discrimination legislation (in the UK, at least) means that employees can be compelled to retire although a recent High Court judgment – while accepting the current situation – recommended that the government address the issue as compulsory retirement ages may conflict with age **discrimination** law. These embedded factors all serve to support predictions of how many employees are likely to stay with the organisation over a period of time.

Organisational variables

The more complex the organisation is, the greater is the number of job types, and the longer it takes to train and develop employees. By extension, it becomes thus more difficult to make accurate predictions of job needs using HRP. A straightforward organisation (e.g. one engaged in retail or fast food provision) might be able to conduct a detailed and accurate HRP process for the near future, as it is unlikely that there will be rapid changes in consumer demand or in the supply of unskilled labour. However, and even for these less complex organisations and occupations, attempting to predict too far into the future is likely to undermine the HRP process.

Although modern **information systems** enable more detailed HRP processes to be modelled, users must not confuse detail with accuracy. Finely tuned HRP can demonstrate the number and types of human resources needed over a long period. However, changing conditions within the ILM and ELM can make these detailed plans inaccurate or irrelevant. In times of rapid change many organisations decided to forgo HRP and rely on ad hoc predictions of human resource needs. This was the case in the UK and in the USA in the 1970s and 1980s, when 'boom and bust' replaced the stability and predictability of the 1950s and 1960s; it is true also in response to the turbulence of ELMs in India and China in the 2000s. By downplaying the importance of HRP, some organisations believe that the money saved from HRP investment can contribute towards buying in extra human resources when business demand causes an HR need for these. Generally, however, the use of HRP techniques with an emphasis on producing general predictions of needed job numbers and job types related to organisational plans remains common.

WH

See also: **development; diversity management; information systems; international HRM; job planning; labour markets; outsourcing; recruitment; resourcing; strategic HRM; talent management**

Suggested further reading
Hendry (1994): A standard and widely respected text in the field.
Lam & Schaubroeck (1998): Develops a detailed perspective on how to integrate HRP with organisational strategy.
Scullion & Collings (2006): A wide-ranging collection of perspectives linking HRP to issues relevant to global HRM.
Sisson & Storey (2000): An updated reappraisal of HRP/HRM 'realities' by two prominent UK-based HRM scholars.
Turner (2002): A concise 'how to' HRP guide for HRM practitioners.

INDUCTION

It is during the first few weeks and months that a new recruit settles into a new job and a new employer and begins to add value to the organisation. Alternatively, it is during this initial period that he or she fails to settle and so is underproductive and may soon leave the organisation. In such cases, the time and cost spent on **recruitment** and **selection** is wasted (CIPD, 2008). Induction is key in reducing the risk and impact of such waste and avoiding or, at least, reducing unplanned **organisational exit**.

Induction processes

The first stage in induction is the offer of employment. As discussed in the concept entries for **contracts of employment** and **legal aspects**, in some situations a verbal offer is sufficient contract to start employment and in some countries no contract of employment is ever issued – employment at will being the standard in places such as the USA. A well-organised employer wishing to have settled and productive employees will make sure that the stages from selection, through offer of employment, then introduction to the new organisation and new job and on to being a settled member of staff are well handled. If the HRM department, or line managers, mishandle the induction a demotivated employee (or a rejection of an offer) is the result (cf. Davis, 2005).

It does not take much effort to communicate well with the successful candidate (and even with the unsuccessful candidates who may be customers or even future employers of those who dealt with the selection process). Following up on the interview, sending a properly thought out (and up to date with employment legislation) offer of employment with a comprehensive employee handbook (or link to an intranet site) with details of day-to-day employment matters including how to apply for various benefits will create a good impression and make the recruit feel that they are welcomed to the organisation.

On the first day of service, although various administrative processes have to be undertaken, such as presenting proof of right to work in the UK, bank account details, next of kin information for emergencies or insurance provision, these matters should not dominate the introduction to the new employer. Time must be set aside (and been organised beforehand) to brief the recruit on their role and the organisation properly, some confidential matters may have been withheld until the person has formally joined, and introductions made to the most relevant people within the organisation such as work colleagues and important members of the expected network to be dealt with. Ideally a mentor should be appointed to guide the new recruit during their early service and the mentor should make contact at regular intervals to make sure that all is going well. Certainly the new employee should not be left to get on with the job, learning as they go or be given a set of files to read 'to get to understand the place'.

The induction process is intended not only to establish a settled commitment on the part of the employee but also to aim at inculcating the organisational culture of 'how we do things around here'. Invariably the newcomer will make some unintended errors (usually connected with not knowing who does what or not being able to find the correct location for material or meetings) but the more organised the induction the fewer the errors.

The first few days of the induction period should include briefing on **health and safety** matters, where the fire exits are, etc., and then an explanation of the main administrative matters the job holder will be concerned with, such as being issued with a computer identification and email address or a site ID security card. One area to be covered early on in the induction is the legal responsibilities of the new employee to make sure that along with health, safety and environment factors the person is fully aware of the employer's attitude to bullying, racist, sexist and religious **discrimination** and other matters in which the employee's actions can harm the employer (cf. ACAS, 2006). Some organisations have a formal session explaining the organisation's history and what its vision and mission are. Early on in the induction are formal **training and development** sessions on skills or capabilities needed for the job being undertaken. Even if the recruit has experience in similar roles it is wise to have training to ensure that work practices learned elsewhere are compatible with those applied in the new location.

Types of induction

Different types of induction programmes need to be arranged for different types of recruits, such as school leavers, new graduates, employees returning after a career break, experienced recruits from other similar organisations, internal transferees or promotions from other locations. Different types of jobs will also need different induction programmes such as those for airline cabin crew, process operators, restaurant serving staff, receptionists, skilled specialists, managerial and executive staff. These programmes will all benefit from having a system of feedback to ensure their relevance and effectiveness at making the recruits fit in or highlighting any problems with the new recruit that the **selection** process missed (cf. Thomas, 2003).

Building a successful employment relationship

No matter what induction programme, the aim is to help the organisation and the recruit work better together. The induction is part of the ongoing resourcing of the organisation making sure that unplanned turnover is reduced and that as many as possible of the best employees are retained in service.

WH

See also: **contracts of employment; development; diversity management; job planning; knowledge management; organisational exit; organisational learning; psychological contract; recruitment; resourcing; retention; selection; training and development**

Suggested further reading
Fowler (1996): A practical 'how to' evidence-based guide to induction policies and practices.
Torrington et al. (2008): A standard UK/Europe-oriented HRM textbook that emphasises induction as one of an integrated series of HRM processes, e.g. selection and retention (resourcing).

INFORMATION SYSTEMS

Organisations run on data. Sales, customers, production, accounting and financial data acquisition, storage and retrieval systems are critical if the organisation is to survive. While manual systems can work for small organisations, it is hard to imagine a global organisation existing without extensive automated systems in place. For a long time, HRM – with the exception of payroll – held out against automation, in part because of the extent and complexity of data relative to the human capital of the firm. As technology has developed, systems can now handle much larger quantities of more complex data, and human resource information systems (HRIS) are now common in large organisations.

The original argument for HRIS development and implementation was based on cost reduction: fewer people would be needed to create and maintain employee-related records. In addition, reports demanded by regulatory agencies could be compiled more quickly and more cheaply. While unit costs have gone down, the increase in the amount of data collected and stored, along with the increased demands of government for employee-related reports, have resulted in much larger costs for human resource data collection, storage and information generation.

The implementation of a HRIS in most organisations has followed a predictable pattern. The first stage has commonly been the collection of data that allows for production of government-required reports. In the United States, for example, the EEO-1 affirmative action report was one of the first outcomes of HRIS implementation. The second stage was the automation of processes that were already being done by hand. In general the automated process was simply a duplication of the manual process.

The third stage occurred when more data were entered into the HRIS and managers could get new reports related to the human capital of the organisation. Some of the projects at this stage hinted at new ways of managing human resources. One example is the skills bank. An organisation would try to collect the skills and experience of every employee. Reports could then be generated at will locating people in the organisation that had a specific skill set. With a few exceptions, these projects were failures. Skills and experience data turned out to be much harder to codify than had been thought. One result was that reports had too many hits that were not really matches for the desired skill set. A second major problem was that the data in the system were impossible to keep up to date. Employees saw no reason to enter new skills acquired into the database or enter in skills that dissipated; consequently, employees rarely did update. Perhaps the only exception to the skills bank failures was the language bank, especially in service organisations such as hospitals or police departments where such skills could be critical in an emergency. In such work contexts employees understand the need for such a database and are thus motivated to enter the appropriate data. The data required are fairly specific and straightforward, e.g. the data entry 'fluency in Bulgarian' is not ambiguous and is unlikely to be confused with skills in any other language. Similarly, language skills rarely dissipate. So, once entered, the data remain useful for the employee's tenure.

The fourth stage occurs when managers do not simply duplicate a manual process with an automated one. Rather, they find a new way of carrying out a human resource process based on the characteristics of HRIS. Unfortunately, few organisations are fully at this stage. HRIS and applications vendors have created and developed new processes that have been adopted by most large organisations. However, few organisations have taken advantage of the power of the HRIS to recreate human resource management. The following sections in this discussion note some of the ways HRIS can and have been used to change processes.

Resourcing employees

The first automation of the staffing process was the scanning of résumés and then the application of artificial intelligence techniques to those résumés to screen out unqualified applicants. As a by-product, letters could be sent to all applicants using the addresses on their résumés. This letter could provide a notice of receipt and, if the résumé was screened out, a rejection letter. This process is largely a duplication of what recruiters did previously. As the internet developed, it became possible to post openings on the organisation's website and employees could apply online, avoiding the scanning of résumés. In a sense, part of the recruiter's job has been transferred to the applicant. Skills tests can be administered online, either directly or indirectly. Authorised line managers can review applications without delay.

HRIS data contain much of what is needed for an analysis of recruiter effectiveness. The hire rate can be calculated for each recruiter, the mean acceptance rate can be calculated per recruiter, as can turnover rates and performance levels. The organisation can then know who its best recruiters are and try to duplicate their success. Similar analyses can be done for the sourcing, recruiting and selection of overqualified or under-qualified candidates, assessing the usefulness of job specifications in differentiating high and low performers. While these are fairly straightforward analyses, few organisations apply them routinely, or at all.

Employee training and development

Training needs analysis lends itself particularly well to intelligent use of the HRIS and other information systems. Gap analyses can be run using organisation level, group level and individual level information. These analyses can provide insights into areas of **training and development** needs.

To the extent that organisational long-term plans are available, career development needs can be also addressed. HRIS data analysis supports estimates of future retirement and staff turnover. National occupational projections can provide estimates of available replacement stocks. Areas of shortages can be tied in with developmental plans for employees. Since few organisations do formal **career development** planning for employees (except for selected high potentials or talent) intranets with appropriate software can allow employees to do career planning on their own.

Employee rewards

HRIS has actually done more to revise HR practice in the area of rewards than any other area. Even so, much of what has been done is merely automating current practices rather than changing practice to utilise the strength of the HRIS and the intranet.

An example of this revision is **performance management** linked to rewards. In many organisations the whole process is now automated. Performance plans are developed online, managers (and employees) can enter information online during the performance period, and the summary appraisal itself can be done online. Manager training in the performance management process is done over the company intranet with asynchronous education techniques. Appraisal data are transferred to compensation applications and then used to generate suggested merit increases and to generate training applications for suggested remedial training and developmental training. However, all of this happened before, only manually and more slowly.

The **pensions and other benefits** arena provides an example of how HRIS can be used to create new processes. Much of the benefits process has been transferred from HR practitioners to employees and outsourcers. Employees can go on line, see what benefits are available, make choices (e.g. between a flexible plan or one offering dependent benefits that require co-pays or other people to contribute), file claims, check status with respect to specific benefits eligibility, make changes to their family status (e.g. new dependent, divorce, change of address, change of beneficiary, etc.). Armed with this information, employees can then seek advice. Many organisations have outsourced their benefits administration processes and the outsourcer has access to all employee benefit and other relevant records in the HRIS. An employee can call or have live web communication with the outsourcer, who can answer questions based on specific and real-time employee information.

Another area in which practice has changed in some organisations is in support of **compensation strategies** and the awarding of merit pay. Compensation managers developed the merit budget and set up constraints on the size of increases managers could give their direct reports or subordinates. Under a paper-based system, this was necessary to ensure budget control and some degree of equity for employees. New information technologies allow merit pay increases to be handled almost entirely within managerial hierarchies, like other budget and expense issues. A manager receives information from the compensation function noting labour relevant market salary shifts and suggestions for increases for each employee in his or her unit and based on performance data. The manager is free to accept or reject the recommendations. When the manager has decided on increases, the budget goes to his or her line manager, just as any other suggested budget would. The senior manager may accept it as it is or suggest/ require changes. Thus, HR still plays a role in checking for biases in the rewards system as a whole, but is no longer a gatekeeper. This is a significant change in practice made possible by technology.

There has been much talk of the importance of HRM metrics in the last few years. Not enough of that discussion has focused on the information that can be constructed from the data in the HRIS, nor how technology enables managers to develop very different approaches to HRM.

Author's note: EEO-1, or Equal Employment Opportunity Form 1, is a report that all government contractors in the US are required to file annually. The form requires data on the number of employees from each major racial/ethnic group broken out by job family. It also requires analyses of compensation to test for systemic compensation discrimination. The Office of Federal Contract Compliance Programme uses the information on these forms to determine whether affirmative action on the part of the contractor is required and may disqualify the contractor from doing business with the federal government. The definition of 'government contractor' is so broad that nearly all large organisations are included.

CF

See also: **compensation strategies; development; human resource planning; knowledge management; legal aspects; organisational learning; outsourcing; performance and rewards; performance management; resourcing; training and development**

Suggested further reading

Guetal & Stone (eds) (2005): HRIS in a new digital age.

IHRIM (2001, 2002, 2003): These 'how to' guides cover the design and implementation of the HRIS and include chapters on specific HR areas, such as 'e-recruiting'. IHRIM is the professional organisation of HRIS managers and consultants.

Kavanagh & Thite (eds) (2008): This text/professional book contains chapters by leading academics and professionals covering design, implementation and administration of HRIS, and chapters on HR area applications.

Walker (ed.) (2001): Walker, a former manager of HRIS at A&T and a long-time consultant in the field, describes in detail web-based HRIS applications.

INTERNATIONAL HRM

In the mid–1980s international human resource management (IHRM) was described as a field in the infancy stage of development (Laurent, 1986). The majority of research was on multi-national enterprises (MNEs) and focused on highly visible activities, such as international production and international marketing and IHRM was one of the least studied areas in international business (Scullion, 1995).

The main reasons for the growth of interest in IHRM over the last decade have been outlined by Scullion (2010). These include the following:

- The rapid growth of internationalisation and global competition has increased the number and significance of MNEs in recent years and resulted in the increased mobility of HRs (Young & Hamill, 1992).
- The effective management of HR is increasingly being recognised as a major determinant of success or failure in international business and it has been argued that the success of global business depends very much on the quality of management in the MNEs (Edwards et al., 1996).
- It is increasingly recognised that the effective implementation of international business strategies will depend on the ability of companies to develop appropriate HR strategies for the **recruitment** and **development** of 'international managers' (Bartlett & Ghoshal, 1992).

- There is growing evidence to suggest that the human and financial costs of failure overseas are more severe than in domestic business and that many companies underestimate the complex nature of the HRM problems involved in international operations (Tung, 1984).
- The movement away from more traditional hierarchical organisational structure towards the network MNE organisation has been facilitated by the development of networks of personnel relationships and horizontal communication channels. It has been argued that HR plays more significant roles in network organisations.
- There is growing evidence that HR strategy has a more important role in implementation and control in international firms. It has been suggested that in a rapidly globalising environment, many MNEs have less difficulty determining which strategies to pursue than how to implement them and it has been argued that the success of any global or transnational strategy has less to do with structural innovations than with developing often radically different organisational cultures.

Defining IHRM

Typically, HRM refers to those activities undertaken by an organisation to utilise its HR effectively. These activities would include at least the following six: HR planning, staffing (**recruitment**, **selection** and **placement**), **performance management**, **training and development**, remuneration and benefits, and **employment relations**. The question is: 'which activities change when HRM goes international?'

One model, developed by Morgan (1986), defines IHRM as the interplay among three dimensions: HR activities, types of employees and countries of operation (see Figure 3, overleaf). The broad HR activities of procurement, allocation and utilisation can be easily expanded into the six HR activities listed above. The national or country categories involved in IHRM activities are the host country where a subsidiary may be located, the home country where the firm is headquartered and other countries that may be the source of labour, finance and other inputs.

Differences between domestic HRM and IHRM

The complexities of operating in different countries and employing different national categories of workers is a key variable that

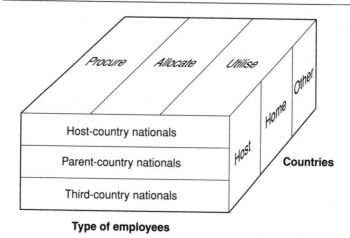

Type of employees

Figure 3 A model of IHRM. *Source:* adapted from Morgan (1986)

differentiates domestic HRM and IHRM, rather than any major differences between the HRM activities performed. Dowling (1988) argues that the complexity of IHRM can be attributed to six factors: more HR activities, the need for a broader perspective, more involvement in employees' personal lives, changes in emphasis as the workforce mix of expatriates and locals varies, risk exposure and broader external influences.

Many firms underestimate the complexities involved in international operations and there has been consistent evidence to suggest that business failures in the international area are often linked to poor management of HR. In addition to complexity, there are four other variables that moderate (that is, either diminish or accentuate) differences between domestic and IHRM. These are: the cultural environment, the industry (or industries) with which the multi-national is primarily involved, the extent of reliance of the multi-national on its home-country domestic market, and the attitudes of senior management.

IHRM in the literature

The literature on IHRM tended initially to focus on the management of expatriates (Ivancevich, 1969; Mendenhall & Oddou, 1985; Torbiorn, 1982; Tung, 1981). A stream of research into cross-cultural issues (Hofstede, 1984, 1993; Laurent, 1986) and comparative HRM

(Brewster et al., 2004; Brewster et al., 1996) has also developed. In line with a growing literature on international business strategy (Bartlett & Ghoshal, 1989; Porter, 1986; Prahalad & Doz, 1987), more interest was shown in the issues of managing people in international organisations.

Boxall (1995) highlighted the distinction between comparative HRM (how people are managed differently in different countries) and IHRM (how different organisations manage their people across national borders). The comparative HRM field analysed practices within firms of different national origin in the same country or compared practices between different nations or regions (Pieper, 1990). IHRM addresses the added complexity created by managing people – probably the most nationally specific resource (Rosenzweig et al., 1994) – across a diversity of national contexts of operation and the inclusion of different national categories of workers (Tung, 1995). Although originally comparative and IHRM were distinct fields of study, the increasing reliance on strategic partnerships and joint ventures, coupled with a trend towards localisation, has made the need to understand how HRM is delivered in different country contexts more important. Consequently there has been a degree of convergence in thinking between comparative and IHRM (Budhwar & Sparrow, 2002).

Some of the early models of IHRM focused on the role of MNEs and argued that finding and nurturing the people able to implement international strategy is critical for such firms. IHRM was considered to have the same main dimensions as HRM in a national context but to operate on a larger scale, with more complex strategic considerations, and co-ordination and control demands and some additional HR functions. These latter functions were considered necessary to accommodate the need for greater operating unit diversity, more external stakeholder influence, higher levels of risk exposure and more company involvement in employees' lives and family situations (Dowling et al., 1999). The field focused on understanding those HR functions that changed when the firm went international and also began to identify important contingencies that influenced the HR function to be internationalised, such as the country that the MNE operated in, the size and life-cycle stage of the firm and the type of employees.

The development of IHRM research can be divided into three categories as follows:

1   studies that look at the management of firms in a multi-national
    context, that is, the international aspects of management that do
    not exist in domestic firms, such as the internationalisation pro-
    cesses, entry mode decisions, foreign subsidiary management
    and expatriate management
2   comparisons of management practices across different cultures
3   studies that look at management in specific countries within the
    domain of international management.

More recent research into IHRM has acknowledged the importance of linking HR policies and practices to organisational strategy (de Cieri & Dowling, 1999; Schuler et al., 1993). The ways in
which MNEs organise their operations globally has been the subject
of extensive research by international management scholars (Bartlett
& Ghoshal, 1989; Porter, 1990; Prahalad & Doz, 1987). A recurring
theme in the literature is the link between strategy – structure configuration in MNEs and the demands for global integration (Adler &
Ghadar, 1990; Ashkenas et al., 1995; Bartlett & Ghoshal, 1989; Birkinshaw et al., 1995; Evans et al., 2002; Hamel & Parahalad, 1985;
Hu, 1992; Levitt, 1983; Sera, 1992; Yip, 1995) as against the need for
local responsiveness. An element of both is required in most organisations but, where global integration and co-ordination are important, subsidiaries need to be globally integrated with other parts
of the organisation or/and strategically co-ordinated by the parent.
In contrast, where local responsiveness is important, subsidiaries will
have far greater autonomy and there is less need for integration.

Globalisation and HRM

Globalisation is generally then seen as an economic process, but is
not one that is well defined. Political economists tend to use economic models to establish who the relevant 'actors' are and calculate
their relative interests. However, HR professionals need to adopt a
broad view of globalisation. There is a distinction between IHRM
and global HRM. Traditionally, IHRM has been about managing
an international workforce – the higher-level organisational people
working as expatriates, frequent commuters, cross-cultural team
members and specialists involved in international knowledge transfer. Global HRM is not simply about these staff. It concerns managing all HRM activities, wherever they are, through the application
of global rule sets. The added-value of the HR function in global
HRM lies in its ability to manage the delicate balance between

overall co-ordinated systems and sensitivity to local needs, including cultural differences, in a way that aligns with both business needs and senior management philosophy.

QW & CR

See also: **best practice; cross-cultural training; diversity management; employment relations; expatriate pay; frames of reference; labour markets; management styles; outsourcing; strategic HRM**

Suggested further reading

Brewster et al. (2005): Addresses the debates about the nature of SHRM and argues that the IHRM field is changing significantly and rapidly and that there is a need for better understanding of these developments.

Harzing & van Ruysseveldt (2004): Addresses the contemporary development of HRM in the international context.

Rowley & Warner (2008): Contains a wealth of relevant works, bringing together leading scholars in the field from around the world to give a broad cross-national overview.

JOB PLANNING

Without a prediction of the likely numbers of jobs and the type of jobs required by an organisation, HR **resourcing** – together with associated processes such as **recruitment** and **selection** – becomes a haphazard undertaking. If the outcomes, in terms of jobs, are unknown then the inputs, in terms of employees, will be confused and unproductive. For all the possible weaknesses associated with **human resource planning** (HRP), most organisations and their managers attempt to predict and plan for the types and numbers of jobs they are likely to require in the future (Bechet, 2008). Job planning and analysis is closely linked to HRP and many practitioners include these all under the heading of HRP, but we treat this as a separate concept as job analysis and planning tends to be concerned with the micro issues applying to specific jobs while HRP is more interested in the macro aspects of large numbers of jobs and many jobholders in an organisation.

There is usually some variation on how the processes of job prediction and planning evolve. For example, small and medium-sized enterprises (SMEs) as well as rapidly changing organisations in Asia tend to rely on managers' estimates of jobs needing to be filled. In contrast, most large organisations rely on fairly systematic means of

predicting job needs, usually driven by strategic business plans showing what the organisation intends to accomplish in set periods or
terms of time. Thus, job planning might be relevant for the organisation's staffing needs for one year (short-term) and/or in three or five
years, i.e. in the medium- and long-terms respectively.

Comparing methodologies

In relatively straightforward business contexts, existing matrices (i.e.
numbers and types of jobs in relation to the business needs) can be
used. Here the organisation starts by examining the current number
and types of jobs it already has in order to accomplish current activities. For example, a retail bank branch may typically need 10 tellers,
one assistant manager and one manager available in order to service 10,000 customers with total deposits of £10 million and loans of
£5 million. If the bank decides to open another branch with a similar customer profile then the HR resource needs will be assumed to
be similar. The business requirements for smaller branches are likely
to vary, e.g. a need for second signatories for branch transactions.
However, even the smallest branches must be able to calculate
minimum requirements in terms of job numbers and types, e.g. all
branches will need a manager and an assistant manager. Economies
of scale may also allow larger branches (e.g. with up to 25 tellers) to
require only one manager and one assistant manager. Similarly, an
aircraft capable of taking 12 or 400 passengers will need both a cap-
tain and at least one co-pilot.

In less straightforward business contexts, standard HR and job-
planning systems and practices might not be sufficient. For example,
if an organisation moves its business and thus strategic HRM focus to
a location where the education or previous training of staff appears
to differ significantly then the HR matrices used will also be different. The change in business requirements leads to the introduction of
different job types, e.g. the organisation might have reached a stage
in its business cycle where a specialist HRM function is required in
order for localised HRP to be effective.

One quick and easy way to determine job requirements in such
situations of change is to seek benchmark data, either by asking
similar (and even competing) employers or by buying-in comparative data from consultants and other agencies. In the case of the
retail bank invoked earlier in this discussion, benchmark data from
the new location might show how the sophistication of technology
used and customer expectations expressed are such that the bank

needs only half the number of tellers expected in the home business environment. Alternatively, they might discover that one HRM specialist is sufficient – or, perhaps, is only available – for every 100 employees in the new location. The use of benchmarking in relation to staff recruitment and reward is discussed elsewhere in this book under the concept entry **labour markets**.

Comparing traditions

A more systematic means of predicting the job needs of organisations is to combine use of method studies – which originated in the Scientific Management School – and job analysis, which is an aspect of industrial engineering or work study methodology. These techniques analyse all aspects of tasks to be undertaken within the definition of 'a job' and often break down these tasks into simple components, indicating set times to complete the task. This process focused mainly on tasks designed for unskilled workers, which was a driving force in scientific management – an approach to HRM developed in the United States in the early decades of the 20th century and one that underscores an employer's power in relation to the mass of unskilled migrant labour available.

Taking a more international HRM perspective highlights similar developments. For example, in Asia – and particularly in China and India where large numbers of internal migrants impact on localised job-planning processes – these method-based techniques remain attractive to both international and domestic employers (cf. Rowley & Harry, 2010). Here again the business plan determines what the output requirements are (e.g. the number of customers to be attended to, meals to be served or widgets produced) while the method study or job analysis shows what the input should be. The input in this case will be the number of jobs and the type of jobs required, e.g. 50 unskilled operators, four skilled workers, and two supervisors.

In more sophisticated activities such as those involving multi-skilled employees or where there is a need for a flexible allocation of work (e.g. defined as managerial roles), it becomes more expensive to apply detailed method studies and job analysis. Consequently, a more general description of the job requirements is built up with more emphasis placed on the type of capability (often called competencies) required of jobholders together with the likely number such jobholders required. This form of job analysis demands a more sophisticated application of management and specialist HRM skills. The analysis will be systematic; however, without aiming to be too precise in setting requirements. The job analysis may involve inter-viewing existing jobholders and their supervisors, observing work being carried out, or seeking information from consultants or other specialists. The job analysis will outline the expected responsibilities and accountabilities of a job, likely deliverables, and the qualifica-tions and experience required of jobholders. As an example, after job analysis the local resourcing requirement will stipulate that a factory manager will be responsible for factory operation involving the per-formance of 50 machine operators producing 10,000 widgets a day. This manager will be a university graduate with five years of relevant industrial experience.

As mentioned already in this discussion, the available technology and the training and expertise of the employees will have a crucial impact on the numbers and types of jobs deemed to be required by the organisation. Unskilled workers with few resources will be much less productive than skilled workers supported by machines or other resources. Hence, within the **human resource planning** process it is necessary to be aware of these factors. Sometimes business plans will suggest the hiring of many unskilled workers, e.g. in fast food retail outlets working in standardised ways. Other business plans will prefer skilled workers with significant supporting technology (equipment) together with maintenance staff working to ensure that the logistics systems ordering ingredients for the same retail fast food outlets works effectively.

Job planning and radical change

Attempts to improve an organisation's ways of working radically lead to radical changes in the numbers and types of jobs required. Such changes occur in processes of 're-engineering', where human labour becomes substituted by machines or information and com-munications technology (ICT) is used to replace human thought (cf. Hammer & Champy, 1993). In general, **trade unions** and work-ers prefer to keep to the current levels of staffing and so commonly attempt to prevent employers from gaining the advantages implied by introducing new ways of working.

Links to other HRM processes

It should be noted that the more expensive the labour costs then the more effort that HRM specialists will tend to invest in making accurate predictions of the jobs that their organisation requires. In reality, however, the more expensive jobs are those requiring flexibility in delivery and are thus less easily measured. Consequently, most organisations rely on benchmarking or **best practice** comparisons to decide on the job types and numbers. In these contexts, the job type is fed into **information systems** that then describe the basis of a job description and a candidate specification, which outlines the qualities a jobholder should bring to the job. These job-planning processes then feed into processes for HR **recruitment** and **selection**.

Whatever method is used to decide on how many and what type of jobs are needed by the organisation, it is important to introduce a system of feedbacks to compare the expected and needed jobs at different stages in the business planning and development processes. Thus, the job-planning process feeds into processes of **performance and rewards** management in that it advises business managers about the extent to which their assumptions concerning being able to attract and retain needed employees at assumed rates of pay (and so on) are or have been accurate, and can be achieved in the future.

To summarise, job planning represents a systematic approach towards establishing the number and type of jobs and employees that an organisation needs to operate competitively. As such, job planning is a core aspect of **human resource planning** and informs **training and development** activities together with succession and **career development** planning. It also supports **recruitment** and **performance management** systems as well as the foundation of the employment relationship between employees and employers.

WH

See also: **development; human resource planning; information systems; international HRM; labour markets; organisational learning; outsourcing; performance management; resourcing; strategic HRM**

Suggested further reading
Becker et al. (2001): Develops a performance-oriented approach to the job-planning process.
Boxall & Purcell (2003): Develops a strategic HRM perspective on job planning.
Lam & Schaubroeck (1998): Develops a detailed perspective on how to integrate job-planning processes with business strategy.
Rowley & Harry (2010): Connects job-planning issues to the 'global/local' HRM debate.
Turner (2002): A practical 'how to' guide linking processes of job planning with human resource planning (HRP).

KNOWLEDGE MANAGEMENT

Knowledge-based business has become a major strategy for an organisation to sustain its growth. Application of knowledge management (KM) facilitates organisations to maintain their competitive advantage through leveraging intellectual capital or knowledge residing in the mind of organisational workforce.

Definition of knowledge

In general, KM is concerned with the identification, acquisition and maintenance of organisational knowledge. Definitions of knowledge range from the practical to the conceptual to the philosophical views, and from narrow to broad in scope. Woolf (1990) in *Webster's Dictionary* defines knowledge as organised information applicable to problem-solving. Van der Spek and Spijkervet (1997) believe knowledge is a whole set of insights, experiences, and procedures that are considered correct and true. Similarly, Nonaka and his colleagues (1996) describe knowledge as a meaningful set of information that constitutes a justified true belief and an embodied technical skill.

There are also definitions of organisational knowledge centring on intellectual capital. Meyers (1996) refers to organisational knowledge as 'processed knowledge' embedded in routines and processes that enable action. Brooking (1996) defines it as the collective sum of human-centred assets, intellectual property assets, infrastructure assets and market assets. Organisational knowledge can be spilt into two dimensions, so-called explicit knowledge and tacit knowledge. *Explicit knowledge* is knowledge that can be documented or codified. It can be easily classified, categorised, combined, and distributed to others (Mládková, 2007). This assumes that much of the knowledge of individuals that is useful to an organisation can be articulated and thereby made explicit and available to others. *Tacit knowledge* is knowledge held by human beings. It is based upon personal experience that is accumulated over an extended period of time, perhaps even over a lifetime. This type of knowledge is influenced by intangible factors such as personal beliefs, perspectives, and values. An organisation's tacit knowledge takes the form of rules of thumb, intuition, tips and techniques, internalised skills, best practices, etc. Tacit knowledge is relatively difficult to communicate or share (Mládková, 2007). Any attempt to communicate tacit knowledge is complicated further by the fact that even those people who hold a great deal of personal knowledge have a hard time expressing exactly how they do what makes them experts in their fields. Yet, the sharing of tacit knowledge can be significantly important to an organisation's ability in highly challenging and competitive markets or in the management of highly complex processes.

The KM process

Why is KM important? Global competition has been increasing at a greater pace; what is useful today may become obsolete tomorrow. Under such rapidly changing environments, only the learning organisation can survive, it is asserted. Organisations have to update themselves constantly in changing environments. The formalisation and access of experience, knowledge, and expertise in the KM process can create new capabilities, enable superior performance, encourage innovation and enhance customer value. KM is often treated as the systematic, explicit and deliberate building, renewal and application of knowledge to maximise an enterprise's knowledge-related effectiveness and returns on its knowledge assets.

KM consists of three components: knowledge creation, sharing, and transfer. *Knowledge creation* can be through four different modes (Nonaka & Takeuchi, 1995):

1 socialisation which involves conversion from tacit knowledge to tacit knowledge
2 externalisation which involves conversion from tacit knowledge to explicit knowledge
3 combination which involves conversion from explicit knowledge to explicit knowledge
4 internalisation which involves conversion from explicit knowledge to tacit knowledge.

The second component, *knowledge sharing* or learning, can occur in both formal (e.g. classroom events) and informal (e.g. mentoring, coaching) situations, involving either structured, explicit knowledge ('know-what') or non-structured, implicit knowledge ('know-how', 'know-who', 'know-where'). Knowledge sharing that occurs during formal learning in the corporate setting tends to focus on some structured courses led by a trainer or facilitator. In contrast, knowledge sharing that occurs during informal learning in a corporation usually involves interactions during coaching and mentoring or communication that take place within communities of practice. Many scholars (e.g. Collins, 2001) believe that tacit knowledge is embedded in the 'mental models', ways of solving problems, and routines of an organisation, which involve continuous social interaction. It is clear that knowledge sharing is not simply a matter of managing information; it is essentially a deeply social process, which must take into account human and social factors, as well as cultural issues (Clarke & Rollo, 2001).

Additionally, *knowledge transfer* involves the distribution and dissemination of knowledge from one (or more) person to another one (or more). Although knowledge can be acquired at the individual level, to be useful it must be transferred to a group or a community, often described as a 'community of practice'. An ideal climate for such transfer is:

1   maintaining 'learning loops' in all organisational processes
2   systematically disseminating new and existing knowledge throughout an organisation
3   applying knowledge wherever it can be used in an organisation.

A 'learning loop' is any learning process that tries to improve another process, whether incrementally or radically. A Quality Circle is an example of an incremental learning loop designed to transfer knowledge steadily to raise the quality of a production process. In the international business situation, knowledge transfer generally involves downloading technical information from headquarters to local partners in international joint ventures, or some international managers sending or teaching knowledge while local managers receive and learn knowledge (Clark & Geppert, 2002). Some forces and trends (for example globalisation, internationalisation, technological advancement) may also trigger transfer of HRM knowledge from Western developed countries to other countries, such as the Asian economies (Rowley & Poon, 2008).

Knowledge is a key component of all forms of innovation. However, the deliberate effort of KM to support innovation has still not found its way into all companies. Some commentators would argue that this is because organisations try to use too many structured approaches and tools to capture and diffuse knowledge, and hence stifle the development of innovation. More recent approaches to innovation management have shifted to focus more on managing the supporting structures and climate that allow individuals to engage in interaction and communication. This approach eventually results in new knowledge and innovation (Murray & Blackman, 2006).

Innovation management is critical for both practitioners and academics, yet the literature is characterised by a diversity of approaches, prescriptions and practices that can be confusing and contradictory. Innovation can be thought of as a process involving little change, fine-tuning, incremental adjustment, modular transformation, system transformation (Dunphy & Stace, 1993) and continuous improvement methodologies (Murray & Blackman, 2006). Conceptualised as a process, innovation evaluation emphasises a series of stages and phases. Conceptualised as a product, companies emphasise the impacts and results derived from innovation activities and the performance of these innovations can be measured according to the product. This activity view of innovation focuses on the technological implications and the managerial implications (Liu & Tsai, 2007). After all, innovation comes from the acknowledgement of vicious circles and dead ends and the investment of positive and action-led approaches. Innovation management approaches taken by companies should consider the need for balance between what has to be stable, structured and systematised and what has to be creative, dynamic and open.

Innovation management and KM

Adams et al. (2007) propose that the three KM areas important for innovation management are idea generation, knowledge repository, and information flow. The early stage of the innovation process is a somewhat fuzzy period, including idea generation, opportunity identification, data analysis, idea selection and concept development. Then, if knowledge is fundamental to innovation, it should be possible to measure the accumulated knowledge of the firm, in other words its knowledge repository. One aspect of innovation relates to the combinations of new and existing knowledge (including explicit and tacit knowledge). Central to this perspective is the idea of 'absorptive capacity', the firm's ability to absorb and put to use new knowledge, recognise the value of new, external knowledge, assimilate it, and apply it to commercial ends (Cohen & Levinthal, 1990: 128). Firms with strong absorptive capabilities are more likely to acquire knowledge and learn effectively from outside. Higher levels of absorptive capacity appear to be positively related to innovation and performance (Chen, 2004). Finally, innovation management involves information flow into and within the firm, as well as information gathering and networking in KM.

IP & CR

See also: **assessment; development; cultural and emotional intelligence; employee involvement and participation; information systems; models of HRM; organisational learning; teams; training and development**

Suggested further reading

McInerney & Day (2007): Explains the fundamentals of KM in organisations and societies as well as knowledge processes.

Pauleen (2007): Presents the views of a diverse range of academic researchers, industry leaders, and public policy experts on how knowledge and KM perspectives vary across different cultures, in different contexts, using different processes for different purposes.

Renzl et al. (2006): Presents perspectives on knowledge and learning, including modes of knowing in practice, transactive knowledge systems, organisational narrations, and challenges conventional wisdom. It deals with emerging issues in knowledge and innovation embracing models of distributed innovation and forms of co-operation.

LABOUR MARKETS

One of the major shifts in HRM research and practice in recent years has been the increased attention given to strategic factors generated outside the organisation such as the influence of market fluctuations and of stakeholder (e.g. customer and shareholder) interests and expectations on **human resource planning** and decision-making. One of the major shifts in **performance and rewards** management research and practice over the last decade or so has been the move to benchmark as many jobs as possible in the labour market. In the 1970s and 1980s most organisations still relied on internal value hierarchies to create a salary structure and then priced that structure using a few 'key' jobs in each grade. Now many organisations benchmark as many jobs as possible. This has resulted in a new emphasis on market surveys covering wages and other parts of the rewards and compensation mix.

Demographic, technological and organisational changes have impacted work value during this time. The increased participation of women in labour markets, for example, has increased the supply of many professional skills. Automation has deskilled (and lessened the demand for) many jobs while at the same time creating a demand for new highly skilled jobs. The move of many organisations towards **outsourcing** jobs to lower-cost labour markets has lessened demand for jobs in some geographical areas while increasing demand for the same jobs in other areas. All this roiling and turbulence of labour markets has changed perceptions of the value of labour in local, regional, national and global labour markets. At the same time, changes in work have made jobs less static and more ambiguous, resulting in greater difficulty in finding matches for many jobs. This has left compensation professionals less certain about benchmarks and seeking guidelines for evaluating surveys and other sources of market rate information.

Against this background, this discussion looks first at current approaches towards determining market values for work, and then focuses on the questions raised by the resulting survey data. Unfortunately there are not, at this time, many convincing answers to such questions.

Wage and benefit surveys

The traditional approach towards developing benchmark information on job worth or work value uses a fairly straightforward methodology. A survey form is developed that has short job definitions (typically no more than five or six sentences) and requests information on several reward forms for each current holder or incumbent of a particular job. At one point surveys asked only for base wages for most jobs but most surveys now ask about a variety of reward types, including base wage, any incentive payments, and other job rewards. Some job family surveys (e.g. IT, sales, executive jobs) ask questions about pay policy and practice and seek other reward-related information particular to members of the job family.

Survey questionnaires or forms are sent out to clients of the surveying company and to mailing lists from professional associations and other sources likely to include a high percentage of compensation professionals. The use of a convenience sample requires survey providers to do extensive data editing. Survey data are increasingly collected over the internet and are also made available to survey subscribers online.

The wage or salary differential literature – in conjunction with practical experience – has led most survey users to look for those aspects of the data that most closely resemble their own organisation. At the very least, someone pricing a job needs to do so on a total reward basis rather than a simple base wage. Some of the major classifying variables are geographic location, industry, size (e.g. in terms of number of employees or level of revenues), **trade union** status, and organisational reward policies. While arguments can be made for rewards convergence – and especially in terms of HRM policies and practices – wage differentials remain significantly great. Thus, taking a single global benchmark for a job would result in over- or under-paying most employees. The practical implication is, of course, that market data are no more adequate to specify 'true' work value than are procedures designed to generate an internal value hierarchy. At most, market data can reveal only what competitive pay levels are, and what the organisation may need to offer in terms of rewards to attract and retain employees for specific jobs – more discussion on this issue appears under the concept heading **retention**.

With the rise of the internet has come a proliferation of websites claiming to offer good market data about wage levels for many jobs. These sites usually work with volunteered data, and the results are questionable at best. Nonetheless, employees access these sites and HR professionals have to contend with these data and be prepared to counter the information offered by web data sources with their own market data.

Problems with market survey procedures

While rewards professionals have significant problems with the popular websites that employees use for comparing wage or salary data, they also have problems with the wage surveys they use routinely to set actual wages within the organisation. This is a recent development, at least in terms of stated concerns among HR and rewards professionals. However, some of the concerns they raise were discussed in detail by academic researchers more than 20 years ago. For example, Rynes & Milkovich (1986) noted four areas of research needed on market wage surveys:

- Employer and consultant surveying practices.
- The impact of variation in measurement procedures on survey outcomes.
- The basis of policies on the usage of wage data.
- The impact of wages on attraction, retention and labour quality.

More than 20 years on there has been little research focusing on any of these areas.

The problems raised by many professionals include the reliability, quality and breadth of data available generated by surveys. In many cases, the surveys available for some jobs include data from only a few organisations, and in some cases one employer provides most of the incumbent data. Data rarely come from a large-enough cross-section of organisations that cuts or relevant outtakes from specific industry data can be made with confidence.

Job planning descriptions are sometimes so brief that professionals wonder whether it is possible for survey respondents to make good job matches. Few surveys capture all parts of the rewards package, so it is difficult to know whether higher levels of one part make up for low levels of another part of the reward package. Data on incentive payouts are particularly hard to interpret without detailed knowledge of the specific incentive generating the payout. See the concept entry **motivation and rewards** for a more detailed discussion linking incentives and job performance.

Surveys eliciting data about benefits and other **non-monetary rewards** present additional problems. An employer trying to cost labour will want to know what organisations actually pay for the benefits package received by a job incumbent. Since organisations have different workforce demographics, are of different sizes, and have different qualities of negotiating skills within the organisation, non-cash benefits costs can differ considerably for very similar packages. An organisation worried about attracting and retaining employees might be more interested in the level of service provided to the incumbent, and what the incumbent would have to obtain it externally. Finally, a researcher might well want to know the actuarial value of a specific benefits package for a hypothetical incumbent. All three measures of value are valid, but are rarely provided in surveys. Level of service tends to be the main set of data provided.

Benchmarking from survey data

Aside from the reliability and quality of the data, rewards professionals have difficulties in analysing the survey data in order to come up with a benchmark, even assuming that the survey data represent a valid and reliable sample of the market. The most fundamental problem arises from the fact that any survey returns a picture of a distribution of wages. Which survey statistic should rewards professionals match against? Typical choices are median, average, 60th percentile or 65th percentile, and others. All these choices are a means to represent job value in the market.

Another problem facing rewards professionals is how to price hybrid jobs, team jobs, and other jobs for which job surveys do not provide an exact match. A typical hybrid job is a maintenance mechanic/electrician. The market rates for maintenance mechanics and electricians are readily available. Is the hybrid job worth an average of the two, or is it worth more than either? Similarly, the market value of a work–alone production expediter is accessible, but the rate for one who is part of a large customer service team may well be worth more; or, indeed, less. The most common problem occurs when the survey job differs slightly from the organisation's job. How much more is the job of an HR VP position worth when the incumbent is also responsible for the organisation's fleet of corporate jets?

The unresolved problems of rewards surveys make them a poor (but the only available) source of determining and, by extension, benchmarking job value. Most organisations rely on rewards surveys to construct the rewards package relevant to their own employees. As long as organisations recognise that surveys provide flawed answers to questions of job value and processes of **valuing work**, their use is appropriate. A benchmark, though flawed, is better than no data at all, especially when the professional using it recognises that it is a guideline and not an absolute truth.

CF

Editors' note: Each year the UK-based Chartered Institute for Personnel and Development (CIPD, at www.cipd.co.uk) offers downloadable results from an annual survey of UK practice in rewards/compensation management. The survey is designed to provide benchmarking data in respect of current and emerging practice.

See also: **compensation strategies; diversity management; executive rewards; expatriate pay; information systems; international HRM; performance and rewards; resourcing; strategic HRM; valuing work**

Suggested further reading

Armstrong & Mitchell (2008): Offers a British perspective on HRM that takes into account labour market impacts on staffing, rewards and other processes.

Bjorndal McAdams & Ison (2006): Outlines the leading rewards association's take on analysis of market data for rewards purposes.

Bovbjerg & Dicken (2007): A paper prepared for the US Government Accountability Office giving practical advice on how to control employer costs such as health and retirement benefits.

Fay & Tare (2007): A study outlining market pricing concerns for the influential WorldatWork journal.

McMahon & Hand (2006): Guidance on how to design and conduct a salary survey.

Parus (2002): Marks a direct application of labour market data to job pricing and building salary structures.

Perkins (2006): Offers a British perspective on rewards that considers labour market influences on wages.

Rynes & Milkovich (1986): A scholarly study aiming to 'dispel some myths about the market wage' concept.

WorldatWork (2006): Provides data from surveys focused on North America; also includes major surveys from other countries. Provides instructions on how survey data can be applied to build salary structures.

LEADERSHIP DEVELOPMENT

Leaders in today's organisations face a number of significant challenges as their jobs and the world around them become increasingly complex. Trends such as rapid technological advance, proliferation of team-based organisations and cross-cultural operations require that leaders adapt their leadership styles to meet these new challenges. In the face of all these changes, researchers and HRD specialists are working to find methods to develop more effective leaders.

Definitions

There are several schools of thoughts concerning leadership. 'Leaders are born, not made' is perhaps one of the most common assumptions about leadership. Those who hold this 'qualities' approach maintain that there are certain inborn qualities or traits, such as initiative, courage, intelligence and humour, which together predestine a person to be a leader. However, there is no agreement upon what these qualities may be and this approach hardly favours the idea of training at all. On the other hand, leadership can be viewed as a system embedded within a larger social organisational system. Leadership systems include the quality of dyadic interactions and relationships, collective leadership characterising group interactions, and ultimately leadership culture characterising an organisation system. The functional approach, however, stresses that leadership is essentially an interaction between a leader, the group members and the situation. Another school of thought is that leadership involves relationships that exist between persons in a social situation. People who act as leaders in one situation may not necessarily act as leaders in other situations (Stogdill, 1948). A more contemporary view is that leadership is a process that induces others to pursue a common goal (Locke & Associates, 1999). Leaders (as opposed to dictators) must influence people through persuasion as well as induce people to go above and beyond mechanical compliance with routine directives of the organisation (Katz & Kahn, 1978). This perspective emphasises personal power rather than position power, such that followers are intrinsically motivated and will perform extra-role behaviours.

Although a vast number of leadership definitions have been offered over the years, there appear to be some common denominators for leadership development. Most of the organisational leadership development approaches are oriented towards building capacity to engage organisational members in leadership roles and processes so as to anticipate unforeseen challenges (McCauley et al., 1998). It is the stage of development in the career lifecycle that promotes, encourages and assists the expansion of knowledge and expertise required to optimise one's leadership potential and performance (Brungardt, 1996).

Leadership development is different from management development. Management development primarily includes managerial education and training with an emphasis on acquiring specific types of knowledge, skills and abilities to enhance task performance in management roles (Day, 2000), whereas leadership development is increasingly global in outlook, using a variety of **development** experiences, diverse activities and real-time organisation problems. Another feature of management development is the application of proven knowledge to known problems, which gives it mainly a training orientation. The goal of leadership development, however, involves action not knowledge. Therefore, leadership development means providing people with opportunities to learn from their work rather than taking them away from their work to learn.

Leadership development programmes

In addressing leadership development programmes, McCauley et al. (1998) identify the three main components of **development** programmes: assessment, challenge and support. *Assessment* provides an awareness of the level of an individual's performance at a given time. It provides identification of leaders' strengths and weaknesses. **Development** cannot take place if one does not know at what level he or she is performing compared to the standard or ideal. Consistent *support*, in terms of time and commitment, should be gained from the executive and board of the companies for effective development programmes.

Key features to design, develop and deliver leadership development programmes are summarised below in a five-stage process.

1 Select target audience

Leadership development activities focus on demonstrating to individuals how they may generate influence to create positive change. In this way, organisational members should understand that leadership is a behaviour, not a role, and therefore can be exhibited regardless of the position one occupies (McCauley et al., 1998). The programme should not be reserved for those in managerial positions but should be offered to all organisational members.

2 Develop organisational competencies and the leadership pipeline

A core set of organisation-wide competencies are defined (vertical columns), and then translated into their practical application for employees at different levels of management (the crossing pipes). Organisation-wide competencies are defined by a committee of the company's senior executives. Within the different hierarchical levels, these competencies are tailored to meet the appropriate needs for employees at each level of the pipeline. One of the complications is determining what competencies should be used. It may be confusing to determine the competencies to be used for leadership development purposes given numerous theories about leadership and leadership development.

3 Build individual development plan

Various tools, such as 360-degree feedback, multi-source feedback and multi-rater feedback, are typically employed. Rating sources can include peers, direct reports, supervisors and, occasionally external parties such as customers and suppliers. The advantage lies in obtaining a more comprehensive and accurate picture of an individual's performance. At the core of multi-source feedback is the cognitive process of self-reflection and self-awareness. It is triggered by the comparison of ratings from different sources (direct reports, supervisors, peers, customers, etc.) to self-evaluations (Day, 2000). Individual assessment and a development plan are contingent on discovering the discrepancies among self- and other ratings. The plan is built to capture employees' awareness and motivation, identify individuals' competency gaps and map out the development path.

4 Employ development initiatives

Although a variety of approaches have been employed to facilitate the **development** needs of managers, the most common development initiatives are as follows. First is *executive coaching*, which involves practical, goal-focused forms of one-on-one learning and behavioural change. The objectives of coaching are improving individual performance and personal satisfaction and, consequently, enhancing organisational effectiveness (Kilburg, 1996). Second is *networking initiatives*, which develop leaders beyond merely knowing 'what' and 'how', but knowing 'who' in terms of problem-solving resources. It is about investing in developing social capital and building support. Third is *development through job experience*, which pertains to how managers learn, undergo personal change, and acquire leadership capacity as a result of roles, responsibilities, and tasks encountered in their jobs (McCauley & Brutus, 1998). Fourth is *action learning*, this is a set of organisation development practices in which important organisational problems are tackled. This helps people learn effectively when working on real-time organisational problems (Revans, 1980).

5 Implementation and ongoing maintenance

It is generally believed that performance improves most when managers hold employees accountable for their growth. For the **development** to stick, the programme should focus less on the learning event and more on ongoing practice and reinforcement. Performance assessment and alignment with organisational goals and individual skill gaps are important.

Change in leadership development programmes

In face of rapid change in the business world, there seems to be something of a shift in leadership development programmes that have been popular for the last several decades. First of all, there has been the increasing use and recognition of a variety of **development** initiatives. Classroom-type leadership training has been for long the primary formal **development** mode (Hernez-Broome & Hughes, 2004). Activities, like executive coaching, mentoring, networking, action learning, etc., are gradually becoming key elements of **development** initiatives. Besides, the field is moving away from viewing leadership and leadership development solely in terms of leader attributes, skills and traits towards critical reflection about the competencies and social relationships of leaders. Moreover, the availability of technology in **training and development** allows individuals access to learning opportunities when it best suits their schedule and enhances knowledge management and sharing among participants via such venues as e-learning, e-mentoring, chat-rooms and so on (Hernez-Broome & Hughes, 2004). Finally, the field of cross-cultural leadership has become much more complex and strategically important than previously. The ability to lead and make sense across cultures and institutions and adapt to local expectations is changing the paradigm of leadership development programmes. While there may be many ways to develop cross-cultural leaders (like with business travel, multi-cultural teams, temporary international assignments and expatriate assignments), a leader cannot learn cultural adaptability and the competencies associated with it without actually living and working in another culture and successfully coping with the accompanying discontinuities (McCall & Hollenbeck, 2002).

IP & CR

Editors' note: Readers are also referred to the Global Leadership and Organisational Behavior Effectiveness Research Programme (GLOBE) and to publications derived from this research such as House et al. (2004).

See also: **career development; cross-cultural training; cultural and emotional intelligence; development; employee involvement and participation; executive rewards; management styles; talent management; training and development**

Suggested further reading
Conger & Riggio (2007): Stresses the complexity and complication of both transactional and transforming leadership.
Murphy & Riggio (2003): Explains how changes in business, such as organisational delayering, rapid technological advances and increased employee empowerment impact on the leader's skills, techniques and styles to meet these new challenges.

LEGAL ASPECTS

Many commentators regard **contracts of employment** as the beginning and the end of **employment relations**; what Kahn-Freund (1967) described as the cornerstone of the edifice. As a distinct perspective on HRM generally, and on employment relations in particular, this view is concerned with understanding the HRM policies and practices that result from the legal obligations enshrined in property and contract legislation. Of course, laws governing employee relations are derived from a variety of sources: *statutory legislation, judge-made laws, government policy* and *European directives and regulations*. It is the capacity of these sources of law to affect the contract between an employer and employee that is crucial. The contract of employment as a discrete entity is discussed elsewhere in this book. This current discussion serves to develop a broader understanding of the legal aspects of employee relations.

Origins of the legal contract of employment

Contracts of employment can be traced back to social and political reforms in master–servant legislation that took place in 19th-century Britain. They were often driven by **trade union** campaigns to remove some of the powers bestowed on a 'master' to control the activities of a 'servant' (Wedderburn, 1986). The idea of a legal contract of employment replaced previous systems of work relations based on servitude between a landowner and peasant. Even though these were regarded as wide-sweeping reforms at the time, they maintained and further strengthened the fundamental nature of capitalist markets. As with other contractual rights and obligations such as property ownership, the law assumes that the employment contract is made freely between two equal parties: in this case the employee and employer. For the former, the contract of employment is essentially a legal promise to be available for work under a set of agreed terms and conditions. For the employer, the contract expresses a reciprocal promise: in return for the employee's service, the employer will pay the employee an agreed amount in a certain way. Legally, when someone accepts an offer of work, they have entered into a binding contract. This means there are (or will be) certain fixed terms and conditions, often categorised in a number of ways.

Terms of employment contracts

First, there are *expressly agreed terms*; the things that the parties agree to from the outset, such as wages and holidays. The UK Employment Rights Act of 1996 stipulates that an employer should provide these terms in writing to the employee within two months of starting work.

Second, *implicitly agreed terms* cover statutory rights and common law judgements that may not be undermined by the terms of an agreed contract – for example, an employer's duty to take reasonable care of the employee's health and safety or to pay no less than the national minimum wage (implied terms of law). A court can also be persuaded to recognise that, where there is a gap in the expressly agreed contract, then other terms can be implied, i.e. implied terms of fact (Lewis & Sargeant, 2004: 18).

Third, the terms of a contract may be derived from *collective agreements* that, once negotiated and agreed, are then incorporated into an individual employee's contract of employment. An example is a new rate of pay. Practical implications of such agreements are discussed elsewhere in this book under the concept entry **performance and rewards**.

The fourth category that determines the terms of a contract is *works rules*. While collective agreements are made between two negotiating parties, works rules are often made at the discretion of management. For example, failure to comply with a revised or even new works rule can be deemed a breach of contract, and thus provide the employer with a significant power advantage to unilaterally alter the terms of the wage-effort bargain (Lewis & Sargeant, 2004: 17).

One final set of terms defining the employment contract involves workplace *customs and practices*. These can affect the terms of a contract in much the same way as collective agreements or works rules (Brown, 1972). In order for these practices to be interpreted as contractual they must be definite, accepted and understood by both managers and employees as a legitimate practice, and followed for a substantial period of time (Lewis & Sargeant, 2004: 17).

Problems of managing legal employment contracts

Of the range of approaches to the study of **employment relations** discussed elsewhere in this book, the legal contract is perhaps the most problematic, for two very fundamental reasons. First is the assumption that the contract is made between two parties in an individual and unambiguous way. However, except perhaps for some leading premiership soccer players, employees seldom have their own personalised contract of employment. In most situations the employment contract is a standard document that applies to almost everyone in a company. Indeed, it has been shown that even when individual contracts exist they are no more than 'individually-wrapped', which creates only an impression that they are personalised (Evans & Hudson, 1993).

A more fundamental flaw is that most firms are structured in terms of a hierarchy of departments and workgroups. This means that employees are ultimately bound by a collective rather than individual identity (Fox, 1974). Indeed, some of the key aspects that make up the contract are derived from group-based dynamics, such as collective agreements and customs and practices that have evolved and shaped work relations over time (Rollinson & Dundon, 2007). For these reasons it has been argued that the contract of employment is not even tantamount to an agreement as such, but rather an understanding about the employment relationship, for which the detailed terms and conditions can only fully emerge at some point in the future (Honeyball, 1989).

The legal implications of this point are now being realised as organisational structures and boundaries have changed with the growth of flexible and non-standard forms of work. For example, in the case of agency and temporary employees, the courts have found it difficult to decide who the actual legal employer is (Rubery et al., 2004). This is because many temporary employees do not work on a day-to-day basis for their employer but are based at a client company elsewhere, and often for substantial periods of time. Consequently, defining the actual employer can be ambiguous and difficult to pinpoint.

Another weakness of the legal view is its inadequate treatment of the indeterminate nature of employment relations (Blyton & Turnbull, 2004). Essentially, many other dimensions than those captured by the legal contract can shape the terms of the wage-effort exchange. These include the social and psychological aspects associated with paid employment, both dimensions discussed in detail elsewhere in this book under the **psychological contract**. In other words, the employment contract is more than a simple economic exchange. The indeterminacy of employee relations means that while workers and managers will have some objectives in common, on other issues their interests are likely to diverge (Edwards, 2003).

For these reasons, the employment relationship is fraught with tensions and contradictions that are never expressed (implicitly or explicitly) in the legal contract. Related to this is the fact that the employment contract is hardly ever made between two parties of 'equal' bargaining strength. In reality, it is management who have at their disposal all the resources of the employing organisation, while the individual employee is often a lone voice in a bureaucratic recruitment and selection process. In practical terms, this means it is easier for an employer to simply offer a vacancy to someone else than it is for an individual employee to try to secure a higher wage or to negotiate better terms and conditions when being interviewed for a job. Moreover, upon entering an employment relationship the employee has to submit to the authority of management and obey works rules (Fox, 1974). The argument that the contract of employment cannot capture this dimension of power and authority has been more eloquently expressed by Kahn-Freund: 'In its operation it is a condition of subordination, however much that submission and subordination may be concealed by that indispensable figment of the legal mind known as the contract of employment' (Kahn-Freund, in Davis & Freedland, 1983: 18).

Despite the concerns outlined above, the legal contract of employment is real and important in employee relations, with its origins traced to master–servant legislation during the 19th century in Britain. Today, there is a range of both *explicit* and *implicit* sources that affect the terms of a contract, including statutory laws, collective agreements and works rules. The major limitations of the legal view concern its inability to capture and express the complex indeterminacy underpinning the employment relationship. Indeed, it is because of these limitations that many workers join trade unions and seek to redress the inherent imbalance of power in the employment relationship (Kahn-Freund, 1977: 10). Because of these major criticisms with the legal view of employee relations specifically and of HRM generally, it is important to examine alternative perspectives, namely the **psychological contract** and the debates concerning employment, as outlined elsewhere in this book under the heading **frames of reference**.

TD

See also: **best practice; contracts of employment; employee involvement and participation; employment relations; frames of reference; grievance and disciplinary procedures; health and safety; management styles; performance and rewards; psychological contract; valuing work**

Suggested further reading
Edwards (2003): An analytical chapter that considers, among other things, the legal and contested nature of managing the employment relationship.
Lewis & Sargeant (2009): An important employment law resource and update on legislation and cases.
Wedderburn (1980): A discussion from one of the world's leading employment law experts, written in a highly engaging way that explains the role, importance and critical aspects of the legal system to industrial relations.

MANAGEMENT STYLES

The notion of 'management style' is an enduring industrial relations concept for understanding different approaches to the management of labour at an individual and collective level. Most **employment relations** textbooks will include a discussion of 'management style'. The concept has been developed by John Purcell and colleagues and draws inspiration from the work of Alan Fox's frames of reference and ideal types of industrial relations management. The concept has been adapted and modified over time.

Definitions and types

Management style can be defined as 'a distinctive set of guiding principles . . . which set parameters to and signposts for management action in the way employees are treated and particular events handled' (Purcell, 1987: 535). In an early formulation, Purcell and Sisson (1983) identified five main ideal type styles of labour management:

1 *Traditionalist:* hostility to unions and exploitation of employees.
2 *Sophisticated paternalist:* hostility to unions and paternalistic attitude to employees.
3 *Sophisticated modern constitutionalists:* extensive union/management involvement codified in extensive collective agreements outlining rights and obligations of parties.
4 *Sophisticated modern consultative:* extensive union/management partnership in joint problem-solving and integrative bargaining with less emphasis on legalistic agreement-making.
5 *Standard moderns:* union recognition but industrial relations essentially a reactive, fire-fighting approach to resolving disputes as they arise.

In 1987 Purcell extended this initial classification schema by arguing that there were essentially two dimensions to management style: individualism and collectivism. Individualism refers to 'the extent to which the firm gives credence to the feelings and sentiments of each employee and seeks to develop and encourage each employee's capacity and role of work'. On the dimension of individualism, at one extreme, employees can seek to develop employees as a resource. At the other extreme, employees can be treated merely as a business cost to be minimised. The intermediate position between these two extremes would be a paternalistic management approach.

Figure 4 Classification of management styles. *Source:* adapted from Purcell and Ahlstrand (1993)

Employee development (resource)	Sophisticated human relations		Sophisticated modern consultative
Paternalism	Paternalist	Sophisticated modern constitutionalist	Modern paternalist
Cost minimisation (commodity)	Traditionalist	Standard modern	
	None (unitarist)	Adversarial	Co-operative

Individualism (left axis)

Collectivism

Collectivism refers to how employers deal with collective or representative institutions at work such as unions. At one end of the collectivism dimension, employers could be anti-**trade union**. At the other end, management may have a co-operative approach to unionism. The intermediate position on this dimension can be labelled 'adversarial collectivism' where unions are recognised and tolerated rather than encouraged or avoided.

By combining the dimensions of management style with the early approach to ideal types, a matrix of management styles was developed (see Figure 4). This framework utilises the ideal types identified earlier plus additional management styles including 'sophisticated human relations' (anti-union but with a strong employee development approach) and 'modern paternalist' (co-operative union relations with paternalistic treatment of employees). While such classification schemes are an oversimplified version of reality, they are useful in helping us understand the main types of employee relations climate in different organisations (Hollinshead et al., 2003). Organisations may display different styles at different times and in response to different circumstances. Firms may also exhibit different management styles to different groups of workers.

Storey and Bacon (1993) have extended the concept of management style and suggested that the terms individualism and collectivism

Table 7 Individualism and collectivism in employment relations. *Source:* based on Storey and Bacon (1993)

	Individualism	*Collectivism*
Industrial relations	Non-unionism	Union/management bargaining
Work organisation	Low trust work systems with high managerial control	Group-based work systems with employee autonomy
Personnel/ HR	Market-based arrangements with weak employee attachment to the firm	Internal labour markets with job security, promotion prospects and fair treatment of employees

can be applied to different elements of the employment relationship. They contend that the terms 'individualism' and 'collectivism' relate to three separate realms of the employment relationship: industrial relations, work organisation and personnel. The main elements of their classification are shown in Table 7.

In addition to this work, other authors have also adapted and extended the management style framework. For example, McLoughlin and Gourlay (1994) and Dundon and Rollinson (2004) have explored classification of management style in non-union organisations.

Usefulness of styles

One of the main contributions of the management style approach is that it identifies that managers not only have characteristic ways of dealing with employees but they also have distinctive approaches to dealing with collective employment relations and unions. As a result, the management style concept has a broader application than other management constructs such as 'transactional' versus 'transformational' leadership styles.

The management style construct has also influenced border debates about the declining collectivism and the growth of individualism in many economies. While there is evidence that there has been a decline in adversarial collectivism in some countries, there is less evidence to suggest it has been replaced by sophisticated HRM approaches or union/management 'partnership' initiatives.

Traditional management approaches based on managerial prerogative and cost-minimisation predominate.

Problems with styles

One of the main problems with the management style construct is measurement and unit of analysis. Should management style be measured by interviewing or surveying senior managers or human resource managers or line managers or individual employees? Senior managers may report the existence of formal management policies but there is often a large gap between stated policy and actual implementation by line managers. Lower-level managers commonly do not fully understand or in some cases circumvent formal policy such that lower-level management style in action is sometimes quite different from the management style espoused by senior managers (Rollinson & Dundon, 2007).

More work needs to be done to clarify the unit of analysis and develop appropriate survey research instruments to measure the characteristics of management style statistically. To date, most research about management style has been restricted to case study analysis where management style is used as heuristic classification schema. As a result, management style has not been used as a validated construct in multivariate analysis. More sophisticated statistical factor analysis needs to be conducted to establish the validity and the characteristics of the management style construct. Such work is important if the construct is to be used effectively in cross-national studies and in contexts for **international HRM**.

CA

See also: **best practice; cultural and emotional intelligence; diversity management; employee involvement and participation; employment relations; frames of reference; international HRM; leadership development; trade unions**

Suggested further reading
Bacon (2008): Provides a succinct overview of the management style and management choice literature and its applicability to industrial relations.
Budd & Bhave (2008): This chapter outlines the values, frame of reference and ideologies that influence how employers act in employment relations matters.
Kessler & Purcell (1995): Introduces the distinction between the dimensions of individualism and collectivism in management style.

Purcell (1987): This important early contribution establishes the basic elements of the management style construct and provides a rationale for its importance.

Storey & Bacon (1993): The management style construct is developed further by extending its applications to the domains of industrial relations, work organisation and human resources.

MODELS OF HRM

In contexts for business and management research, a 'model' represents a 'systematic description which maps or represents some state of affairs' (Jankowicz, 2000: 181). By extension, models of HRM represent a scholarly attempt to reduce – *systematically* – complex processes of HRM theory and practice to perceived simplicity. However, and as many scholar-practitioners of HRM point out, there are practical dangers of relying too much on the apparently clear and simple solutions and decision-making paths that models of HRM suggest. Using as an example the so-called 'HRM cycle' model (cf. Fombrun et al., 1984), Torrington et al. (2008: 39) emphasise how such models too often depend 'on a rational strategy formulation rather than on an emergent strategy formulation approach' – in other words, the model appears to assume that all will go to plan. Torrington et al. (2008) go on to suggest that many designs for models rest on 'unitarist' assumptions. In other words, there is a danger of relying too much on the welcome simplicity that models of HRM offer and thereby of underestimating some of the 'specific employee behaviours' (Torrington et al., 2008: 39) that are likely to complicate attempts to interpret and implement such models in contexts for HRM practice. However, models of HRM exist and serve to lighten up many standard texts on HRM theory and practice. This discussion suggests ways in which models of HRM can guide practice and, more importantly here, act as vehicles for professional reflection and **development**.

Working with models of HRM

As a minimum contribution, management models should help HRM researchers and practitioners describe and explain how certain complex management situations might be interpreted. Ideally, reference to models should also inform predictions of how these complex situations might evolve. Interpreted thus, the design of HRM models might support hypothetical attempts to measure the impact of HRM

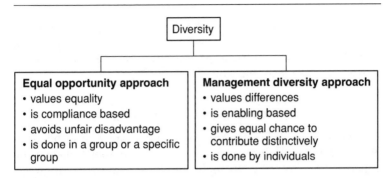

Figure 5 Diversity management. *Source:* adapted from Millmore et al. (2007)

interventions; indeed, this measurement potential of models connects with the origin of the term 'model': Latin *modus*, meaning 'measure'. Echoing Jankowicz (2000), referring to models of HRM facilitates the prediction of how one 'state of affairs' might evolve subject to influences of context. A 'context' represents the semantic space within which to interpret – both universally and particularly – the meaning of a patterned series of connected concepts or symbols, e.g. as represented by words and images. Figure 5 serves to illustrate this effect.

Figure 5, discussed elsewhere in this book under the heading of **diversity management**, clusters various concepts into boxes. It thereby assumes – and guides the reader towards accepting – that these concepts are somehow related and together form some kind of mini-discussion or argument. The argument is driven mainly along the lines that connect between concept clusters and, as a premise, by the concept ('Diversity') that appears to stand as a superordinate concept and thus start this particular argument off – an interpretation that fits the particular context in which this diagram is presented. It is through reference to context that this diagram and its arrangement of elements becomes coherent; and it is this coherence that supports the development of an argument or explanation, thus fulfilling the description, explanation and prediction conditions for HRM and other management models highlighted above. Connecting with the inevitable uncertainty that attempts to predict how the 'state of affairs' illustrated here might evolve, readers are able (if not explicitly invited) to speculate. Given the stable point of reference offered by the model, readers are able to do this collectively and individually – the model thus supports processes of reflection, discussion and learning. For example, one test of the coherence suggested in this particular diagram might be to ask: 'What if the "equal opportunity approach" were set as the superordinate concept and thus a starting point for discussion? What shape and direction might the explanation process take then, and why?'

The cultures of HRM modelling

Echoing Bratton and Gold (2007), working to and with such models presents HRM practitioners and researchers with some coherent and collective sense of 'certainty and control'. As a collective or group-oriented experience, this sense of certainty and control relies on each reader's sense of perception and, by extension, of how information might be communicated in order to achieve some abiding sense of coherence and relevance (cf. McKenna, 2000). However, by invoking notions of in-group identity and, by extension, intra- and inter-group communication, the concept of 'culture' becomes relevant to an understanding of what a particular model appears to be 'saying' to us (cf. Hofstede, 1991). In other words, reference to culture becomes relevant towards understanding the context that appears to afford one or other model its communicative meaning and thus its potential to describe, explain and predict the emergence of a given state of affairs. The following depiction of the **psychological contract** (Figure 6) illustrates this effect.

At face value, this model tells a relatively clear story. A series of HRM concepts are clustered into three distinct boxes, each box connected by an arrow. The causality suggested by these arrows can be interpreted as a theory, thus reinforcing the status of the

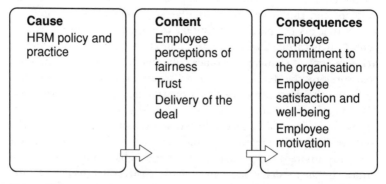

Figure 6 The psychological contract. *Source:* adapted from a reading of Guest and Conway (2002)

psychological contract as a 'theoretical framework' (cf. Conway & Briner, 2007). As a theory, this model should support the generation of various hypothetical statements. These might include:

- HRM policies and practices that are perceived by an employee to be fair will influence that employee's sense of satisfaction and well-being.
- If HRM practitioners are able to persuade employees to trust them during times of economic crisis, employees will commit to the organisation.

Before proceeding with such conceptual and (potentially) empirical investigations, it is as well to examine the culture-specific assumptions upon which such hypothetical statements are based. To illustrate: the model depicted above suggests a left-to-right causality, made explicit by the connecting arrows and the three individual box headings highlighting 'cause' through 'content' (of the contract) to 'consequences'. In terms of assumed 'value-added', an incremental progression through time and place is suggested; for example, from the formulation and implementation of 'HRM policy and practice' through 'trust' to (employee) motivation and (by implication) expectation of reward. Inferring the salience of reward in this way can serve to reconnect with the nominal beginning of the sequence and the concept of (employee) expectation, and so the sequence – or cycle – can continue. This appears to be a coherent interpretation of this particular model and one that appears to connect with our general experience as both employees and as HRM practitioners and researchers: it appeals to our sense of shared culture; it 'speaks our language'. Thus, the causal coherence suggested by this and similar models of HRM appeals to our learned or (echoing Hofstede, 1984) 'pre-programmed' culture-specific expectations.

A closer examination of the causality suggested in the model serves to highlight how embedded these culture-specific expectations are. To illustrate, the model confirms much of what has been developed in the field of social scientific enquiry: it is positivistic in that it suggests a constancy of relationships between events and, relevant to this current discussion, HRM interventions. To illustrate further, the 'delivery of deal' (however defined in practice) appears to derive from some sense of (managed) employee expectation that leads to some sense of commitment (or otherwise) on the part of the employee. Albeit a simplistic interpretation, reading the model thus should support the aforementioned sense of certainty and control among HRM practitioners and researchers. The causal nature of the model is similarly embedded in social scientific enquiry; as, indeed, is the 'rule of three' arrangement depicted in this particular model – an arrangement formalised as a 'law of three' by what many scholars regard as the founding father of social scientific enquiry: Auguste Comte. However, the model as it stands appears so fluidly coherent that HRM practitioners in any one organisation might feel encouraged to apply it narrowly to their own situation and thereby lose sight of other more external and strategic factors (cf. Torrington et al., 2008: 39). With more critical thought, the model does support more strategic scenario analysis and application. For example, what if the larger box around the model were defined as the organisational boundary and the 'delivery of the deal' subject to definition from an imagined future (i.e. potential) employee perspective and in respect to current thinking on **motivation and rewards**?

Conflicting interpretations of models

As discussed elsewhere in this book, invoking culture and the assumptions and beliefs that serve to distinguish one culture from another serves also to invoke cross-cultural dimensions for HRM communication (cf. Mead & Andrews, 2009). This is particularly evident in contexts for **international HRM** (cf. Briscoe et al., 2009). This holds true also for more general considerations of how people's expectations and assumptions might differ in HRM processes of managing diversity. Attempting to work with diverse interpretations of what a model of HRM might mean in reference to over-generalised assumptions of culture-specific homogeneity or convergence emerges in phrases such as 'As we can all see, . . .' or 'obviously, this model shows us how . . .'. The 'obvious' nature of the (arrowed) left-to-right incremental progression through time represented in many process-based models of HRM is, when examined closely, highly contestable: just because members of many Western cultures are socialised into forms of writing and reading that imitate a left-to-right progression does not mean that thinking and expectations of coherence shaped by learning other languages (Arabic, traditional Chinese, Japanese, and so on) need to follow suit. Invoking metaphors can have a similar effect. For example, in the introductory discussion to this book, it was suggested that the so-called 'paradigm shift' from PM to HRM might be questioned on the basis that it represented (merely) putting 'old wine into new bottles' (cf. Armstrong, 1987). This metaphor, though memorable, is an example of culture-specific assumption and, as with many models of HRM, the assumptions of 'certainty and control' such metaphorical statements express are markedly 'Western' in origin (cf. Harry & Jackson, 2007).

Taking this potential for divergent interpretations of the model further allows us to predict that competing ambitions for certainty might well collide, lead to a lack of certainty by one party or other, and thus (potentially) towards a context for interpretation imbued with an expectation of conflict (cf. Avruch, 2004; Griffiths et al., 2002). To illustrate, the psychological contract is well established in studies of industrial relations, **employment relations** and, by extension, HRM theory and practice. However, and as Conway & Briner (2007) remind us in their highly accessible review of research into the psychological contract, up to 80 per cent of this research focuses on perceptions of contract violation or breach. Despite – or, perhaps, because of – the model's apparent conceptual stability and causal familiarity, together with its implicit claim to represent **best practice**, interpretations of this and other HRM models are informed by diversity and disagreement when subject to more multi-perspective questioning.

Learning from models of HRM

Working to expressions or illustrations of best practice is valuable just as working to models of HRM is useful because doing so sets formalised benchmarks against which to measure observed and inferred HRM reality and complexity. As highlighted in the introduction to this book, HRM is an aspect of management activity that all working people have direct experience of: we are all consumers of HRM. Indeed, negative experiences of HRM – such as a perceived breach of the psychological contract – often spur people to learn more about how their experience of employment and career development is or might be structured and so, for future reference, better understood. Examining and interrogating the assumptions that inform the design and discussion of models of HRM creates a potential source of professional learning and **development** – a source that can be sustained by ongoing curiosity and enquiry. As also stated in the introduction to this book, there is no one 'correct' answer in discussions of HRM, and even the concept of best practice in HRM is and remains contentious (cf. Rowley & Poon, 2008). Drawing on traditions of open-minded scientific enquiry, this is as it should be.

KJ

See also: **best practice; cultural and emotional intelligence; diversity management; frames of reference; knowledge management; organisational learning; psychological contract; training and development**

Suggested further reading

Brockman & Brockman (1996): An accessible collection of thought-provoking essays about how we experience social reality and how scientists try to explain this reality to us.

Giddens (2009): An eclectic synthesis of sociological thought and enquiry, including reference to Comte and to a full range of topics relevant to people's experiences of employment.

Rapport & Overing (2000): Another title in the Routledge 'Key Concepts' series that offers a detailed insight into how processes of human thinking and enquiry are shaped and structured.

Saunders et al. (2007): An excellent resource and guide for students embarking on research into business and management.

MOTIVATION AND REWARDS

There have been discussions over the years about whether money can motivate employees to increase their performance. Maslow, Herzberg, and modern critics such as Alfie Kohn (Kohn, 1993) argue either that money does not motivate work performance or that it motivates people to focus on money rather than performance. Most rewards scholars argue that money does in fact motivate performance and that properly designed reward systems will motivate employees to organisationally desirable performance levels.

This section focuses on the intersection between motivation theory and rewards systems. A brief summary of the rewards/relevant parts of selected motivation theories is provided, along with the implications of those theories for rewards systems and, in practice, to the formulation of **compensation strategies**. A summary of major incentive schemes is provided, followed by the relevance of the different motivation theories to each incentive scheme. To make the linkage between motivation theory and rewards more complete, this last section also looks at the relationship between motivation theory and other non-incentive parts of the rewards system.

Motivation theories

Not all motivation theories are included in this review. Coverage is restricted to those theories that purport to explain work-related

Table 8a Motivation theories

Motivation theory	Basic assertions relevant to rewards
Maslow's Hierarchy of Needs (Maslow, 1987)	Money generally considered at physiological or safety/security levels of hierarchy, but may satisfy social/affiliation or esteem/recognition needs for others. Not a great motivator. Requires individual employee motivational analysis and plans.
Herzberg's Two-factor Theory (Herzberg, 2008)	Money is a hygiene, not a motivating factor. Money is a necessary but not sufficient condition for motivation. Data contradict assertions.
Equity Theory (Adams, 1963)	Individual compares outcome/input ratio with that of relevant others. If ratios similar, equity is felt; if ratios dissimilar, individual will seek to correct situation.
Expectancy Theory (Vroom, 1964)	Individual considers probable performance associated with different effort levels, probable rewards associated with different performance levels, liking of different reward sets; then makes effort believed likely to achieve preferred reward set.
Goal-setting Theory (Locke & Latham, 1990)	When people have high, specific, accepted goals they perform better, although they do not necessarily reach their goal.
Reinforcement Theory (Skinner, 1953)	When consequence of a behaviour makes it more likely to be repeated, we say the consequence is reinforcing. Reinforcement immediacy is important. Continuous reinforcement schedules are good for training; variable ratio reinforcement schedules best for sustained behaviour.

motivation and have been traditionally tied to rewards systems. Table 8a provides a summary of these theories.

Maslow's and Herzberg's theories are classified as needs theories; that is, they argue that innate needs drive behaviour. While some have argued that rewards can serve to meet many different needs (e.g. a large bonus might satisfy self-esteem needs), both Maslow and Herzberg argued that money was not motivating in terms of work performance. If in fact rewards could meet all needs, then the theory is not very useful to rewards specialists in designing and implementing rewards systems. Equity theory, expectancy theory and goal-setting

Table 8b Motivation theories

Motivation theory	Implications for rewards systems
Maslow's Hierarchy of Needs	None: money doesn't motivate
Herzberg's Two-factor Theory	None: money doesn't motivate
Equity Theory	The basis for traditional reward systems: job evaluation promotes internal equity, wage surveys promote external equity, merit systems promote individual equity. Organisation needs to specify which inputs are valuable with respect to rewards and make sure employee is aware of all reward outcomes.
Expectancy Theory	Managers need to make sure direct reports understand probable required effort level to reach various performance levels, and probable rewards outcomes of achieving various performance levels. Organisations must make sure rewards outcomes are, in fact, primarily a function of performance levels. Employees need to know the 'rules of the game'.
Goal-setting Theory	Rewards need to be based on performance, not goal achievement. Anyone achieving all their goals probably didn't have stretch goals.
Reinforcement Theory	To be most effective, rewards should be immediate and delivered on a variable ratio schedule.

theory are process theories, that is, they focus on the process whereby workers may be motivated without specifying which need may be satisfied. Reinforcement theory specifies neither need nor process.

More specific implications of motivation theories for rewards systems are shown in Table 8b.

Traditional wage systems (where most of an employee's reward is given in base pay founded on job planning and evaluation and labour market benchmarks, with increases given through merit pay systems) are founded on notions of equity. These systems rarely utilise the findings of expectancy, goal-setting or reinforcement theories. This is one reason that as motivation theory and rewards systems have evolved, newer rewards systems try to make use of the findings of motivational research.

Incentive pay

The newer forms of rewards are usually referred to as *incentive pay*. A summary of the different types of incentive pay is provided in Table 9 (p. 150).

Incentive schemes are generally divided into long- and short-term plans, with one year being the dividing line between the two. All have one thing in common: any reward received is not added to base pay, and must be re-earned every year. When properly designed, all (but the lump-sum bonus) are self-funded; that is, there is no payout unless the metrics driving the reward are achieved.

Motivation and rewards

The relevance of each of the motivation theories described above to incentive schemes and to other parts of the rewards package is shown in Table 10 (p. 151).

A rating of 'high' indicates that most of the motivational conditions proposed by the theory are met. Thus, base pay, merit pay, lump sum bonuses and benefits programmes generally meet the conditions set forth under equity theory. No rewards programme meets the conditions set out by Maslow's Hierarchy of Needs, thus that theory is 'n.a.' or not applicable. Goals-setting theory has only limited application to base pay, thus base pay is marked 'low' in that category. A 'mixed' rating may occur because different kinds of a particular incentive scheme may be high while others are low. Some small-group incentive schemes, for example, might include formal goal-setting procedures while others would not. Other bonuses are marked 'mixed' with respect to equity theory because such programmes rarely apply to all employees, and those not eligible might feel they have valuable inputs not recognised by the programme.

In spite of the comments of critics of incentive rewards, most organisational rewards specialists, along with academic researchers, understand that establishing incentive schemes is a critical part of motivating employees to achieve high individual, group and organisational performance.

CF

See also: **assessment; compensation strategies; cultural and emotional intelligence; diversity management; employee involvement and participation; non-monetary rewards; performance and rewards; psychological contract**

Table 9 Incentive schemes

Short-term incentives

Lump sum bonuses	Identical to merit pay increases except that base pay is not changed. Usually an introductory incentive used in moving employees to other incentive schemes.
Other bonuses	Targeted rewards for specific achievements, e.g. quality increase, accident reduction. When desired achievement level reached, may drop bonus programme or replace with a different target.
Gain sharing	Gains in reduced labour costs per unit produced shared with employee teams responsible. Gains made through working smarter rather than harder. Formula-driven, requiring information sharing and consultative, decision-sharing management style. Acceptable to unions. Primarily used with production workers.
Goal sharing	Extra profits resulting from exceeding standards (e.g. reduced time to market, increased market share) shared with employee group responsible. Primarily used with professional workers.
Small group incentives	Similar to individual bonuses but earned and distributed at the group level.
Profit sharing	Some portion of profits is shared with employees, almost always pro-rated by salary level. An incentive only when there is a cash payout.

Long-term incentives

Stock options	Employee (usually executive) is awarded right to buy some shares at a strike (fixed) price (the market price of shares the date of the set-aside). The employee usually cannot exercise the options for five years. Designed to align interests of the employee with long-range interests of shareholders.
Stock and unit plans	Actual shares awarded to employee but employee restricted from selling for some period and awards are subject to forfeiture under some circumstances. In a performance unit plan the employee is granted 'units' entitling employee to cash payments or equivalent in stock (as valued at time of award) if company achieves predetermined objectives.
Project plans	Some projects have longer than one-year cycle; incentive plan would reward based on overall success of multi-year project, as well as at project milestones.

Table 10 Rewards

Reward schemes	Maslow's Hierarchy of Needs	Herzberg's Two-Factor Theory	Equity Theory	Expectancy Theory	Goal-setting Theory	Reinforce-ment
Base pay	n.a.	n.a.	high	low	low	low
Merit pay	n.a.	n.a.	high	low	low	low
Lump sum bonuses	n.a.	n.a.	high	low	low	low
Other bonuses	n.a.	n.a.	mixed	high	mixed	mixed
Gain sharing	n.a.	n.a.	mixed	mixed	mixed	low
Goal sharing	n.a.	n.a.	mixed	high	high	low
Small group incentives	n.a.	n.a.	mixed	mixed	mixed	low
Profit sharing	n.a.	n.a.	mixed	low	low	low
Stock options	n.a.	n.a.	mixed	mixed	low	low
Stock and unit plans	n.a.	n.a.	mixed	mixed	low	low
Project plans	n.a.	n.a.	mixed	mixed	low	low
Low cost/ no cost	n.a.	n.a.	mixed	mixed	low	high
Benefits	n.a.	n.a.	high	low	low	low

Suggested further reading

Cameron & Pierce (2002): Focuses on the arguments for and against money/ pay as a motivator of job performance.

Kanfer et al. (2008): A detailed study of work motivation past, present and future.

Latham (2007): Contains a review by a leading expert in work motivation of various theories and their implications.

Latham & Pindar (2005): A new millennium perspective on work motivation.

Locke & Latham (1984): A standard study of goal-setting techniques and motivation.

Porter et al. (2003): A standard text that covers motivation theory in detail.

NON-MONETARY REWARDS

Non-monetary rewards are known by many names: recognition awards, low cost/no cost awards, and 'hugs and mugs' are just several of the many titles given to this kind of reward programme. In some cases, money is a part of the reward, but the emphasis is on the recognition received by the employee rather than the nominal amount of money involved. The earliest non-monetary rewards were perquisites or 'perks', i.e. special rewards that were related to job status and which reinforced status differences in the organisation.

The great strength of non-monetary rewards is their immediacy. An award can be given to an employee immediately following the triggering performance, reinforcing the employee's commitment to that level of performance in the future. Similarly, because an integral part of many non-monetary rewards is celebration of the performance and presentation of the reward in front of work groups it strengthens contingencies between **performance and rewards** among other employees.

While non-monetary awards have always existed in organisations, they have typically been arbitrary, capricious, and not integrated in any way with the rest of the rewards system. From an HRM perspective, the change in recent years has been not so much towards an increase in the number of awards or the amount of individual awards. Rather, change has been concentrated on the rationalisation of non-monetary rewards programmes and their integration into the rest of an organisation's rewards system. This discussion focuses on the range of non-monetary rewards that exist in organisations today and the way organisations are attempting to integrate them with other parts of the reward system. Integration is not necessarily a simple issue. Most rewards are designed and administered by the HR department, with input from other (e.g. line-) managers. HR may design most non-monetary rewards. However, implementation and administration is much more in the hands of other managers. Since performance celebration is a critical part of non-monetary rewards, managerial behaviour can make or break the effectiveness of these rewards.

Perquisites

Perquisites – also commonly referred to as 'perks' – include any non-monetary reward that is a function of the job rather than the incumbent. Initially reserved for executive jobs, perquisites include such things as special eating areas, use of the corporate jet for travel (or first-class travel), club memberships, cars (sometimes with driver), larger office space (perhaps in a restricted area, and with lavish furnishings) and unsupervised time. These rewards reinforce the status of the person receiving them. In some countries perquisites were also one way of getting around high marginal income tax rates.

Many organisations have dropped perquisites except for the most senior executives, and argue that some are required for security purposes and others allow the executive to spend more time in productive work. Other organisations have turned some perquisites (especially reserved parking spaces and first-class travel) into performance rewards. Further examples of this approach are discussed elsewhere in this book under the concept entry **executive rewards**.

Perquisites have received considerable criticism from social activists on moral grounds. Similarly, some management theorists argue that they reinforce the status differences between those receiving them and other employees. It is hard for a senior manager to argue that 'we're all in this together' to employees when she has a car and driver, retreats to the executive dining room, and works in an office protected by former Secret Service guards. However, if the culture of the organisation and its workforce strategy are both based on status differences, perquisites are an effective way of emphasising those differences.

Recognition awards

Most incentive programmes are based on plans to reward deserving employees prospectively; recognition awards acknowledge contributions retrospectively. The emphasis in most of these awards is on the psychic rather than the monetary value of the award. Typical recognition programmes include: spot awards – small amounts of cash of up to (for example) US$1,000; achievement medals or trophies; an all-paid night on the town for the employee and a significant other; T-shirts and other logo clothing; electronic or athletic equipment; choices from a merchandise catalogue; gift certificates, travel awards, and so on. Many of these award programmes were first used by sales managers for top performers, and were designed to make the rewards process more distinctive and interesting. Public celebration of the award is also a tradition drawn from sales compensation.

Integrating recognition awards with other compensation programmes means that most recipients of recognition awards would be expected to also receive incentive rewards and more substantial merit increases (on average) than non-recipients. Since most recognition rewards depend on nomination by the employee's manager or peers, it is critical that nominators be trained in the purpose of recognition awards and that favouritism neither occurs, nor is believed to occur.

Psychic pay

Psychic pay also started with sales compensation. The prototype of psychic pay is the Million Dollar Club. Sales personnel whose sales exceeded US$1 million were publicly recognised, sometimes in advertisements placed in trade journals.

Other forms of psychic pay include employee-of-the-month programmes, special parking privileges, letters of commendation from management, and stories and features in company newsletters. A practice which has had mixed results – depending on the quality and purposes of the executive doing it – is 'lunch with the CEO' or other senior executive. In these programmes, managers nominate high performing individual contributors to have lunch with the CEO or other senior manager. During lunch the CEO talks about the company's business plan, and then asks each employee what changes they believe need to occur in his/her unit to make it possible to achieve the plan. The CEO then follows up on each suggestion and either makes the change or informs the employee why the change is not feasible. Other processes of psychic rewards are illustrated elsewhere in this book under the heading of the **psychological contract**.

Worksite policies

Worksite policies were not seen as a part of the rewards system until recently. Many of the innovations noted here started in technology companies where employees worked relatively long hours. The emphasis on worksite policies as a part of the reward system has become more common among organisations whose competitive advantage lies in the intellectual power of their employees. Consequently, high technology companies, companies offering professional services and other similar organisations are much more likely to use worksite rewards than traditional manufacturers. Break rooms with game tables, computer games, and other forms of recreation were among the first of these programmes, followed then by casual dress codes, gardens and break areas together with an allowance and provision to bring children to work (occasionally) or animals to work (frequently). More employees were given their choice of office furnishings. Most of these companies threw out the time clock (if they ever had them) and focused on achievement rather than physical presence at the worksite.

The rationale behind worksite policies is that employees spend so much time at work that it is appropriate to reward them for this by making the workplace a pleasant place to be, and to provide relief from work settings within the office. Organisations located in office parks or isolated areas frequently now offer support services: dry cleaners, laundries, post offices, gift shops, massage tables, barbers and hairdressers, banks and any other services that save employees having to leave for long periods to conduct personal business. Some organisations even arrange for company dining rooms to sell takeout food in the afternoon so an employee can take an entire dinner home without having to stop anywhere on the way home and later cook.

Like benefits, worksite policies are not related to performance. Rather, they are membership rewards, available to all employees regardless of performance level.

Family friendly policies

In line with the type of worksite policies noted above, family friendly policies apply to all employees. The goal is to have the entire family of the employee connect with the employer, and thus render employee **retention** more likely.

Frequent open houses for relatives of employees are one form of family friendly policy. Flexible work hours and temporary or permanent part-time work or job sharing is another. Other initiatives supported by many organisations include support of educational and charitable concerns, often by matching employee gifts; child and elder care referral together with other community information service referrals; and, last but not least, general support of work–life balance expectations.

CF

See also: **assessment; best practice; compensation strategies; diversity management; employee involvement and participation; motivation and rewards; performance and rewards; psychological contract; retention**

Suggested further reading

Barton (2006): Focuses on low-cost recognition programmes and their integration with other rewards.

Gostick & Elton (2007): Develops a popular approach, with many examples of how managers can use recognition programmes.

Hay (2004): Outlines how to develop a recognition programme.

Hundley et al. (2007): Explores reward and recognition approaches to building a committed and engaged workforce.

Jensen et al. (2007): Offers a popular treatment of all rewards, but focuses on things managers can do rather than broad recognition programmes.

McAdams (1996): Remains the definitive book on developing rewards plans emphasising recognition programmes.

ORGANISATIONAL EXIT

People leave or 'exit' organisations – and particular positions within particular organisations – for a variety of reasons. These include reasons of transfer, promotion, retirement, redundancy, maternity/paternity leave, ill health, vacation, extended or repeated absenteeism, sacking, quitting (e.g. as a stage in an individual's career development), and death. Key variables here include the nature of the exit, the length of the exit (it might be temporary or permanent) and the HRM response to the exit, given that all these forms of exit need to be managed in some way. For example, employers might choose to conduct exit interviews in order to learn why certain people are leaving at a particular time and at a particular juncture in the employment market. Unfortunately, it seems that many employers and their agents lack the confidence or competence to conduct such interviews in a constructive manner and thus miss an opportunity to add to **organisational learning**. Similarly, employers might choose to present the fact of employee exit as planned or unplanned, expected or unexpected, and 'dress up' the fact to pacify, for example, key shareholders with reference to terms (or euphemisms) such as 'restructuring', 'downsizing', or the 'redeployment' of human resources.

For no matter how well the organisation works at effective **performance management** and targeted staff **retention** there comes a time in each employment relationship when the organisation and employee go their separate ways. The reasons might be natural – such as death in service or reaching a statutory retirement age if one exists. Or the reasons could be organisationally driven – such as a business downturn or relocation leading to a lay-off of employees. Or a change in personal circumstances might lead to a departure such as winning the lottery or a desire to give up work to care for family members. More usually the ending is due to the employee finding a different job that suits them better. For some it is a lack of perform-ance that leads to disciplinary action and loss of employment.

Means of ending the relationship

No matter what the cause of the end of the employment relation-ship the way the separation is handled has an important impact on **resourcing** – a concept discussed separately elsewhere in this book. If the end is predictable such as for those on fixed-term **contracts of employment** (which are now severely limited by employment protection legislation) and retirement (in the UK age-related dis-crimination legislation has led to most retirement schemes having a flexible retirement age) then these should be accounted for in **human resource planning** processes. Even if it is not possible to predict individual retirements it is likely that demographic trends can be used to construct plans so that if it is known that 50 per cent of the senior or specialist staff will reach 60 years of age in the next five years replacement resources should be put in place in plenty of time.

If the person is leaving for a job which suits them better, or other voluntary reason, a period of notice will have to be served during which time the employee's thoughts will be on the new job or new situation so will be unlikely to be motivated to work at their best – although many employees will want to ensure that they leave with a tidy workstation in which all tasks have been completed or handed over to their successor. Employees in sensitive positions or with access to key resources (such as access to sensitive data from HRM **information systems**) will be asked to leave immediately and all passwords and access facilities will be withdrawn. If the person is leaving at the employer's request (dismissed for a cause or made redundant) it is even more likely that the employee will not be making the required effort to undertake needed work at the required standards so in many cases those leavers will be asked to go immediately – although care must be taken in redundancy sit-uations that sending home straight away does not breach proper **legal aspects** of exit (cf. acas.org.uk). In all cases (except where an employee is being dismissed without notice for a serious offence) the period of notice included in the employment contract must be served or the employee paid for the notice period.

Impact on morale

It is not just in planning for retirees and voluntary leavers that the organisation will be judged but in the way it handles the more difficult situations. If employees are treated as commodities (or as resources and not as people!) to be bought and sold, then the recruits will be focused upon money and benefits, not on loyalty and commitment. If the employer makes efforts to communicate business plans and progress to their fulfilment then the employees, and potential recruits, will be more committed and their work efforts more directed at helping their employers even in business downturns.

Organisations which dismiss employees in ways which are perceived to be unfair, in terms of the application of disciplinary systems, display of racial, religious or other discriminatory activities, bullying or victimisation will gain a reputation which will demoralise existing staff and discourage potential applicants. It is much harder to gain a good image as an employer than it is to destroy a good image. With media attention on employers the reputation for dismissing staff unfairly can impact on wider business activities and customers may shun the organisation's products or services.

Redundancy programmes occur occasionally in almost all organisations as a result of rapid changes in the business and social environments. There are statutory regulations for handling redundancies (cf. ACAS, 2003). But just adhering to the letter and not the spirit of the legislation will mark out the employer who cares little for staff from those that do care to maintain a co-operative and mutually respectful relationship.

Trying to retain employees

Retention represents an attempt to manage exit to the organisation's strategic benefit. Where the employee has personal reasons for leaving, if the employer has attempted to meet the change in the individual's circumstances such as more flexible hours, sabbaticals or other extended periods of time off work, or sought job-sharing, the other employees and potential candidates will think this is a generous employer who will try to treat me well if I need help. Even where the reason for leaving is to get a better job it is worthwhile treating the departing staff well in the hope that they will speak well of their former employer to others who might want to work there. Or in a future job the departing employee might be a customer or supplier whose good will could be of great value to the organisation.

In all cases some attempt should be made to understand, and record the reasons for the departure to help choose suitable candidates to replace them or to feed back relevant information into the **human resource planning** and **resourcing** processes; for example, graduates find a particular well paying but highly demanding job good to be in for two to three years but not one which they want to hold for more than three years. So that for two- to three-year typical length of service could be used to drive the recruitment and graduate training programmes. The usual way of gaining the departing employee's views is through an exit interview or an online survey. In the case of an exit interview, interviewers other than the line manager to whom the departing employee reported should be selected – one reason being that it was perhaps this supervisor who caused the person to leave (cf. MacAfee, 2007). Most employees will be reluctant to give negative reasons for departing, hence the preference for confidential and anonymous reports either on paper or on an intranet system.

Community of employees

Assuming that those employees who commit for a longer or shorter time to entities defined as organisations or teams, contribute also to some sense of collective identity or community, the exit of individuals or groups from these entities raises the profile of the 'community'. This sense of community can be expressed in various ways. To illustrate, sports teams might talk about 'team spirit'. In other contexts the community feel might take on mythical proportions as in the *unmei kyodotai* (community of faith) concept long held to be typical – and, latterly, a significant constraint to innovation and change – for HRM in large Japanese organisations (Jackson & Debroux, 2009).

In whatever defined community context the exit occurs, the ending of one or many employment relationships will have some impact on those left behind. Those left may have a greater workload, may start to think of moving themselves, may want higher pay and benefits to stay or may have a reduced (or even a higher) level of morale. Some may see more positive prospects for individual **motivation and rewards** such as promotion. Just as an organisation is continually changing, the employees of the organisation will have changing needs and wants which they will expect the employer to contribute to. Most of these wants and needs will be linked to the community aspect of being workers within the organisation but some of these will be linked to the pay and benefits which they expect the employer to provide.

KJ & WH

See also: **best practice; career development; contracts of employment; grievance and disciplinary procedures; human resource planning; labour markets; legal aspects; psychological contract; resourcing; retention**

Suggested further reading

Dolan et al. (2000): A reappraisal of 'downsizing' processes that emphasise the securing of HRM/organisational value.

Gomez et al. (2002): A useful discussion emphasising mandatory retirement as a process that can be managed rather than as an event that HRM practitioners (merely) react to.

Incomes Data Services (2008): A practical insight into retention strategies and processes.

Rankin (2008): A UK perspective on trends and costs generated by staff turnover.

Taylor (2002): A 'how to' guide to staff retention.

Taylor (2006): A top-down perspective on 'keeping your employees happy'.

ORGANISATIONAL LEARNING

Traditionally, the concept of learning was applied to individuals in different settings (e.g. school). More recently, learning has become more organisational-related. Intense global competition and technological advances, as well as a growing knowledge-based economy, have all pressurised organisations to try to respond quickly to changing environments. Organisations need to become good at learning and managing knowledge to sustain their competitiveness. This has changed the focus of learning from a mechanism for achieving individual aspirations to a mechanism for creating organisational values. In other words, the organisation does not only facilitate learning for individual employees, but it is also a learner. The development of a capacity to transfer knowledge across the organisation, to share expertise and information combined with an emphasis on continuous adaptation, all lead to the emergence of organisational learning (OL).

From learning to a learning organisation

Knowles (1990) identifies the defining characteristic of learning as change, by either acquiring something new or modifying something that already exists. The change must be long lasting to ensure learning has really occurred. The focus of learning can include behaviour, cognition, affect, or any combination of the three. Learning outcomes can be skill based, cognitive, or affective. Argyris and Schön (1978) distinguish between single-loop learning and double-loop learning, which relates to Bateson's (1972) concepts of first-order and second-order learning. Single-loop learning or first-order learning occurs when errors are detected and corrected without altering the organisation's present policies. Double-loop learning or second-order learning occurs when, in addition to detecting and correction of errors, the organisation is involved in the questioning and modification of existing norms, procedures, policies and objectives.

Senge (2006) uses this concept and creates a management tool called the 'learning organisation', which is a set of principles of associated techniques applicable to the management of organisations. A learning organisation is one where people continually expand their capacity to create the results they truly desire, where new expansive patterns of thinking are nurtured, where collective aspiration is set free, and where people are continually learning how to learn together. Pedler et al. (1997: 3) concur with the view and suggest that a learning organisation can 'facilitate the learning of all members and consciously transform itself and its context'. Sharing knowledge, experience and ideas become a habit in a learning organisation. In a nutshell, all organisations learn, whether they consciously choose to or not – it is a fundamental requirement for their sustained existence (Kim, 1993).

The learning organisation is an instrument for connecting learning and **knowledge management** so as to enhance and maximise OL. According to Marquardt (2002), the most important core element of the learning organisation is the learning itself as it has the power to change people's perceptions, behaviours and mental methods. This, then, facilitates, encourages and maximises learning at individual, team and organisational levels. HRM practices can be the primary tools to facilitate learning. HRM practices, through **training and development**, can be considered as the first step to build organisational learning capabilities. Investments in **training and development** are likely to have a positive impact in developing the skills and knowledge of people. These learning programmes can help employees learn and recognise specific contexts and prepare them for future changes (D'Netto & Sohal, 1999). When people have the ability to learn within an organisational setting, this will in turn enable organisations to adapt more quickly to environmental changes than their competitors (Hodgkinson, 2000).

Various perspectives of OL

OL has been increasingly recognised as a critical factor for an organisation's ability to create ongoing economic value and to maintain competitive advantage (e.g. Garvin, 1993; Senge, 2006). The OL process consists of the way people learn and work together to overcome changes and leads to better knowledge and performance improvement. It involves experimentation, observation, analysis, willingness to examine both successes and failures, and knowledge sharing among individuals (Watkins & Marsick, 1993). OL is also a human process involving individual willingness and social interaction to detect and correct the errors for continuous improvement. Consistent with the knowledge management (KM) literature, knowledge can be codified, stored and shared. When the knowledge transfer occurs, organisational knowledge is then created. OL becomes part of KM procedures to process, interpret and improve representation of reality through knowledge.

How does the OL process occur? There are lots of debates in the literature about learning in an organisation. According to the sociocultural perspective, learning is always embedded in local organisational cultures, norms and values that influence activities and OL is a highly contested concept embedded in power relations within organisations (Contu & Willmott, 2003). Nevertheless, cognitivist theory assumes individuals as processors of information. Given limited capacity to process information, individuals rely on representations of an outer environment to learn. Learning takes place through a negative feedback mechanism of adaptation through trial and error. Apart from these views, the behavioural perspective supports the view that organisations become more efficient at doing something by repeatedly doing it. The problem is that organisations can become constrained by their own experience. A more recent practice-based view suggests that knowledge and know-how are shared through activities where individuals tell and show how certain operations are carried out in the best way. OL is always examined in terms of being based on practical undertakings and standard operating procedures (Gherardi, 2000). These various perspectives of OL are useful in that they encourage organisations to pay attention to different aspects of OL. If either of these views is adopted in isolation, the full picture of OL cannot be seen.

According to Senge (2006), the practices of OL can be expressed through five lifelong OL disciplines. A discipline is a development path for acquiring certain skills and competencies. These five disciplines are:

1 *Personal mastery* is described as learning how to generate and sustain creative tension. It continually expands one's ability to create the results in life one truly seeks.
2 *Mental models* are illustrated as deeply ingrained assumptions, generalisations, or even pictures and images that influence how people understand the world and how they take action.
3 *Shared vision* is described as the capacity to hold a shared vision of the future of 'what we seek to create'.
4 *Team learning* is vital because working together to gain insights from many team members can take innovative and co-ordinated action and engage in dialogue.
5 *System thinking* is the discipline that integrates the first four disciplines and fuses them into a coherent body of theories and practices to enable collaborative interactions among organisation employees.

It is acknowledged, however, that there exists a growing literature that raises some issues regarding the OL concept. This is illustrated by the fact that organisations are a collection of people who each has a unique learning style and motivation to understand and plan for his or her interactions. Some other studies (O'Connor, 1997) show that there are at least 32 different learning styles and hence, not all the people would concur in the same learning perspective.

Electronic learning (e-learning)

The widespread availability of the internet has revolutionised the way organisations train their employees, transfer knowledge, and hence promote learning. The term 'technology' usually refers to the development of hardware; when using technologies for HRD, they are often referred to as e-learning. Today, technology makes it possible to facilitate traditional training tools, combine learning methods and deliver them as an integrated learning system that combines computer-based quizzes, video, interactive simulations, among others (Derouin et al., 2004). E-learning usually involves the use of the internet or an organisational intranet to conduct training online.

The role of e-learning in OL can be viewed in many ways. First, e-learning enables more employees to access training in a convenient manner. This is likely to facilitate organisation knowledge transfer and sharing, even to those beyond the formal boundaries of the organisation at relatively low cost. Second, e-learning systems have the potential for speeding up communications within large corporations, ensuring consistency of presentation and allowing flexibility in delivery, pace and distribution of learning. While e-learning is good for communicating facts, areas of complexity and feedback might be better left to human trainers (Angel, 2000) through traditional instructor-led training, or e-learners may be unable to sustain their momentum and motivation. Recently, organisations have attempted to capitalise on the benefits of both e-learning and traditional instructor-led training by creating training programmes that involve a combination of both classroom- and computer-based training techniques. In these programmes, learners are able to interact in classroom settings while working on training tasks at any time and at any place via e-learning methods.

No matter what type of organisational learning methods are adopted, certain critical questions have to be answered. Is OL a solution to enhance people skills and hence improve organisation performance? Is there sufficient top management support and funding to develop and implement the OL process? Are current HRD methods adequately meeting OL needs? Are potential learners geographically separated and hence travel time and costs are concerns?

IP & CR

See also: **cultural and emotional intelligence; development; employee involvement and participation; information systems; knowledge management; leadership development; models of HRM; teams; training and development**

Suggested further reading
Chawla & Renesch (2006): Contains essays about some key ideas of an emerging new management paradigm and captures the depth, breadth, vision and challenges inherent in modern organisations.
Easterby-Smith et al. (1999): Provides a synthesis of the debates surrounding two different concepts of OL and learning organisation. It provides

an integrated framework of concepts and theories that draw in current insights from management cognition, theories of knowledge and learning, as well as work psychology.

Yoo et al. (2008): Covers important relevant aspects of OL across Asian contexts.

OUTSOURCING

Many activities are currently being outsourced all over the world. In services, production and consulting, outsourcing is growing dramatically. Business process outsourcing (BPO), for example, was predicted to yield over US$50 billion in revenues worldwide by the end of 2004 (Dearlove, 2003). Evidence from professional and practitioner publications indicates that HRM outsourcing has increased substantially over the last decade (Woodall et al., 2000). However, the academic literature on outsourcing the HR function is almost non-existent (Lilly et al., 2005). Few academic researchers have investigated empirically how decisions on outsourcing are made, the manner in which these decisions are implemented, how effective HR outsourcing is, and so forth. This concept entry defines HRM outsourcing, outlines its advantages and disadvantages, the extent to which organisations might trust HRM outsourcing, and aspects of the process they should try to control.

There are many definitions of outsourcing. One recent study defined it as a process in which a company contracts with a vendor and rents its skills, knowledge, technology, service and HR for an agreed-upon price and period to perform functions the client no longer wants to do (Adler, 2003). Information technology and management information systems led the way in outsourcing, but recently outsourcing has been expanded to other operations. Outsourcing is now of major importance in the HRM area; it has come to the foreground as the role of HRM in the contemporary business environment has gained particular emphasis. HRM is the second most likely corporate business function to be outsourced, according to a study by the American Management Association (*HRM Focus*, 1997). Outsourcing activities initially encompassed only small segments of HRM such as payroll functions (Adler, 2003), but has gradually grown to encompass many human HR functions (Lever, 1997).

Advantages and disadvantages of HRM outsourcing

HRM outsourcing has received considerable attention from companies and many articles have investigated its different aspects, such as managerial motivation, company performance, HRM business processes, service providers and how outsourcing affects organisations. Lever (1997), for example, identifies four stages of outsourcing: discovery, negotiation, transition and **assessment.** Cooke (2004) cites the growing complexity of the **legal aspects** of the environment, technology, and organisational changes as the main factors conducive to the decision to outsource. Adler (2003) adds to this list, with intense competition, industry changes, globalisation, restructuring and downsizing. Additionally, outsourcing is mandated quite often by the need for specific expertise, a new developmental stage of organisational HRM that has exceeded the firm's existing capacity, advances in HR **information systems** (HRIS), cost savings (Babcock, 2004) and increased risk exposure (Greer et al., 1999).

Among the advantages of HRM outsourcing are decreased costs, a better focus on HRM issues directly tied to the company's success, and higher quality customer service (Greer et al., 1999). HRM outsourcing can be an important value-added activity when combined with effective restructuring. Marinaccio (1994), for example, claims that HRM outsourcing along with improved engineering processes may increase the efficiency of business processes while maintaining product quality. In Gainey et al.'s (2002) study, companies reported that they outsourced approximately 30 per cent of their HRM training functions closely connected to core capabilities, and in most cases this outsourcing led to improved performance as well as improved **training and development** design. Greer et al. (1999), however, asserted that **employment relations** and **performance management** should not be outsourced at all, unlike some related functions, such as payroll administration and benefits, which are sometimes outsourced simultaneously as a bundle. The value-added activity that HRM outsourcing brings should ultimately enhance strategic capabilities and benefit the firm's performance with respect to maximising returns, gaining a competitive edge, managing market risks and strengthening internal capabilities, it is argued (Lever, 1997).

However, HRM outsourcing has pitfalls that should not be ignored, including factors such as high transaction costs, potential lower service quality and loss of control over outsourced processes. Therefore, a careful analysis is always required to determine the wisdom of outsourcing. For instance, Brenner (1996) believes that

HRM functions are no longer viewed as a core value-adding corporate component, but rather as a process that can be measured on the same scale as other business processes and, consequently, changed to become merely more efficient. The HRM department may risk losing the human element of the HRM function and thus downgrading the value of activities of the HRM generalist. In this event outsourcing becomes a dilemma between strategic value and cost savings. Outsourcing of HRM may be directly aligned with core strategic competencies for a positive impact on the company's performance, yet not lead to an effective HRM system overall (Brian & Gerhart, 1996). Outsourcing can also fail due to either managerial unwillingness to scrutinise the exact need for outsourcing or excessive control of the outsourcing implementation process (Quinn, 1999).

HRM outsourcing, therefore, can fail for several reasons: high costs and an unforeseen need of additional resources (Lawler et al., 2003), lack of a proactive educational approach on the vendor's part, incompatibility of vendor and client cultures, contract ambiguity, technological incompatibilities (Laabs, 1998) and lack of trust between the vendor and HRM customers (Hammond, 2002). Furthermore, heavy reliance on an outsourcing vendor may lead to a loss of internal expertise, skills and strategic competitive advantage by the customer organisation (Adler, 2003; Ulrich, 1996).

Reasons for HRM outsourcing

There are a number of reasons, at both strategic and operational level, why firms may want to outsource HR activities (Greer et al., 1999). First, demands for increased productivity, profitability, and growth have forced organisations to examine their internal HR processes, resulting in a move towards strategic outsourcing services and away from discrete services. HRM outsourcing decisions are frequently a response to an overwhelming demand for reduced costs for HR services. Second, outsourcing HRM is seen as a way of 'liberating' HR professionals within the client organisation to perform the more consultative and strategic role of designing and implementing programmes aimed at retaining the workforce and enhancing its performance. Third, outsourcing HRM also is seen as an effective way to bypass organisational politics and improve efficiency.

In short, the main reasons for outsourcing HRM appear to be fairly consistent. Typical reasons include seeking specialist services and expertise, cost reduction, and enabling HR specialists to take on a more strategic role. In general, most commentators are convinced that outsourcing HRM is seen not only as a cost-cutting exercise but also as a strategic tool.

Types of HR activity to be outsourced

The major issue in HRM outsourcing is to decide what types of HR activities should be outsourced. In making this decision, organisations need to distinguish 'core' and 'non-core' HR activities. Finn (1999) notes that the former includes top-level strategy, HR policies and line management responsibilities (e.g. appraisal and discipline), while the latter include specialist activities (e.g. **recruitment** and outplacement), routine personnel administration (e.g. payroll and pensions) and professional HR advice (e.g. legal advice related to employment regulations). Ulrich (1996) suggests that core activities are transformational work that creates unique value for employees, customers, and investors. Non-core activities would be transactional work that is routine and standard and can be easily duplicated and replicated.

Hall and Torrington (1998) found that management **training and development**, **recruitment** and **selection**, outplacement, **health and safety**, quality initiatives, job evaluation and **compensation strategies** and systems were the likely HR activities to be outsourced, either because they were considered non-core or because the organisation lacked the expertise to handle them internally. The Human Resource Outsourcing Survey Report by the Society of HRM (2004), found that HR functions that are entirely outsourced are generally background checking, employee assistance/counselling, and flexible spending account (FSA) administration. The functions that are partially outsourced include administration of health care benefits, **pension and other benefits**, and payroll.

Trends in HRM outsourcing

This survey conducted by the Society of HRM (2004), in which over 2,000 members participated, concluded that the HRM outsourcing trend is presently proving useful, practised to an increasing extent by companies with large workforces, and more likely to be utilised in the future by larger organisations than by smaller ones. Larger organisations have the additional advantage of having a sufficient resource pool to afford multiple outsourcing, so they can enjoy certain economies of scale. However, smaller companies appear to experience fewer negative outcomes from outsourcing.

Apart from cost concerns, however, HRM outsourcing could also trigger major changes in the future role of HRM managers, substantially altering the very essence of the profession. Cost savings is the primary concern when companies consider outsourcing with international offshore opportunities that move operations and functions across borders. Nevertheless, when HRM functions require a high degree of specialisation, they may resist outsourcing. The following were among the major findings from the Society of HRM research study (2004).

- About 60 per cent of organisations use outsourcing for at least one HRM function.
- One-third of US companies do not outsource.
- Over half of the respondents partially outsource one or more HRM function.
- Areas of most frequent outsourcing use are background checks (49 per cent), employee assistance programmes (47 per cent), and administration of flexible spending accounts (43 per cent).
- HRM areas cited as most frequently outsourced, at least partially, are administration of health care benefits (36 per cent), pension benefits (36 per cent) and payroll (35 per cent).
- The most frequently mentioned reasons for outsourcing are reducing operating costs (56 per cent) and controlling for legal risks by improving compliance (55 per cent).
- Most of the respondents (64 per cent) believed that the level of outsourcing HRM functions will stay the same in the next five years; more than one-third (32 per cent) thought it will increase, and only 4 per cent believed that outsourcing will decrease in the future.

Monitoring and measuring HRM outsourcing

The effectiveness of HRM outsourcing as a management strategy has rarely been explored, especially with work that involves in-depth, firm-specific knowledge and great autonomy. In certain HR activities it is often difficult to specify the requirement in a manner that leads to observable and verifiable outcomes (Domberger, 1998). Effective HRM outsourcing requires enormous resources and expertise from an in-house monitoring team.

One danger with outsourcing HRM is that the service provider may have a vested interest in standardising all parts of its service in order to achieve economies of scale across clients. Standardisation may lead to a detrimental loss of the client company's unique organisational characteristics. In addition, many problems may arise from a mismatch in culture between the host operation and the supplier (Pickard, 1998).

Ulrich (1998) argues that outsourcing transactional HR activities that are heavily reliant on expensive IT systems frees internal HR professionals to engage in strategic decision-making. However, this result cannot be easily achieved. Any attempt to develop HR **information systems** would face many operational problems which in-house HR must control. HRM outsourcing should also be used in conjunction with an internal HR team that focuses on core competencies to produce solutions in partnership with an external HR service provider. HR departments are being challenged to change their bureaucratic culture, to be more customer-focused and to deliver value-added services.

QW & CR

See also: **contracts of employment; employee involvement and participation; human resource planning; information systems; knowledge management; organisational learning; strategic HRM**

Suggested further reading
Hunter & Saunders (2007): Provides updated solutions and key processes.
Millmore et al. (2007): Discusses current issues and future directions in HRM outsourcing.

PENSIONS AND OTHER BENEFITS

Benefits differ from other compensation or rewards programmes because of their varying nature across countries. In the United States the two most expensive parts of the benefits package are pensions (and other capital building programmes) and health care. In contrast, many other countries (such as the UK and Canada) have public pension programmes and some version of public health insurance. Thus, benefits issues in the United States differ significantly from those in other comparable national contexts for HRM.

To some extent, there are similarities in relation to the end impact on US-based organisations with employer provided pensions and health care and on organisations in countries with government supplied pensions and health care, or the many permutations of these two situations. In the US, the organisation bears direct expenses as servicing benefit commitments to aged employee populations increase; in countries with government supplied pensions and health care, an aging population requires higher tax contributions to support government obligations.

In both cases the solution includes having employees work longer – thus reducing the length of time pensions must cover – and encouraging healthier lifestyles, so that health care expenses are reduced. Other measures include some form of rationing of healthcare, either by reduced coverage, increased co-insurance and co-payments, or limiting the availability of health care resources. Similarly, benefits frequently receive favourable tax treatment by governments in the United States and elsewhere – the aim being to encourage organisations to take on the responsibility for socially desirable programmes.

Regardless of the mix of benefits offered by organisations, employers and HRM professionals worldwide face many of the same questions. These include the following:

- Why offer benefits at all? Why not just offer higher wages and let employees buy the services they want?
- Should there be differentiation among job families in benefits types and levels offered?
- Should the organisation commit to defined levels of service or commit to some contribution level for benefits?
- To what extent should the risk generated by any benefit provision be borne by the employer or the employee?
- Can benefits be strategic in the same way other parts of the reward package are?

In effect, all benefits are biased towards one group or another. Paid time off for new parents does not benefit those who have no children or who have older children; allowing employees time off to go to children's soccer games not only fails to benefit the childless. It also penalises them, as they are frequently expected to fill in for those using family-friendly benefits.

Further globally relevant questions include:

- As cash compensation becomes more performance driven, should benefits become so as well?
- Benefits have been shown to be a factor in employee attraction and retention considerations; can they be a factor in performance decisions as well?

Against this background, this discussion will first look briefly at a typology of benefits offered, and then focus on the type of questions listed above.

Benefit types

Benefits programmes are typically divided into five categories: retirement and other capital accumulation programmes, income protection programmes, medical and other health benefits, paid time off, and services and other miscellaneous benefits. Table 11 shows these benefits and gives typical examples of each.

In many cases company benefit plans have grown in bits and pieces, with little thought given to overall cost or how they interact with other parts of the rewards system. Consider, for example, paid time off. Given a 40-hour working week, there are 280 working days per year in the United States. According to figures provided by the US-based Employee Benefit Research Institute (EBRI, 2005), vacation time for employees with service of 10 or more years ranges from 10 to 20 days per year, and paid holidays range from nine to 11. Even excluding all the other forms of paid time off, employees are given between 24 and 31 days of paid time off, or 192 to 248 hours. This amounts to between roughly 9 per cent and 12 per cent of payroll that goes to paid time off. Few managers are concerned with paid time off, perhaps because it is not an out of pocket expense. However, it does add to the total cost of labour by requiring more employees than would be the case with lower levels of paid time off. Every benefit has costs associated with it, and too many organisations have not thought carefully about those costs when expanding old benefits or offering new ones. Further thought on these issues is offered elsewhere in this book under the concept entry **valuing work**.

As a minimum HRM strategy, employers could offer only those benefits mandated by government and offer higher wages to employees. This is unlikely to occur, since most organisations and employers compete for labour. Those that offer benefit packages will probably find it easier to attract and retain staff. Bulk purchasing from among competing benefits providers allows employers to offer more benefits and higher levels of benefits than an individual employee could purchase with the same amount of money. Furthermore, some employers feel a moral obligation to offer benefits even when not required to by law. For while labour economists argue that employers look at the labour bill and pay lower wages when paying higher benefits, evidence from private sector surveys suggest that employers who pay

Table 11 Examples of benefits types

Benefits type	Examples
Retirement and other capital accumulation programmes	Obligatory government programmes Individual savings programmes Company pension plans
Income protection programmes	Workers' compensation Unemployment insurance Disability coverage Life insurance
Medical and other health benefits	Hospitalisation/medical care Surgery and major medical Health management organisations (HMOs), preferred provider organisations (PPOs), managed care Long-term care Dental care Prescription drugs Vision care Hearing care
Paid time off	Vacation Holidays Personal days Special purpose days (jury duty, bereavement) Family leave Sabbaticals Rest periods Community service Paid time off banking
Services and miscellaneous	Dependent care (child care, elder care) Family leave programmes Employee assistance programmes Legal services Financial advisory services Property and liability insurance buying co-ops Paid or subsidised meals Discount on organisation's products, services Parking Gymnasium and other health/recreation facilities

high wages also have larger and better benefits packages. American employers, at least, see benefits as a supplement to – rather than a substitute for – wages.

Differentiation

In practice, reference to job family or hierarchical level within the organisation does generally not differentiate benefits packages. In the United States this is due to **discrimination** regulations that deny tax-favoured status to benefits that are offered only to more highly paid employees or are utilised by more highly paid employees. There are specific non-qualified (i.e. for favourable tax treatment) benefits available only to executives. It is easiest to have the basic benefits package open to all. One exception is benefits packages negotiated with **trade unions**; these may be restricted to the **collective bargaining** unit, although an equivalent benefit may be given to non-bargaining unit employees.

Trends in benefit planning

Initially most benefits were given to employees as a level of service. These defined benefits programmes specified what benefit the employee would receive rather than cost to the employer. Because of the increasing costs of some benefits, and especially the increasing costs of medical or health care, US employers have moved towards defined contribution benefit programmes, where the employer commits to spending a defined contribution level. If costs rise faster than the employer can afford, the employee is faced with choices between increasing his/her contributions to the benefit, accepting a lower level of service, or (most usually) both. This trend has also supported the growth of flexible benefits plans, where the organisation commits to a specific total contribution for an employee, but allows the employee some choice in the benefits received. Such plans typically have some core set of benefits the employee must take but then allow the employee to choose higher levels of those benefits or additional benefit categories. These programmes usually allow the employee to 'buy' higher quality levels or more amounts of benefits by increased payroll deductions.

With the move towards defined contribution benefits plans, a shift in risk and reward has occurred. As an example: when organisations offered defined benefit pension programmes, the organisation committed itself to offering a certain pension level to each employee.

When the pension fund made investments, the organisation was obligated for specific pension payments whether those investments lost value or increased by large multiples. All the risk (and reward) went to the organisation. Under a defined contribution pension plan, the organisation makes some specified contribution to the plan of each individual employee. All the investment risk lies with the employee, and employees who invest wisely (and luckily) will end up with a much larger amount of capital to fund retirement. Similarly, the poor investor may end up with very little funding to finance retirement.

A key question facing benefits managers is whether benefits can become strategic; that is, used to further the strategic objectives of the organisation. There are two ways employers have been trying to make benefits more strategic. One way is to make sure that the benefits available are attractive to high potential applicants and high-performing employees. A second way is developing a benefit specifically to attract a desired set of employees. Day-care centres and tuition/**training and development** reimbursement programmes have been developed specifically for these purposes. These programmes are not restricted to target applicants and employees. However, they may appeal to them more than to other employees, thus impacting attraction and retention in desirable ways. This approach harnesses the bias in most benefits programmes, but does so in a defensible way.

Organisations have flirted with making benefits performance driven, but have not been very successful. Perhaps because most benefits are future- (pensions) or need- (health care) oriented it is difficult to make a linkage between **performance and rewards** and performance and benefits.

CF

Suggested further reading
Benefits and Compensation Glossary (2005): In its 11th edition, this glossary provides detailed definitions of benefits terms.
Dulebohn et al. (2009): A useful review of current and emerging research into employee benefits.
Fundamentals of Employee Benefit Programmes (2009): In its 6th edition this offers the best source for information of United States benefit programmes. It is also available free online (www.ebri.org) and chapters are updated on a regular basis.
Markowich (2007): Offers the leading discussion on employee benefits from an organisational rewards perspective.
Martocchio (2006): A college-level textbook that tries to place benefits in a framework of human resource strategy.

Murphy (2010): Develops an up-to-date strategic perspective on pensions, benefits and health care issues.

Rosenbloom (ed.) (2005): A practical handbook about employee benefits.

See also: **collective bargaining; compensation strategies; executive rewards; expatriate pay; labour markets; motivation and rewards; non-monetary rewards; performance and rewards; valuing work**

PERFORMANCE AND REWARDS

Merit pay has always depended on the quality of performance ratings and **assessment**. Until recently, most discussion about performance in organisations focused on the performance appraisal process. The emphasis was on getting the *best* appraisal format and training managers to rate employees using the format. Most research, whether by scholars or professionals, was on rating formats, rater error and the training of raters – the assumption being that, if the correct format could be developed and managers were trained, the resulting ratings would be accurate.

During the 1980s HRM professionals and some scholars became interested in a different goal: improving performance. This led to a reconsideration of the whole performance process, whereupon attention shifted to **performance management**. The performance management process consists of three parts: performance planning, observing performance and providing positive and corrective feedback, and developing periodic performance summaries. The summaries serve both as a basis for performance planning for the next period and provide data for a variety of human resource decisions focusing not only on merit pay but also including staffing/**resourcing**, **training and development**, together with other decisions affecting the employee's relationship with the organisation.

Performance planning

Like most management processes, performance planning must be constructed in such a way that any manager can do it, regardless of management style or skills. Better managers involve the employee collaboratively in all phases of the performance management process. However, the system needs to be designed such that even directive managers can follow the process. Even directive managers have to recommend merit increases, and if the process can't improve the ratings they give it is of little value.

The manager must first define what performance means in the case of a specific subordinate or 'direct report', i.e. the person for whom a manager is responsible when entering performance plan and evaluation data into the performance tracking system. At the broadest level, this refers to what the manager would have to do if the direct report were terminated and a replacement could not be hired. Ideally this definition is based on a cascade of goals beginning with the organisational strategy and operating plan, with the immediate source being what the manager is expected to accomplish during the period and ending with the direct report's expected part of that accomplishment. The manager must then move from the general to the specific, usually expressed in terms of desired outcomes. This constitutes the performance dimensions for the direct report.

Where outcomes are difficult to observe or measure, behaviours that are expected to lead to desired outcomes are added. For each performance dimension the manager must develop specific outcomes and behaviours that will be used to measure the direct report's performance. As an illustration: for a performance dimension of customer service, an outcome might be 'Maintains close contact with key customers', while a behaviour on the same dimension might be 'Sets up regular customer contact schedule'.

After the measures are determined, the manager must set appropriate standards for each measure. The standard for 'Sets up regular customer contact schedule' might be 'Checks in with key customers twice monthly'. After defining standard performance, definitions for 'exceeds standards' and 'fails to meet standards' are compiled. The exceeds standards level for 'Sets up regular customer contact schedule' might be 'Checks in with key customers monthly; when complaints or problems occur checks in with customer daily until problems resolved'. In contrast, the 'fails to meet standards' level might be 'Misses expected check in with customer; allows problems to continue without any follow-up'. It should be noted that performance dimensions, measures and standards are unique to each position, although attempts should be made to develop common standards for employees with identical job titles.

Communicating performance expectations

When performance dimensions, measures and standards have been developed, the manager must communicate them to the direct report. The manager must make certain that the direct report understands measures and standards. The manager then gets the direct report to set goals for performance for the coming year. Note that goals and standards are not the same thing. The standard is what is expected of a fully job-knowledgeable employee who exerts normal effort. One purpose of performance management is to encourage employees to set stretch goals, i.e. to exceed the norm or standard. At the end of the goal-setting discussion, the direct report should have agreed some performance level as a goal. The set of performance measures, with standards and goals, becomes the performance 'contract' for the period. This discussion of 'performance contract' is developed elsewhere in this book in discussion of the **psychological contract**.

Performance context

Most organisations define the performance instrument differently depending on the type or level of the employee. For example, a non-management or clerical position may have a relatively standard set of criteria that requires little or no change year over year. On the other hand, management employees tend to utilise a format that combines both goals and objectives together with a competency evaluation.

For the management format, the goal portion and the competency components might be weighted, e.g. 60 per cent of the overall rating might be based on the goals results while 40 per cent reflects the competency ratings. Within each section, each goal or competency might also be rated. Therefore, the overall result could be pure weighted calculation of each goal, competency and section result. Web-based performance systems can easily perform these calculations for the user.

Even if the organisation prefers that the employee and/or the manager actually determine the overall rating, the system can provide advice and act as a shared reference point in determining the perceived reasonableness of the entered rating versus the underlying ratings.

Performance period

During the performance period the manager uses the performance contract as a benchmark for observing the direct report. When performance above standard is observed, the standard becomes the basis of positive feedback. When performance is below standard or below the goal set by the direct report, corrective feedback is used. Again, this is done by relying on the standard and goal set as the benchmarks for the performance observed. When discussion about performance is couched in terms of known measures, standards and goals performance feedback can be much more objective, and thus less likely to be seen as criticism of character. The conclusion might be that the subordinate or direct report is not a bad person; s/he is simply not performing at the agreed upon level on one or more measures.

Periodic performance summaries

At some point, a summary of performance during the period is provided to the direct report. In most organisations this is an annual event, but some organisations have quarterly or semi-annual performance summaries. At this point the manager provides a summary of how the direct report has been doing against each performance measure, and whether standards and goals have been met. Consequences of achieving various performance levels are communicated, and planning for the next period's performance begins. If performance management has been conducted correctly, the summary appraisal should have no surprises for the direct report.

Managing and rewarding team performance

The process described above applies to **performance management** at the individual level. Yet most employees today work as an integrated part of one or more **teams**. The performance management process does not change significantly for a team. It is usually easier to get outcome performance measures for a team than for an individual and more difficult to get individual performance measures for a team member. Some organisations have elected to use team output as the primary outcome measure of performance for all team members. One method to achieve this is to develop a 'team citizenship measure' for each team member.

Linking performance criteria and rewards: the merit matrix

Most use of performance-rating systems depend on ratings of multiple criteria. For example, training-needs analysis requires ratings on many individual criteria so the employee can be directed into training that speaks to specific shortcomings or areas for improvement. Similarly, staffing uses of performance ratings require measures of various strengths and weaknesses so that proper decisions on employee assignments – or de-assignments – can be made.

Table 12 A sample merit matrix

(% in each performance category)	Performance	Comparatio				
		(percentage in each comparatio category)				
		0.050	0.380	0.260	0.210	0.100
		<0.85	0.85–0.95	0.95–1.05	1.05–1.15	>1.15
0.13%	5	18	16	14	12	10
0.35%	4	16	14	12	10	8
0.41%	3	14	12	10	8	6
0.12%	2	12	4	0	0	0
0.00%	1	0	0	0	0	0

Merit pay requires a single performance measure that is equivalent across jobs. That is, a 5-rated administrative worker must be equivalent (in terms of value-adding performance) to a 5-rated research scientist. This is because a merit pay matrix – the predominant form of awarding merit increases – will, all other things being equal, award a 5-rated secretary and a 5-rated research scientist the same percentage merit increase. The other primary source of inequality is place in range (also known as 'comparatio'), usually measured as the ratio of actual salary to range midpoint.

Using the type of matrix shown in Table 12, a target percentage increase for the entire group of employees eligible for merit increases (the budget increase percentage) can be determined. The function of the merit matrix is to allocate that percentage across employees based on merit (performance) and place in range (comparatio). Actual percentages of employees in each performance category and each comparatio category are calculated from employee records. Appropriate percentage increases are then determined for each cell in the matrix.

The matrix is 'proved' by multiplying each increase percentage by the percentage of employees with that level of performance and falling in that comparatio range, and then summing these values. This weighted average equals the total payout of the matrix for that employee set. Percentage increases in the matrix are adjusted until the proved matrix percentage equals the budgeted percentage increase.

The merit matrix is still the predominant means of increasing salaries in most large organisations. The merit process does not appear to have much motivating impact and is largely divorced from the business strategy of the organisation. Any increase earned one year becomes an annuity to the employee as long as employment continues. For that reason, many organisations are putting less money into merit increases and budgeting more for one-off incentive schemes.

CF

See also: **assessment; collective bargaining; compensation strategies; executive rewards; expatriate pay; information systems; motivation and rewards; performance and rewards; performance management**

Suggested further reading
Aguinis (2007): A US scholar of performance appraisal, this summarises a broad array of research and practice.
Armstrong & Baron (1995): A practical guide to job evaluation from the London-based IPD/CIPD.
Armstrong et al. (2003): As above, and with a sharper focus on achieving equal pay.
Chingos (2002): This is oriented towards measuring and rewarding the performance of executives.
Cokins (2009): An up-to-date study integrating performance management to strategy (risk and analytics).
Heneman (1992): The best summary of research on the way merit pay is done and its impact (or lack thereof) on performance, along with what it takes to have an effective merit programme.
Milkovich & Wigdor (1991): While somewhat dated, still the best scholarly work on the linkages of merit pay and performance.
Seltz & Heneman (2004): The leading compensation association's take on merit pay.
Varma et al. (2008): A useful resource for developing an international perspective on performance management systems (PMS).

PERFORMANCE MANAGEMENT

Organisations vary in the extent to which they emphasise individual accountability for job performance, typically expressed in the performance management process. Traditionally, performance appraisal (PA) or **assessment** has been the responsibility of the immediate supervisor. However, changes in the workplace, such as decentralised workforces and remote work sites, have made it harder for supervisors to be effective managers of others' performance. Performance management (PM) and valuing and evaluating performance, can all have significant cultural dimensions.

Overview of PM programmes

PM can be defined as a strategic and integrated approach of increasing the effectiveness of organisations by improving the performance of the employees and developing the capabilities of **teams** and individual contributors (Armstrong, 1998). PM is not simply the appraisal of individual performance: it is an integrated and continuous process that develops, communicates and enables the future direction, core competencies and values of the organisation. It identifies 'what' (objectives, targets and performance standards) and 'how' (behaviour, competencies and processes) to deliver the critical performance with respect to business strategy and objectives (Beardwell & Holden, 2001). Appraisals can provide management with supporting information for promotion, transfer, and compensation decisions. The underlying theories of a PM model can be tracked back to some motivation theories, goal-setting theory and reinforcement theory – a line of discussion developed in the concept **motivation and rewards**.

PM is different from the more traditional PA. Conventional PA programmes allow for the formal exchange of performance-related information once or perhaps twice a year, whereas PM programmes emphasise ongoing regular feedback provided by the supervisor to the employee and a climate of continuous employee improvement (Costigan et al., 2005). Besides, while PA is concerned with unrelated performance indicators (such as time-keeping, attendance) and emphasises past performance, PM is often seen as a continuous process involving alignment with a company's objectives and designing a personal development plan.

PM cycle, methods and techniques

Typically, a PM programme includes four phases. These are as follows:

1 *Planning:* At the initiation of the cycle, an employee aligns his or her personal goals with those of the company, identifies core competency improvements and key result areas, agrees with the supervisor the actions needed to accomplish the objectives, and lays out a personal development plan together.

2 *Leading:* This happens during the year whereby the supervisor and employee review the progress on goals and competencies formally or informally and the supervisor gives any coaching and support required to assist the employee to achieve the agreed objectives.

3 *Reviewing:* It is the formal assessment phase that is focused on the achievement of goals and objectives – how performance can be improved as well as developmental needs. A formal review meeting typically happens at the year-end; sometimes a mid-year review may be included.

4 *Rewarding:* Rewarding is the systematic process of linking performance targets with accompanying rewards. This can be as merit pay, commissions, incentive pay, and so on.

A range of methods and techniques for PM exist. The main appraisal methods are work standards, comment boxes, checklists, ranking, forced distribution, rating scales, critical incidents, management by objectives (MBO), behaviourally anchored rating scales (BARS), behavioural observation scales (BOS), 360-degree appraisal, and self-appraisal, among others. While there are many types of PA, those that involve an interview at some stages are common. The choices of different methods and techniques depend on speed, ease and cost versus slowness, complexity and expense.

Kaplan and Norton (1996) famously introduced the balanced scorecard approach (BSC) as a PM framework in the 1990s. The BSC is a framework to align business activities to the vision and strategy of the organisation, improve internal and external communications, and monitor organisation performance against strategic goals. It comprises measures of several key perspectives, including financial, customer, internal business processes, learning and growth. A criticism of BSC as PM framework is that the scores are not based on any proven economic or financial theory and have no basis in the decision sciences.

PM for a global workforce

When companies expand globally, their workforce becomes increasingly diverse, with employees who speak multiple languages, come from distinct cultures, and have different business priorities and ways of working. These differences can place strains on human resource development (HRD) professionals, who then need to consider new strategies for developing, localising and deploying HRD activities (Farrell, 2007). According to some studies, the global workforce has virtually doubled in size (number of persons in the global economy) in the last 15 years. Having twice as many workers places great pressure on HRD initiatives in general and PM programmes in particular.

Global companies face many challenges when conducting PM. One concern is that supervisors are often not able to observe employees' performance directly, making it difficult for them credibly to manage performance in the traditional sense. Another concern is that supervisors do not have enough time to monitor the performance of all the employees in remote work sites. Those decentralised employees may report to more than one supervisor around the world (such as to a business unit manager at headquarters, to a country manager in a local office, or to a project leader), making it even harder to do proper assessment. Without the expertise, knowledge, and understanding of global context, the credibility of feedback is suspect.

Hence, many global companies face the dilemma that exists between the corporate imperative to standardise their PM programme in overseas subsidiaries and the equally important requirement to embed sufficient flexibility to allow local cultural adaptation. Two different views prevail: one view suggests that **best practice** in PM will be universally effective across culture (an universalistic perspective); and hence global companies should adopt an ethnocentric approach. Another view argues that the effectiveness of PM will likely vary due to cultural differences and institutional isomorphic changes; hence global companies should adopt a polycentric or geocentric strategy to balance global integration and local adaptation. Some scholars (e.g. Fletcher & Perry, 2001) have questioned the universality of PM programmes across cultures. For example, giving and receiving feedback in performance review sessions will be very hesitant in a high power distance culture. The extent of participation by employees in setting goals and objectives is low in most high power distance situations. Another example is that PM may be less effective in collectivist societies relative to individualist societies because the employee's focus shifts away from job accomplishments towards the maintenance of in-group relationships. Thus, the in-group collectivism dimension may moderate the relationship between a performance-enhancing strategy and key workplace behaviours (Costigan et al., 2005).

Besides considering the particular contexts in which PM programmes are conducted, a further challenge is the ever-increasing need for speed-to-competency on critical strategic issues. The pressure on global companies to keep their employees on the cutting edge of knowledge, skills and resources is unrelenting (van Dam, 2003). Key questions remain, such as: how to manage the performance of a global workforce quickly, efficiently and effectively? If a global performance standard is set, how can local flexibility be embedded so as to take account of diverse peoples' values, beliefs, perceptions, and background?

Globalisation not only requires the adoption of a cross-cultural perspective in order to accomplish goals successfully in the context of the global economy, but also needs a new and higher standard of training, motivation and evaluation of people (Zakaria, 2000). Since barriers such as time, language, geography, and climate separate people, their values, beliefs, perceptions, and background can also be quite different. The perennial problem remains performance evaluation as the values on which employees are appraised vary between countries (Rowley, 2003). Organisations should be sensitive to this, so as not to underestimate the contribution of various groups of employees.

In sum, the work on PM of a global workforce indicates both the limits to views on universalism and 'one best way' and the importance of contingency and context. The value of PM varies across countries. Global companies need to tailor their PM programmes that recognise these differences.

IP & CR

See also: **assessment; compensation strategies; cross-cultural training; development; international HRM; management styles; motivation and rewards; performance and rewards; talent management**

Suggested further reading
Cheese et al. (2007): Explains the discovery, development and deployment of talent and uses cases to show the importance of talent management.
Rowley & Harry (2010): Considers the influences on HRM, including the political, economic and social contexts, and reviews HRM in Asia in areas such as recruitment and rewards.
Varma et al. (2008): Presents from a global perspective on performance management practices and illustrates the key themes of rater motivation, rate–ratee relationships, and merit pay, and outlines a model for a global appraisal process.

PSYCHOLOGICAL CONTRACT

Although the concept of the psychological contract originates from outside **employment relations**, it has nevertheless become an important analytical tool to articulate both the indeterminacy of the employment relationship, and the limitations of the legal view of employee relations. The use and application of the psychological contract in the HR and employment relations field has grown over the last decade, primarily under the influence of Rousseau (1989, 2010) and Guest (1998, 2004). As a distinctive concept however, it has a much deeper pedigree, with its antecedents evident in earlier work on social exchange theory. Argyris (1960) used the term 'psychological work contract' to describe a set of expectations about what each party (employer and individual employee) can expect from the employment relationship. Significantly, this earlier literature illustrates the point that the employment relationship is shaped and influenced as much by a social as well as an economic exchange (Fox, 1974).

Developing this further, Levinson et al. (1962: 21) saw the psychological contract as 'a series of mutual expectations of which the parties to the relationship may not themselves be dimly aware but which nonetheless govern their relationship to each other'. According to Schein (1978), these expectations between employer and employee do not only cover how much work is to be performed for how much pay, but also a whole set of obligations and anticipated rights. Thus the psychological contract can be defined as a set of 'unvoiced expectations, promises and obligations' of the parties, neither of whom can be fully aware of these until they are not met.

Consequently, this definition alerts us to the idea that conflicts in employment relations may be due to violations of the psychological contract, such as employee dissatisfaction or disagreements over pay, working hours or conditions of employment. The psychological contract is therefore a concept that seeks to capture the intangible needs and wants of individuals, the details of which are difficult to specify.

Visualising the psychological contract

Against this background, some idea of what a psychological contract might look like can be seen in Table 13.

The increasing popularity of the psychological contract in HRM and employment relations can be traced to the changing contours of business and global labour markets (Coyle-Shapiro & Kessler, 2000). For example, Guest (2004) argues that many workplaces have become increasingly fragmented because of the demand for more flexible and customer-responsive ways of working. Managers also seem intolerant of time-consuming negotiations under conventional employment relations processes. With the decline in collective bargaining and the rise in so-called individualist values among employees, informal arrangements are said to be more significant in shaping the employment relations landscape. As a result, the 'traditional'

Table 13 Typical components that make up the psychological contract.
Source: adapted from Rollinson and Dundon (2007: 18)

Employee expectations	Employer expectations
Jobs will be interesting, rewarding and satisfying	Honesty, diligence and trustworthiness
Safe working conditions	Acceptance of the organisation's core values and vision
Fair and reasonable rewards for efforts	Loyalty and dedication to the job and the organisation
Involvement in work-related decisions	Demonstrate a concern for the reputation of the organisation
Opportunities for career progression and personal development	To conform to accepted standards of behaviour
Equality of opportunity	Consideration for other employees, managers and customers

collectivist employment relations paradigm is argued to be out of touch with the changing world of business operations. Given these diverse employment relations contexts, a framework like the psychological contract, reflecting a set of articulate and self-confident individual demands, can easily find favour among practitioners as an appealing 'alternative' employment relations paradigm.

Criticisms

Of course the concept of the psychological contract is not without its critics. To begin with, there is no clear or accepted definition as different authors interpret what the psychological contract is and what it is claimed to achieve in quite diverse ways. Some stress the importance of *implicit obligations* of one or both of the parties involved (employee or employer); others focus on the *expectations* from employment; while a third interpretation views the psychological contract in terms of a *reciprocal mutuality* inherent in the employment relationship (Rousseau & Tijoriwala, 1998; Tekleab & Taylor, 2003). Consequently, some authors seem to be measuring different aspects of the same construct with very little understanding about the relationships between these different meanings and interpretations (Guest, 1998; Roehling, 1997).

A second criticism is the use of the contract metaphor to try to illustrate a very elusive and imprecise concept. In legal terms, the notion of a contract (as in **contracts of employment**) implies some sort of agreement or at least the outward appearance of an agreement. However, given that the psychological contract is based upon unvoiced and implicit perceptions – what Rousseau (1995: 6) suggests is 'agreement is in the eye of the beholder' – it is very difficult to pin down precisely at what point the psychological contract might be successfully negotiated. As Guest (1998: 652) observes, 'where the implicit encounters the implicit, the result may be two strangers passing blindfold and in the dark, disappointed at their failure to meet'.

There are further limitations with the 'contract' implication. A contract implies that the parties have entered into an agreement freely and equally. Legally at least, this type of agreement cannot be changed without some consent between the two contracting parties. However, employment contracts are rarely made among equals; nor are they explicitly negotiated and agreed in the same way as buying a house or a car. In reality the majority of workers enter into a subordinate relationship owing to the employers' power and authority to control and direct organisational resources (Fox, 1974). If, therefore, there is an imbalance of power inherent in an explicit and legal contract, then the prerogative of managers to potentially alter the relationship is magnified when viewed in terms of unvoiced expectations that the psychological contract seeks to capture. When we consider this imbalance of power between management and employee, and its implications for how unvoiced expectations are supposed to be communicated and understood, then it is perhaps not surprising that research evidence surrounding the psychological contract consistently finds contract violation (Morrison & Robinson, 1997).

A third concern is that the concept of a psychological contract ignores other important structural, institutional and community-based dimensions that shape **employment relations** (Cullinane & Dundon, 2006). For example, much of the theory underpinning the psychological contract focuses on the role of the individual. At best, the psychological contract is ambivalent towards the role of **trade unions**, **collective bargaining** or other developments such as social partnership and the regulatory environment for employee voice (Bacon, 2003). Furthermore, the meanings of *mutual obligations*, delivering a *fair deal* to employees, of *promises* implicitly made or a relationship based on *shared understandings* can serve as a distraction to employment insecurity, exploitation or an abuse of the managerial prerogative. It is argued here that in the urge to promote the psychological contract as an attractive conceptual and analytical tool of

HRM and employee relations, advocates have failed to acknowledge that even if a positive psychological contract did exist, this is not testimony to the removal of the structural, institutional and social tensions that exist in the workplace. Arguably, the locus of attention is directed towards individual expectations as being the problem, rather than the system that individuals inhabit (Hollway, 1991).

A work in progress

In conclusion, the psychological contract has emerged from an earlier and deeper intellectual pedigree as a conceptual tool to help understand the complexities of employment relations. At one level it might be argued that the concept of the psychological contract is capable of addressing many of the limitations noted in the **legal aspects** and contractual view of employment relations. However, given the conceptual and practical concerns noted above, it would appear there is much more to do if the psychological contract is to become a viable framework capable of understanding the complex and uneven social interactions that underpin contemporary employment relations.

TD

See also: **collective bargaining; contracts of employment; diversity management; employment relations; employee involvement and participation; frames of reference; grievance and disciplinary procedures; legal aspects; management styles; models of HRM; motivation and rewards**

Suggested further reading
Coyle-Shapiro & Kessler (2000): Uses a comprehensive data set to analyse the implications of the psychological contract and contract violation.
Cullinane & Dundon (2006): A critical review of the theory and literature surrounding the psychological contract.
Guest (2004): An important paper that details the importance of social psychology to further understanding employment relations.
Rousseau (2010): A scholarly source on the individual cognitive structures that affect the employment exchange relationship, with outcomes linked to co-ordination and co-operation in people management activities.

RECRUITMENT

Having identified the number and types of jobs needed the organisation then has to find suitable people to fill these positions (cf.

Roberts, 2005). In the past, a common way of finding recruits was to ask existing staff to recommend family and friends to join the organisation. This is still an accepted method in small and medium-sized enterprises (SMEs) and family businesses in most parts of Asia, but employment legislation discourages this style of recruitment, as those subject to selection tend to be from the same background as the existing staff so potentially discriminating against other groups who are under-represented in the current workforce. Therefore most employers seek candidates through advertising or via employment agents. In the UK public sector external advertising is mandatory for most vacancies even if the employer has already identified suitable internal candidates.

A plan of action

Before setting off to recruit, however, it is essential to develop a plan of action, based on the type of **human resource planning** and **job planning** requirements outlined elsewhere in this book. When drawing up the recruitment plan a number of issues have to be considered including the following five key questions.

1 *What sort of candidate specification will be applied?* The candidate specification will be based on the job analysis and will detail the attributes that the candidates must have (essential attributes – for example three years post graduate work experience) and should have (desirable attributes – for example three years in marketing). A clear candidate specification helps to make objective recruitment decisions.

2 *How many possible candidates are there likely to be?* If there are likely to be many candidates a simple advertising campaign in relevant media will be most appropriate while very few candidates might require using an executive search firm.

3 *Where will the candidates be found?* If the candidates are likely to be far away, for example foreign workers, it might be best to appoint an agent in the originating location to handle the recruitment.

4 *How much will the successful candidate be paid?* The highest paid level of jobs usually requires more careful recruitment due to the cost of employing (and cost of mistakes). If it is not clear what the rate of pay will be (or at least what the pay range could be) it might be that too many or too few candidates will apply. For specialist jobs and senior

level jobs the pay range might be very wide and individual agreements on pay are made while for operative or lower level jobs there will be a fixed wage rate with no scope for negotiations.

5 *When are the recruits to be in post?* If the recruits are to be in place next year but it is likely to take a year to find candidates, select the most suitable and wait for them to serve notice with existing employees, then the recruitment must start soon. If, however, it is expected that there will be suitable candidates able to join in a month, the recruitment will start nearer the time when the employees have to be in post.

Using outside agents

Usually the employer has HRM staff that handle recruitment but recently more organisations have considered **outsourcing** this work to recruitment agents as this recruitment does not fit the strategic orientation of HRM. A useful guide to selecting recruitment agents was produced by People Management (2005). If HRM staff handles the recruitment then the costs are generally fixed (the HRM staff receive their regular salary) while an agent will charge a fee based on a percentage of the successful candidate's salary (usually from 8 per cent for junior staff recruited in large numbers to 33.3 per cent – for top executives identified by selection agents). When the HRM staff conducts recruitment, although their salary costs are fixed the employer will have to pay for advertising costs (which are usually included within the fee paid to an agent). Advertising costs can be substantial – an advertisement in a Sunday newspaper jobs section will cost over £5,000 – so the cost advantage of using HRM staff to recruit can be substantially diminished. But as mentioned in the context of a candidate's pay, the expense of employing staff is substantial and the cost of employing the 'wrong' candidate, especially in senior roles, can cripple a business.

The recruitment plan must include an outline timetable including when to advertise/ brief recruitment agents, what deadline there is to be for candidates to apply by, when to consider the long list and, later, the short list of candidates (these times must fit in with line managers' commitments so that they have adequate time to prepare for selection meetings), when to inform candidates who are to be tested and interviewed, and allowing sufficient time for selected candidates to give notice to existing employers and join the new organisation.

Whether an agency is dealing with recruitment or this is being carried out by HRM staff an advertisement or briefing document must be drafted which contains sufficient details to attract suitable candidates (cf. People Management, 2007). These details will include a job title and brief description of the duties and responsibilities, brief information on the likely attributes of the applicants, taken from the candidate specification discussed above, the salary range or at least an indication of the likely pay and benefits, the name of the organisation (this is sometimes omitted especially if there is a need to avoid alerting competitors to business plans), the location and deadline. In an advertisement there will also be details of how the application is to be made – by completing a paper or online form or by submitting a curriculum vitae (CV) with a cover letter explaining the strengths the candidate has in relation to the position.

Care has to be taken in advertising and briefing agents to ensure that particular groups are not disadvantaged on the basis of their background or beliefs. In the UK employment legislation and possible civil litigation means that if recruitment is mishandled unsuccessful candidates might claim **discrimination** and bring a claim for damages against the potential employer.

WH

See also: **best practice; discrimination; diversity management; human resource planning; international HRM; job planning; labour markets; outsourcing; selection; strategic HRM**

Suggested further reading
Barber (1998): A detailed discussion balancing employer (organisational) and employee perspectives on recruitment.
Incomes Data Services (2006): The London-based Incomes Data Services (IDS) provides regular updates on recruitment trends and statistics.
Taylor (2002): A standard work in the field that connects with regular updates about recruitment policy and practice generated by the UK-based CIPD, a network of HRM professionals (www.cipd.co.uk).

RESOURCING

The field of HRM is often taken to comprise four major areas: employee resourcing, employee rewards, employee development and employment relations (see the introduction to this book). The key initial area is employee resourcing which can be taken as how organisations operationalise and staff their business strategies. This in turn concerns the utilisation of practices such as **human resource planning** (HRP), **recruitment** and **selection** (see these concepts in the relevant places in this collection). For some commentators the concept is even wider and also includes such areas as **induction**, absence, redundancy and retirement. This situation can be seen in Figure 7, giving an overview of the area.

While **induction** and absence are subsumed with the first 'R' in Figure 7 within the redundancy area there are alternatives, such as greater labour flexibility, in terms of numerical, functional and financial. These sorts of strategies have come to more prominence in the post-2008 financial crisis as companies around the world have reacted differently to previous downturns and tried to retain staff and skills and avoid redundancies (see the case study at the end of this entry). Of course, it can be argued that this has been allowed and encouraged as the context is different – this recession is different with already 'lean' workforce levels and low inflation. These alternatives are captured within the three Rs of (re)train, redeploy and reduce.

These phases and activities can be seen within a comprehensive **recruitment** procedure, as outlined diagrammatically in Figure 8.

Each of the main component concepts in the area of resourcing

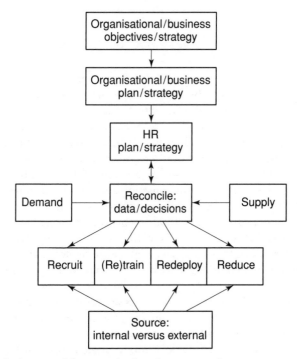

Figure 7 An integrated framework of employee resourcing

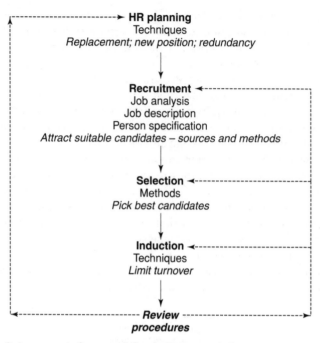

Figure 8 A systematic framework for employee resourcing

are dealt with in more detail in the relevant places in this book. In sum, resourcing can be by using a wide variety of quick and simple, to long and complex methods and techniques.

There is some evidence that organisations often do not take resourcing seriously. Why should businesses bother with sophisticated, but often costly, resourcing? It would seem axiomatic that the resourcing of organisations is crucial to success and one of the key HRM policies to achieve key HRM and organisational outcomes in some **models of HRM**. Indeed, the case for systematic and effective resourcing policies, procedures and methods seems incontrovertible given factors such as the need to comply with laws concerning, for example, **discrimination**; there is a mass of evidence demonstrating the costs of mistakes, which also impact on the image and reputation of the business.

Yet, despite the above, resourcing is sometimes treated as a 'downstream' or 'third-order' decision (by Purcell, see Thornhill et al., 2000: 98–100), that follows on in the wake of the business strategy and which the HRM function simply implements. That is to say, resourcing is not considered in decisions until late on and taken as not that important or difficult. Furthermore, the simple, cheap methods of no HRP or ad hoc plans and use of the continued use of the 'classic trio' (application form + references + interview) prevail in **recruitment** and **selection** of people.

Case study of using the three Rs

It has been argued by commentators that some companies have developed new weapons to fight unemployment in the post-2008 global financial crisis. One is the use of so-called employee leasing, where companies 'exchange' their workforces, lending and borrowing employees. Examples include entrepreneurs in the US and France. Companies rent whole divisions to the company that is upstream or downstream, avoiding dispersion of know-how, lay-offs and dismissals. For instance Cordon Electronics (175 employees), a French company specialising in mobile phone maintenance, agreed to 'borrow' 51 employees from Philips until late 2009. Philips invoiced Cordon Electronics for the work time of its employees, who avoided lay-offs. The questions this idea raises include:

1 Does it represent a possible measure for companies across countries?
2 Are there alternative measures for companies internationally?

In reply to this, there are all sorts of practical issues, problems and implications, for both 'lending' and 'borrowing' companies. These include:

- Which staff would the 'lending' company be willing, and able, to let go?
- What would be the relevance and criticality of such staff?
- Could there be damage to the continuity of business, such as in customer-facing roles?
- Is maintaining confidentiality, trade secrets, etc., vital?
- If the two companies suddenly become competitors, which would staff support?
- Terms and conditions and rewards may differ, what happens then?
- What if staff, especially expensively trained, are 'poached' and leave permanently?
- Who takes responsibility for long-term investment in such staff, such as **training and development**?

- The **legal aspects** of the employment law framework may vary, with what results?
- What about views of not only staff, but also labour organisations and **trade unions**?

As for its widespread use, what rigorous evidence is there of this? By definition we look at cases because they are unusual. How statistically significant are trends in countries with labour forces of 154 million (US), 31 million (UK), 28 million (France), and 25 million (Italy)?

A better tactic would be to negotiate various forms of labour flexibility – numerical and financial – with workers. This could be of two types. First, internal, such as pay freezes, variations in daily, weekly or annual hours, sabbaticals, sending staff on training programmes or redeploying them to other functions or divisions, as Japanese firms do. Also, there could be extended shut-downs, such as Honda's 2009 four-month lay-off at its Swindon, UK plant and BMW's Oxford, UK Mini plant extended four-week Christmas 2008 shutdown; and even maintenance and plant-upgrading during closures. Second, external, such as flexing the periphery – such as those on atypical **contracts of employment**. For example, the Mini factory in Oxford, UK, in early 2009 flexed nearly 300 agency workers with its decision to cut its Friday late shift and then laying off 850 weekend agency staff as the number of production days were reduced from seven to five and permanent staff on weekend shifts were redeployed to the week. About 30 per cent of the plant's workforce were agency employees, alongside 4,300 permanent workers. Of course, these strategies and tactics bring with them their own downsides, for both the individuals and companies, ranging from motivational impacts on all, poor company PR, loss of skills and lack of training encouragement.

In short, it is worth remembering that despite the label of 'human resources', people are not simply 'resources' like others, such as electricity, buildings, etc., to be switched on and off and moved around at a company's whim. Rather they are people, with all the consequences of that, as well as rights.

CR

See also: **diversity management; employment relations; human resource planning; induction; labour markets; organisational exit; psychological contract; recruitment; retention; selection**

Suggested further reading
Taylor (1998): A standard text for the CIPD covering key areas of planning, recruitment, selection, as well as performance, absence and turnover and the oddly titled 'release'.
Taylor (2008): This text provides a comprehensive overview of resourcing and gives practical guidance and theoretical underpinning to students and practitioners alike.

RETENTION

Having invested considerable resources such as time and money in the **recruitment**, **selection** and **induction** of new staff, it is surprising how little effort managers, supervisors, co-workers and HRM staff make to ensure that the recruit's services are retained (cf. Cowie, 2004). It is assumed that the candidate made a definite decision to wish to join the organisation and then when selected they must be happy and content to stay. It is, however, when the reality of working in the organisation mixes with the image – as sold in the advertisement by the recruiting team and (ideally) supported by the inducting team – that problems in **employment relations** tend to occur.

Crucial factors in retention

The retention, or lack of retention, of employees is usually a mixture of 'push' (wanting to leave the employer) and 'pull' (wanting to join another employer) factors. Although managers and leaving employees prefer to emphasise the pull factors (almost everyone likes to say they are going to a better job) it is more often the push factors, which are important (cf. CIPD, 2007).

Often the issues involved in the reward package (pay and benefits) are the cause of problems. The recruit may have been told that 'on target earnings' are £30,000 but discovers that only a small percentage of staff actually achieve this amount. Or the package might have been described as £600 a week but s/he discovers that this includes working the maximum overtime hours at weekends. Or the new employee discovers that although the salary and benefits appeared to be reasonable, they are paid less than their, similarly capable, colleagues. These are issues that could be made clear from the beginning but are hidden because it is feared that there would be few recruits – so resources are wasted in bringing in unhappy employees.

More often the issues are related to poor work practices which senior management or HRM staff are not aware of – such as bullying, harassment, victimisation, overbearing supervision, unsafe or unhygienic working. If the **human resource planning** process has maintained statistics on the internal labour market (ILM) including details of leavers, this should highlight problems in particular work units. If, for example, young females do not stay for more than a few weeks there may be harassment issues or if all new recruits leave in the first six months there may be bullying or unfriendly workgroups. The leavers might also be going because both the ILM or external **labour markets** are buoyant so other opportunities have arisen. But any cases of more rapid then expected departures should be investigated and at least the reasons used to adjust the recruitment and selection processes. The expected rate of staff turnover or **organisational exit** varies between industries and job types. A fast food restaurant might expect to have turnover rates of 200 per cent – each job is filled at least twice during a year. A research institute might expect a turnover rate of below 5 per cent – each job is held for about 20 years. For graduate trainees two years service is expected while, for professors, a 10-year length of service is the norm. The rate also changes due to demographic factors in the ELM – many professors may have reached retirement age so a peak of leavers may occur. Some organisations may also find it worthwhile investigating why there is much less movement than would be expected – are rates of pay much too high, are the conditions much too generous compared to other parts of the ILM and ELM? Or is it that there is a truly committed set of workers producing well for the employer and content to be in the jobs they currently hold?

It is not just the job and the supervision that helps to keep an employee in post. Employers can do a lot to help the employee overcome personal 'pull' factors which might cause them to wish to leave so being able to adjust working hours and use flexitime or job sharing will help staff to cope with domestic pressures. Giving a positive attitude towards job security and the long-term business health of an organisation will help employees feel that they do not have to keep looking out for a job which might last for longer than the current one. Giving opportunities for **training and development** helps people to build up skills and abilities that will be valued by the employer and makes the employee feel more secure. If the job holder can see that there are opportunities for desirable **career development** available, they will feel that any short-term problems are worthwhile being patient about. Each of these factors helps the employee to be committed to the employer (cf. Taylor, 2002).

Value of retaining employees

It is a committed, effective and ideally learning and innovative community of employees that the organisation is seeking to retain. The necessity is to have employees who not only do a good job today but also are capable of doing a better job tomorrow. But such a community does not build itself. It requires appropriate **leadership development**, **management styles**, and working in **teams** to produce and retain such an organisational community. This requires regular attention to the employee making sure they have the resources and support to be effective in their job – and so a basis upon which to conduct **assessment** and appropriate valuing of their work. This regular attention does not mean over concern but sufficient awareness of the employee at work to be able to communicate effectively and to monitor issues and situations to ensure that the employee feels that while they work well they are welcomed and respected. The regular attention does mean that if the employee is unsuitable or is not working effectively and if the employer, after giving suitable training and taking any disciplinary action, is unable to have the worker perform then they should be released from service as protecting non-performers can destroy the motivation of the other employees who have to carry an extra workload.

WH

See also: **career development; diversity management; employment relations; induction; labour markets; motivation and rewards; organisational exit; psychological contract; resourcing**

Suggested further reading
Ramlall (2004): Links processes of retention to theories of employee motivation.
Sheridan (1992): Links processes of retention to analyses of organisational culture.

SELECTION

Most employers, even the largest organisations, use rather unreliable methods to select recruits. Few consider just how much a recruit will cost a company during their service – a fairly standard type of job with a salary of £20,000 will cost the employer £100,000 in wages in just five years and if normal indirect costs such as employer's contribution to pensions and administration of the employee (including

HRM support) it is likely that another £50,000 will be added over that five-year period. However most employers will make a selection judgement on the basis of reading an application form or CV, meeting the candidate for 45 minutes and usually comparing the applicants with an idealised 'job holder' generally based on the personality of a previous post holder.

Processes

The beginning of the selection process is usually an application form or a CV. An application form is the basis for the personal details held in an employee's work file, so many HRM departments like to use this means of gathering data; candidates, however, do not want to spend a lot of time filling in a complex and detailed form for a job which they might not get. A CV on the other hand is quick for the candidate to produce but might exclude information the prospective employers wish to have and maybe the candidate wishes to hide. In the case of application forms, HRM departments should not ask for information which suggests that it can be used to exclude candidates on the basis of discrimination on non-job related factors, so care must be taken about asking questions about age, ethnic background, religion, family status, etc. By whatever means the information is gathered, using a form or a CV is commonly the means of deciding whether to invite the applicant to go further into the selection process. Sometimes employers invite prospective candidates to 'drop in' at a recruitment fair or other event that is aimed at attracting potential employees.

Basing a selection decision on a CV or application form might lead to the 'correct' decision in 10 per cent of cases – a figure given more rigour by the British Psychological Society (see www.bps.org.uk). Basing the decision on a traditional face-to-face interview is also likely to be correct in 10 per cent of cases. Psychometric tests of personality at work maybe are correct in 20 per cent of cases. Tests based on a work-related set of problems or psychometric tests of relevant abilities will lead to better results with 30 per cent being correct. The highest level of results predicting the best candidates for a job score little higher than 40 per cent and these are the **assessment** centres which use a wide variety of techniques including focused interviews, psychometric tests and a range of other exercises to compare candidates against each other and against the job requirements.

The type of results given above may suggest that tossing a coin might be more efficient as a way of selecting people but it is rare for only two people to apply for a job so many coins have to be tossed to get a result – and still the wrong result might emerge. In any case the selection process is a two-way exercise with candidates deciding whether they want to work for the employer and being faced with an interviewer throwing a coin in the air to determine who should get a job is unlikely to cause many candidates to rush to join the organisation.

Methods

What the various methods of selecting staff aim to do is to get the most suitable candidate at an appropriate rate of pay and with sufficient ability to meet the organisation's staffing needs over the period intended in the **human resource planning** process and in the business development strategy. To achieve these selection aims the methods applied have to be reliable (for example it will make no difference to the decision whether the candidate is interviewed first or last on a Monday morning or Friday afternoon – the same results will be achieved) and valid (that is the tests are related to the job requirements so that, for example, a candidate for a fire fighter's job may be asked to climb a ladder but a candidate for a secretarial job will not be asked to go up a similar ladder). Too often those undertaking selection use unreliable methods (such as an unstructured interview) or invalid methods (such as writing an essay for a production job).

Although selection methods used by assessment centres usually offer better results on reliability and, if used properly for validity, **outsourcing** them in this way they are costly and time consuming to administer whereas the face-to-face interview or perusal of an application form are quick and cheap so are more likely to be used for the lower level jobs where a high turnover of staff is expected and accepted. But at not much extra cost, or extra time, improvements can be made to selection by introducing some psychometric tests of ability and of personality at work tests which identify relevant personal attributes such as customer service or quality orientation (cf. Toplis et al., 2004).

Face-to-face selection interviews can be made more accurate predictors of job performance if they are based on job related matters, rather than views about the candidate's personality, and particularly if the views are those by selectors not trained in personality **assessment**. A focused, behavioural or competency-based interview (for simplicity we can assume that each of these interview types is similar) is a much better way of gaining information – better in terms of reliability and, provided the questions are job related, in terms of validity. These types of interview are highly structured so that similar questions are asked of each candidate and the answers should give information on behaviour, motives and attitudes. The questions are also probing and aim to understand in depth what the candidate's capability will be, so closed, leading and prompting questions are not used – see Edenborough (2002) for further discussion on these question types. Even in a highly structured interview some subjective evaluations and biases can creep in so it is wise to have several interviewers ideally undertaking separate interviews to maximise the objectivity of the evaluation of a candidate. If the interviewers are of diverse backgrounds (for example not all men, not all English, not all elderly) this helps to increase objectivity and minimise the appearance and reality of **discrimination**.

A final method used in the selection by many employers is the written and verbal reference to gain an understanding of the person's actual work performance. References are treated with caution in case these are used unfairly, or because it is thought that an applicant would not suggest as a referee someone who would give an adverse report, but a personal view of someone's work ability can be very useful and can help to get a new recruit to fit into the new job.

WH

See also: **cultural and emotional intelligence; discrimination; diversity management; human resource planning; job planning; labour markets; outsourcing; recruitment; resourcing; strategic HRM**

Suggested further reading

Incomes Data Services (2005): One of many useful surveys offered by the London-based Incomes Data Services about trends and emerging practice in selection practices.

Torrington et al. (2009): A standard textbook putting selection into the context of other strategic HRM processes.

Wanous (1992): A standard text linking recruitment selection, orientation (induction) and socialisation under the broad heading of 'organisational entry'. (Organisational entry: recruitment, selection, orientation.)

Whiddet & Hollyforde (2003): Standard text oriented towards practitioners seeking to develop a competency-based approach to selection.

STRATEGIC HRM

According to Armstrong (2006: 115), strategic HRM is 'an approach to the strategic management of human resources in accordance with the intentions of the organisation on the future direction it wants to take'. Strategy is the means of transmitting an organisation's objective, vision and mission into an organised and systematic operational activity. Within a small-scale enterprise the strategy might just be in the brain of the boss or owner and be a simple set of means of meeting targets. Within large organisations, and especially in the West, the strategy is usually incorporated in a plan often stretching three or five years ahead. However, in some industries, such as oil and gas extraction, petro-chemicals or utilities, the strategic plans might seek to work over two or three decades. Such long-term orientation is difficult to achieve in a domestic national or regional context but in the global economy that has developed in recent years it requires much time, effort and information to construct and monitor a strategy. Within a strategy there are regular reviews to ensure that obstacles are dealt with and sufficient resources are allocated to enable the strategy to remain on track or are adjusted to meet changes in circumstances.

At the beginning of the 21st-century, strategy seems to many businesses and organisations to be a management technique of little relevance to those entities struggling to survive. However for survival it is not just tactics and reaction to events that will lead to organisational survival and success. Even if it is not possible to devote resources to long-term plans at least it is essential to develop strategies to give some direction to the organisation and to the people working within the organisation. If there is no strategy then each unit (and possibly each employee) will decide how they will undertake their work. Vision and mission statements are not sufficient to give direction in the required level of detail which strategy provides to guide or direct the organisation and its members.

Organisational strategy

Strategies are often associated with slow-moving large-scale organisations which can predict (or believe they can predict) what will happen in their operating environment. In nation states that believed in central planning, such as countries practising Socialist and Communist ideologies or where 'crony-capitalism' is the dominant means of directing resources, organisations can be fairly sure of the direction of their activities. With the decline of central planning and crony-capitalism strategy lost its lustre and attraction to management. Techniques such as scenario planning (van der Heijden, 1996) gained preference to prescriptive strategies but it may be too soon to discard the views of management experts.

Some experts believe that there are various types of strategy relevant to business. Experts such as Kochan and Barocci (1985) consider that the strategy depends on the life cycle of the organisation – so strategy depends on whether the organisation is at the 'start up', 'growth', 'maturity' or 'decline' phases. Porter (1985) considers that the strategy depends on the focus of a business to be cost reduction, quality enhancement or innovation. Whatever the strategy the business is using, any HRM strategy has to be linked to the business strategy. It is when the HRM function acts as if it is independent of business or organisational objectives that other managers and employees dispute the value of HRM. An HRM strategy must be aligned to the organisation strategy.

HRM strategies

Strategic HRM is regularly linked to change, by which we assume improvement in organisational performance, and seeks to demonstrate that the people aspects of a business strategy are as important as the financial, marketing and resource allocation aspects. Grubman (1998) seeks to link HRM practices to different types of business strategies using the labels 'products', 'operations' and 'customers'. This is a useful perspective as it reminds us that there is not a 'one size fits all' approach to strategy. Each organisation's business plan (whether private or public sector) has to be the driver for the HRM strategy. The different business strategies result in major differences in HRM strategies. The differences are especially marked in rapidly changing economic environments such as is found in China, India, Brazil and eastern Europe. Without the legislative environment and entrenched political and business interests of the developed countries, HRM strategies are much more free, flexible and rapidly changing – with good and bad consequences for organisations and people. Those HRM staff attempting to build a global strategy must be aware of these great differences in strategy needed for separate locations in which the strategy will be applied.

Contents of a global HRM strategy

In general terms, a strategy is a means of achieving medium- or long-term objectives, setting priorities and allocating resources. As mentioned above, a strategy is usually based on the organisation's reason for existing (vision and mission) and is dependent on the environment in which the organisation inhabits or plans to inhabit. So, the strategy might include an element such as 'over the next three years reduce dependence on the home market by creating a presence in a new area'. Such statements are easy to make but have a profound impact on the HRM strategy and operations – meeting challenges of different employment legislation, different talent pools, different expectations of **performance management, compensation strategies**, different attitudes to **organisational learning, training and development**, and so on. The strategy must include expected trends and expected challenges with planned means of dealing with these. Terms such as 'road map' and 'milestones' are commonly used and are helpful by showing that the strategy is a journey not a destination. But it is a journey in a general direction rather than to a specific location so 'strategic direction' is used by some organisations rather than strategic plans, which, according to Dye and Sibony (2007), are inclined to be focused on too much data and information so that they become a hindrance to effectiveness rather than a help to the organisation, Rapid changes in technology and innovation make strategies which are too long term (and the length of the 'too long' varies depending on the industry or sector in which the organisation is involved. However regular checks on progress and obstacles are essential to ensure that the organisation is still moving in the expected direction at the expected rate or to give early warning of problems that are occurring.

To help keep the strategy focused on the important elements it is generally recommended that the strategy should have no more than five or six priority items. No matter how many or how few priorities are included in the strategy, there must be an effective way of ensuring the relevance of the strategy to the organisation and its workers and to communicating that relevance to the managers and employees. If the strategy is now seen as making the organisation better at meeting the objectives and overcoming challenges or if it is clearly understood by, at least, the key levels of management, then most of the efforts at building and monitoring strategy will be wasted.

Contemporary issues impacting on strategy

Following the economic and financial crises of 2007 and beyond, it seems likely that strategies will have to take more pessimistic views of potential risks of any organisational activity. The role of governments and public sector spending is increasingly important even in the most capitalist of countries. To an extent this means that organisational strategies, especially HRM ones, can be more closely aligned with government policies and plans. But in all countries, governments have a habit of dropping plans or putting the brakes on to plans which seemed to be well underway so strategies have to be much more externally focused than pre-2007, as has been demonstrated that even the largest and previously successful businesses can fail if there is a dramatic change in their operating environment. Organisations that moved out of their domestic bases to chase cheaper labour or cheaper resources or higher quality production have found that the global economy has produced not only more workers and more customers but also more competition.

WH

See also: **best practice; human resource planning; international HRM; knowledge management; labour markets; organisational learning; outsourcing; performance management; resourcing**

Suggested further reading
Balogun & Hope Hailey (1999): A standard text linking organisational strategy and change.
Boxall & Purcell (2003): A detailed discussion linking HRM and business strategy.
Fields et al. (2006): A cross-cultural appreciation of strategic HRM during times of perceived uncertainty.
Kaplan & Norton (1996): Details the balanced scorecard – a powerful and enduring tool for translating strategic HRM thinking into strategic HRM practice.

TALENT MANAGEMENT

Reference to 'talent management' has become common across contexts for both domestic and **international HRM**, and notably in contexts for what is becoming termed 'global HRM' (cf. Scullion & Collings, 2006; Sparrow et al., 2004). The concept suggests that HRM professionals should recognise the existence of a 'pool of talent' over which organisations of all types and business sectors compete in their attempts to attract and, where possible, retain the commitment of employees categorised collectively as 'talent'. In strategic terms, HRM professionals are challenged to ensure that their organisation is able to maintain a 'talent pipeline'. As such, the concept has become associated with core HRM processes such as **recruitment** and **selection**, **performance management** and **retention**, together with **career development** and succession management. The fundamental assumption here is that managing talent effectively serves to generate value added to an organisation's business performance. This brief discussion addresses three main questions, which follow.

1   What is talent management?
2   How can or should talent be managed?
3   What are the implications for emphasising talent management over other expressions of HRM or people management?

The meaning of talent

Reference to talent management became prominent during the latter half of the 1990s. A prime driver here was a team of consultants based at the New York office of McKinsey, who announced that HRM professionals and their organisations – wittingly or not – were engaged in a 'war for talents' (Michaels et. al, 2001). In the aftermath of '9/11', this invocation of a 'war' metaphor might have lost some of its appeal. More concretely, some sceptical voices have suggested that adopting an aggressive 'talent mindset' served to nurture several myths about what promoting essentially exclusive notions of a talented 'high performer' or high value employee might lead to, and particularly in the wake of ethical people management disasters – and enduringly popular case studies for discussion on MBA programmes – such as Worldcom and Enron (cf. Gladwell, 2002).

Nonetheless, a quick scan of corporate and recruitment websites highlights how many large organisations continue to highlight the strategic significance of talent in the structuring of their HRM programmes. **Recruitment** drives and job adverts commonly invoke talent; executive headhunters as well as general recruitment agencies trade explicitly in talent. This is a trend that transcends national and regional boundaries and one that appears to follow the internationalisation and globalisation of business strategies as formulated and implemented across business sectors and by organisations small and large.

Consequently, even the word 'talent' has become an established feature of HRM discourse across languages and business sectors, e.g. French *talent*; German *Talent*; Spanish and Italian *talento*; Japanese *ta-re-n-to*. Against this background, it is interesting to consider the origins of the English word. In ancient Greek, a 'talent' described the amount of silver required to pay the monthly wage bill of a crew of a large warship known as a *trireme*. Thus the root of the concept can be interpreted as something denoting quantifiable value (i.e. an *asset*) and – as a measure of silver – as a form of global currency (e.g. 'human capital'), then as now.

From a modern HRM perspective, two main interpretations of the term 'talent' appear to obtain: one broad, and the other relatively narrow. The broad view suggests that all employees have talent, i.e. the potential for professional development and growth and a level of performance relevant to the organisation. Logically, organisations in the education business or health care sectors might be expected to adopt this broader view. However, most business organisations do not have sufficient resources – nor, probably, the strategic intention – to develop all the talents available to them. Consequently, they will tend to adopt a narrower definition and focus their resources on attracting and retaining, motivating, rewarding and committing a chosen few so-called 'high performers', calculating that the return on investment in this narrowed group of employees is likely to be higher and more assured. Thus, in most HRM contexts, reference to talent tends to assume a special case.

Managing 'talent' in organisations

It would be fair to argue that managing talent (however defined) should be no different to the effective management of people or any diverse group of employees. Consequently, it is valid to subsume an analysis of *effective* talent management under discussions of 'managing diversity'. Nonetheless, and given the emerging global currency of the concept, HR professionals are challenged to manage talent effectively. A whole HRM sub-industry has emerged offering practitioners advice about how to do this. To illustrate: Armstrong (2006: 390) defines talent management as 'the use of an integrated set of activities to ensure that the organisation attracts, retains, motivates and develops the talented people it needs now and in the future'. Effective talent management, he suggests further, would 'secure the flow of talent, bearing in mind that talent is a major corporate resource' – and, we can assume, a globally scarce resource. In his 'handbook' of HRM practice, Armstrong (2006) devotes a substantial chapter to talent management, locating it between **human resource planning**, **recruitment**, and **selection**. He identifies various 'elements of talent management'. An annotated selection follows.

- *Resourcing* strategy, i.e. what current and future talent requirements does the organisation have? How do these measure against the talent apparently available in external **labour markets** and the 'internal market' of employees already working for the organisation?
- *Attraction and **retention** programmes*, i.e. what policies and programmes serve to attract and keep talent in the organisation? It is here that metaphors such as (talent) 'pool', 'pipeline' and 'flow' become relevant.
- *Talent audit*, i.e. what are the likely impacts of the above programmes and policies. Perhaps extra resources should be invested in negotiating a **career development** (e.g. promotion or succession) plan for one or more employees identified as 'talent'.
- *Talent relationship management*, i.e. how can managers persuade employees identified as 'talent' to commit to the organisation and its current and emergent business strategy? How might talented employees be encouraged to express their talent more effectively, e.g. by offering them new (creative) tasks and/or structures for work?

One way to visualise the processes associated with talent management in organisations is to imagine the challenges and pressures routinely faced by managers of top-level sports teams, e.g. in football (soccer). International football is a truly global business. The manager tries to fill the team with talent, recognising that some players are more talented than others, that each player's talent is expressed differently, and that they all need to play as a team in order to win games and competitions. Of course, rival **teams** will want to attract – or poach – this manager's more talented players and, at some point, the football club's owners might make a business decision to release one or more talented players either to cash in their return on investment in the player or because the manager wishes to develop a new game plan in which the talents of one or other player might no longer be so suited. In contexts where a change of tactics or playing style is decided on, a change of personnel will follow. The manager will need to work hard to communicate the need for change, and manage talent relationships on both a collective and individual basis. This might mean renegotiating existing **contracts of employment** and the role and stars of one or other team member. This could entail some perceived degree of **discrimination**, perhaps favouritism – invoking de Long and Vijayaraghavan (2003), the 'B players' might choose or appear to lower their commitment to the team. In any case, it will involve the manager in continually renegotiating the **psychological contract** established with each player. The manager might fall short in this regard, such that a team of star talent might fail to deliver: having a team of *galacticos* (stars) does not guarantee success. Wherever success is lacking, clubs usually sack the manager first: teams are judged by their performances; managers are judged by their results.

Implications for HRM activity

From this brief outline it is possible to recognise how emphasising talent management in organisations is likely to impact on established HRM procedures and interventions together with established **models of HRM**. For example, applying a talent management emphasis to models such as the Harvard Framework for HRM (Beer et al., 1984) can generate the following questions:

- To what extent do the organisation's current talent management programmes satisfy shareholder requirements for business performance? To what extent do they attract future employees from the global talent pool? (*stakeholder interests*)
- How does the talent already in the organisation compare (e.g. in terms of skills and competencies) to the talent apparently available in the global market and to competing organisations? (*situational factors*)
- How competent are current line managers and/or team leaders in skills of communication designed to develop and sustain talent relationships? Do these managers need special training? Or should they be replaced? (*HRM policy choices*)
- What is the current rate of talent turnover in the organisation? Is it as planned? How does it compare to rival organisations and to labour/talent market trends? Why do talented employees choose to leave the organisation? (*HRM outcomes*)
- To what extent does the sum of the above HRM activities serve to develop and sustain the organisation as a globally recognised employer of choice, thus (in theory) reducing current and future costs of recruitment and selection? (long-term consequences)

How well do HRM professionals understand talent?

As mentioned at the outset of this discussion, the concept of talent management is attracting enormous attention and investment across national contexts and business sectors for HRM. Indeed, a scan of the titles appearing in the business section at airport bookstores suggests that talent is a concept that is not going to disappear anytime soon: in HRM consultancy terms, it remains a profitable sector. This recognition should give HRM researchers and practitioners cause for thought. To illustrate, more cross-disciplinary research needs to be done into how HRM professionals might identify and define talent and, having identified it, how they might manage talent in ways that can be perceived generally as both ethical and effective.

To give a brief illustration: developmental psychologists offer many established studies on the phenomenon of *gifted* (e.g. musically or athletically talented) children (cf. Albert, 1983; Erikson, 1968). Some of these studies offer distinctive profiles of talented people, e.g. that they tend to appear more willing than their contemporaries to develop an independent perspective on a problem or task. A key insight here is that talented people appear more ready to assume a locus of control over the definition and execution of the task rather than wait for expert help. They appear able to focus on solving a problem despite distractions such as peripheral noise or the pronounced interests of other people/stakeholders. Further studies suggest how talented young people appear to develop these qualities and problem-solving skills over time into a personalised strategy for coping with life, i.e. a level of 'strategic consistency' that, from an HRM perspective, can readily translate into an approach to work and to the development of a career. Elements of **cultural and emotional intelligence** and managed **career development** merge with relation to talent.

This type of psychological insight is important for both HRM researchers and practitioners. It informs how talent might be identified and subsequently managed. It supports some – and contradicts many – psychometric practices currently employed by **assessment** centres claiming to specialise in talent, whether in-house by process of **outsourcing**. In applying the **psychological contract** to HRM interventions, emphasising talent implies the need for a dynamic and critically aware balance to be struck between emphasising transactional needs (e.g. pay) and relational needs, e.g. a sense of security (control) and creativity (risk taking) in the work that talented people are often asked or expected to do. In short, 'talent' provides a focus for exploring a wide and exciting range of paths for scholarly and practitioner approaches to **performance management** and employee **development**.

Emerging issues

However, there are dangers of drawing the path too narrowly; for example, by connecting too narrowly and uncritically between talent and the identification of gifted people, i.e. young people whose gift appears to be 'from the gods'. One danger is thus associating talent too readily with younger people leaving open questions about how to manage the distinctive talents of older, more experienced and (potentially) more emotionally intelligent employees. For example, are age, experience (however defined) and discernible talent hallmarks of effective leaders? Do they add (automatically) more innovative value to the organisation? In order to attract and retain people identified as 'talent' within the organisation, do they need to be offered a special employee value proposition (EVP) (cf. Harris et al., 2003)?

Linking talent to narrow interpretations of performance generates further dangers, e.g. associating it with the explicit (flashy?) displays of limited sets of skills as in the obsessive pursuit of shareholder – as opposed to stakeholder – value. In short, both HRM researchers and practitioners would do well to balance their attention to talent with a systematic consideration of processes discussed elsewhere in this book as **diversity management** and **discrimination**. And given that reference to talent implies by definition a consideration of human potential, identity and self-actualisation, broader issues of HRM and business ethics become acutely relevant, and in both local (i.e. culture- and situation-specific) and global contexts relevant to universal interpretations of talent and of the management of people generally (cf. Harry & Jackson, 2007).

Consequently, drawing more confidently and critically on research into the concept of talent generated in disciplines such as developmental psychology should serve to remind both HRM researchers and practitioners that people have developed as people long before they become significant as employees – deemed to be talented or otherwise – in any given organisation.

KJ

Editors' note: The 'talent management' field exposes the porous nature of the boundaries between scholarly HRM research and commercially oriented

HRM consultancy and book promotion. Readers are encouraged to search widely and critically. Reliable starting points for independent searches can be found by visiting a mix of scholarly and professional HRM web addresses such as: www.cipd.co.uk; www.hbr.org; www.hrmguide.com; www.mckinseyquarterly.com; www.shrm.org; www.talentmgt.com – among many others. Further details of these and other HRM websites can be found at the end of the bibliography in this book.

See also: **career development; cultural and emotional intelligence; development; discrimination; diversity management; international HRM; labour markets; motivation and rewards; psychological contract**

Suggested further reading

Cappelli (2008, 2008a): Peter Capelli has emerged as one of the leading HRM scholar-practitioners in the talent management field. In these texts he attempts to re-examine the strategic HRM value of focusing on talent management 'in an age of uncertainty' and beyond the hype of the 1990s.

Cullinane & Dundon (2006): Offers the opportunity to develop a talent management perspective within the context of an established theoretical framework for describing, explaining and predicting the course of an employment relationship: the psychological contract.

Csíkszentmihályi et al. (1993): Explores sociological and psychological patterns or 'flow' of talent development among teenagers, thus guiding HRM professionals towards developing a broader people-oriented appreciation of the talent concept.

Heller et al. (eds) (2000): An international collection of scholarly essays on human giftedness and talent.

Ohmae (2009): Ohmae is a former director of McKinsey and thus part of the team that popularised the so-called 'war for talents' agenda. Recognised widely as a guru on strategic thinking and the increasingly 'boundaryless' impact of globalisation, his 3Cs model has become influential in guiding HRM practitioners to balance their strategic focus on 'competitors', 'customers' and 'the corporation' within which (according to Ohmae) talent can be identified and incentivised to develop and express itself.

Scullion & Collings (eds) (2006): Linking talent management to processes of global and international HRM generally and to issues of staffing (e.g. selection and retention) specifically. Also highlights related concepts of diversity, e.g. the frequently undervalued talent of female expatriate managers.

TEAMS

In many organisations teams are used to manage complex projects involving research, design, process improvement, and even systemic issue resolution. This is different from organisations with a traditional manager role being responsible for providing instruction, conducting communication, developing plans, giving orders and making decisions by virtue of his or her position. As a generic term, a team is a group of people with complementary skills who are committed to a common purpose, performance goals and approach for which they hold themselves mutually accountable. In the organisational context, team size and composition, member composition, interpersonal dynamics and formation all affect team development.

Characteristics, membership compositions, roles and dynamics

Team size and composition can affect the team processes and outcomes. The optimal size and composition of teams is debated and vary depending on the task at hand. Some argue that the larger the size, the better because they have more resources to address the concerns of the whole system. Besides, cognitive attributes (attitudes, values and beliefs) and demographic characteristics (age, tenure and gender) of team members can moderate team effectiveness (Kang et al., 2006). Are teams better if membership composition characteristics are similar or diverse? Homogeneous groups tend to be more cohesive, whereas the more heterogeneous the team, the greater the differences in viewpoints and the higher the potential for creativity, but also the more likelihood of conflict. Nevertheless, given the more heterogeneous nature of many workforces, choices of 'perfect' team membership may not be available.

Team members play certain roles in the team development processes. Belbin (1993) identifies nine team roles: planner, resource-investigator, co-ordinator, shaper, monitor-evaluator, team worker, implementer, completer-finisher, and specialist. A team member may have more than one role and the degree of balance in a team depends on the extent all nine roles are represented 'naturally'.

Group dynamics is the study of groups and also a general term for group processes. Within a team environment, because team members interact and influence each other, groups will develop a number of dynamic processes that separate them from a random collection of individuals. These processes include norms, roles, relations, development, social influence or group behaviour. It is acknowledged that not all groups are teams. Some people use the word 'team' when they mean 'employees'. A 'sales team' is a typical case of this loose usage. A 'real' team generally goes through a life cycle of development stages.

Team development

Tuckman's (1965) model is a classic team development model. It explains that most teams go through a series of development stages and that there may be conflict and interpersonal issues along the way. It has become the basis for subsequent models of group development and team dynamics and a management theory frequently used to describe the behaviour of existing teams. The assumption is that the team progresses over time towards better communication, maturity in relationships, and better performance. The model incorporates the now famous stages of 'forming', 'storming', 'norming' and 'performing'. The fifth stage, 'adjourning', was later added in Tuckman and Jensen (1977).

1 *Forming:* in the first stage of team development, the forming of the team takes place. The team meets and learns about the opportunities and challenges, and then agrees on goals and begins to undertake the tasks. Team members tend to behave quite independently and are usually relatively uninformed of the issues and objectives of the team. This stage is a good opportunity to observe how each member works.

2 *Storming:* the team addresses issues such as what problems they are really supposed to solve and how to function independently and collaboratively. Team members open up to each other and confront each other's ideas and perspectives. The storming stage is necessary to the team development. In some cases storming can be resolved quickly. In other cases the team never leaves this stage. Tolerance of each team member and their differences needs to be emphasised. This phase can become destructive to the team if allowed to get out of control.

3 *Norming:* team members adjust their behaviour to each other as they develop work habits, making teamwork seem more natural and fluid. A number of dynamic processes develop when team members agree on rules, values, professional behaviour, and shared methods. During this stage, team members begin to trust each other and motivation increases as the team gets more acquainted with the project. However, the team may lose creativity if the norming behaviours become too strong and the team begins to exhibit 'group think'.

215

4 Performing: the high-performing team finds ways to get the job done smoothly and effectively as team members are now competent, autonomous, knowledgeable and able to handle the decision-making process without supervision. The team will make most of the necessary decisions.

5 Adjourning and transforming: adjourning involves completing the task and breaking up the team. The team may transcend to a transforming phase of achievement.

Building on team development research, McFadzean (2002) describes a five-level model of team development associated with group performance in problem-solving and decision-making. Team development can be measured according to their focus or attention to task (level one), meeting process (level two), team structure (level three), team dynamics (level four) and team trust (level five). This model suggests that differing team performances can be associated with varying stages of team development, differences in team processes, structure or activities.

Virtual teams

Developments in communication technologies have seen the emergence of the virtual work team. Virtual teams are groups of people who work inter-dependently with shared purpose across space, time or organisation boundaries using technology to communicate and collaborate (DeSanctis & Monge, 1998). Virtual team members can be located across a country or across the world, rarely meet face-to-face, and include members from different cultures. Many virtual teams are cross-functional to focus on solving specific customer problems or generating new work processes.

Since the virtual team emphasises core capabilities and brings together the requisite set of employees to get work done effectively and efficiently, membership of such teams is more fluid than in a traditional system and evolves according to changing task environments. The virtual team may be either temporary, existing only to accomplish a specific task, or more permanent, used to address ongoing issues.

Duarte and Snyder (1999) suggest seven basic types of virtual teams.

1   A *networked virtual team* consists of members who collaborate to achieve a common goal or purpose.

2   A *parallel team* carries out tasks and functions that the regular organisation does not want to perform and its members are distinguished from the rest of the organisation.

3   A *project development team* has team members moved on and off the project as their expertise is needed in some specific tasks.

4   A *virtual work team* performs regular and ongoing work and has clearly defined membership distinguished from other parts of organisations. Team members may meet face to face once per year for a conference.

5   A *service team* provides continuous operation and work support. Team members, for example technicians, locate around the world, taking turns to deal with network problems.

6   A *management team* members are dispersed across a country or around the world but work collaboratively on a daily basis. Although this team often crosses national boundaries, it almost never crosses organisational boundaries.

7   An *action team* offers immediate responses, often to emergency situations.

The virtual environment does not contain many of the traditional means of managing the task and social aspects of team dynamics. Complicated patterns are more likely to occur in virtual team development during forming, storming, norming, performing and adjourning. Hence, managing a virtual team can be very challenging (Cascio, 2000). There are significant set-up costs associated with creating and maintaining distributed offices. Cross-cultural coordination can be problematic because managers cannot see their members and hence are not in the position to provide accurate and timely assistance. Team members may feel isolated and lose motivation because of not working face to face with other members. Nevertheless, having team members working virtually can bring greater opportunity to leverage knowledge capability and **best practice** (see separate entry) from different sources. Besides, companies have easier access to the global markets for talent rather than primarily to one single location.

In sum, the benefits of teams are propounded to many organisations as they struggle with global competition and search for competitive advantage. In reality, putting teams together, either physically or virtually, and developing an effective team, can be real challenges.

IP & CR

See also: **cross-cultural training; cultural and emotional intelligence; development; diversity management; employee involvement and participation; international HRM; knowledge management; organisational learning; training and development**

Suggested further reading

Gibson & Cohen (2003): Includes case studies and illustrative examples from a wide range of companies on how organisations can put in place structures for virtual teams and improve team effectiveness.

Katzenback & Smith (2003): Covers topics such as optimal size of teams, coping with turnover in team personnel and nurturing extraordinary teams.

TRADE UNIONS

Trade unions are the institutional agent representing the interests of workers both within an enterprise and wider society, and as such they emphasise the collective rather than individual nature of **employment relations**. However, trade unionism can vary quite significantly not only within a firm or industry, but also across countries. In Britain – where trade unionism first developed – union representation has tended to gravitate towards the protection and advancement of vested worker interests through bargaining and negotiation (Flanders, 1970). In contrast, trade unionism in other countries often reflects very different characteristics. In France and Italy, for instance, trade unions have embraced a distinctive working-class consciousness given the particular socio-political environments in these countries (Goetschy & Jobert, 2004; Negrelli & Sheldon, 2004). In other words, they tend to place less emphasis on immediate sectional gains and identify more with class leadership and political ideologies.

As can be seen in Table 14, the trade union movement in almost all countries has experienced significant decline. The extent of these changes varies by country, and for a variety of reasons. For instance in Australia, the UK and the US, employers and government have adopted anti-union policies and laws at different times, and these have constrained union activities to some extent (Gall, 2004), but in Germany and Sweden, governments have felt there was greater value in legitimising the role of trade unions within national policy-making bodies.

Other factors also help to explain the decline in union density. Global market pressures and changes in the structure and composition of the labour force have affected the ability of unions to recruit

Table 14 Comparative trends in union density (%), selected countries.
Source: adapted from Ryan (2004: 379)

	1980	1990	2000
Australia	49	41	25
Canada	35	35	31
France	19	10	10
Germany	35	32	24
Italy	50	39	36
Japan	31	25	21
Korea	15	17	12
Sweden	78	80	79
UK	52	38	29
USA	23	16	13

and represent members. For example, many organisations now out-source jobs to smaller companies, and union recruitment is known to be more difficult among small- and medium-sized enterprises (Dundon & Wilkinson, 2003). In addition, many of the industries and occupations on which trade unionism was based have changed dramatically, such as large-scale manufacturing and engineering operations.

Origins and development

The origins of trade unions can be traced to the emergence of the factory system during the British industrial revolution (Pelling, 1987). As was the case in many other countries, trade unionism emerged from a complex interaction of political, economic and social factors. For instance, trade union organisation was illegal until the turn of the 19th century in Britain. Even with the subsequent social and political reforms that legalised the existence of trade union-ism, many of their activities remained outside the law. For example, industrial action in pursuit of members' interests was deemed to be a form of criminal conspiracy and liable to harsh legal sanctions.

These embryonic forms of unionism first developed among craft workers, and later unskilled and general workers realised they too could achieve more when they organised collectively – a phase referred to as *new model unionism*. During this time trade unions also developed more professional forms of representation including national full-time union officers with a cadre of local activists at the workplace. This system has since been adopted and replicated by many other unions across the globe, with union officials employed on a full-time basis supporting local shop stewards at grass-roots levels.

This form of unionism had particular strengths, not least of which was the ability of craft unions to control the apprenticeship system, and thereby protect wage levels by regulating the supply of workers in an industry. Despite these early developments and the increasing legitimisation of trade unionism, they nonetheless faced legal hostility over both time and space. Even today British unions have to deal with a whole raft of anti-union laws, many of which were enacted during the 1980s and 1990s (Ackers et al., 1996). Similarly, in the US and Australia, trade unions face a neo-liberal political regime that is often pro-business and anti-union (Logan, 2001).

Trade union purpose and function

While trade unions exist to protect and advance the interests of their members, or in some cases articulate a wider political ideology, there remain some important differences in terms of their purpose and function (Bean, 1994). Because the values and beliefs of one trade union, or indeed the trade union movement in a particular country, can vary enormously there is seldom a single or universal purpose. Flanders (1970: 14) explains this by using the metaphor of a double-edged sword. One edge of the sword represents the pursuit of a *vested interest*; for example, recruiting new members and improving their pay and terms and conditions. The other edge of the sword concerns what is known as the *sword of justice* effect. This is the social purpose of trade unions; for example, campaigning for the rights of vulnerable workers or members of society. In recent times, the sword of justice principle can be seen in terms of particular campaigns, such as those which support immigrant worker rights and concerns (Milkman, 2000).

Notwithstanding oversimplification, a trade union may pursue one or more of four broad functions in seeking to achieve their aims and objectives:

1 *Economic regulation:* the first function is economic regulation which, in simple terms, is about securing the highest possible real wages. The rationale here is that trade unions seek to counteract the vulnerability of individuals in the labour market by process of **collective**

bargaining (Hyman, 2001). Clearly this function implies that a trade union may adversely affect the level of profits in a firm, but it has also been argued that the function of economic regulation helps maintain a degree of equitable distribution in a capitalist market economy (Hyman, 2001). Indeed, it has also been shown that trade unions are in fact associated with better firm performance and productivity (Nolan & Marginson, 1988). For example, a trade union can improve management processes and decisions by questioning the validity of change programmes (Cameron, 1987). Moreover, evidence of a direct causal link between the existence of a trade union and its mark-up on wages is almost impossible to verify given the range of other variables that can affect profits; for instance, global trade patterns, international currency fluctuations or investment in new technology (Metcalf, 2005).

2 Job regulation: a second important function is that of job regulation (Hyman, 2001). In this trade unions become the joint authors of rules that govern employment. Examples might include working hours, equal opportunities or employee involvement programmes. In countries like Germany and Ireland, this function can be seen at the highest level through tripartite and corporatist structures involving trade unions, employers and the government in discussing broader macro economic policies.

3 Power and legitimacy: a third function is power and legitimacy. That is to say, irrespective of class leadership or specific vested interests, a trade union is first and foremost based on a collectivist identity. Indeed, this identity is often in stark contrast with the interest of employers. The implication here is that the legitimacy of a trade union ultimately rests on its ability to mobilise workers and impose sanctions against an employer. As Hyman (2001: 4) observes, unions are the power agencies for workers.

4 Political and social change: finally, as unions exist within a broader societal system, political and social change have been a function of many unions since their earliest days (Jackson, 1982). It is this function that is often so evident when comparing unions in different countries. Some opt for diplomatic lobbying while others, say unions in France or Italy, have had a greater tendency to mobilise large sections of the population in support of particular social and economic campaigns. In Britain, trade unions have been quite effective in lobbying government for various legal changes, initially protective-type laws such as equal pay and health and safety in the 1970s and, more recently, trade union recognition rights under the Employment Relations Acts of 1999 and 2004.

Trade union renewal

From the summary information in Table 14, a basic question is what are trade unions doing to try to halt the decline in membership? The simple answer is quite a lot. First, in different countries some trade unions have embraced an *organising model* of unionism. The objective is to implement programmes of renewal based on local grass-roots mobilisation, in which self-confident activists are trained in more assertive organising tactics in order to challenge management. The idea is that, through new organising campaigns, workers will find greater value in membership (Heery et al., 2000). Notable examples include the Justice for Janitors campaign in the USA, promoting issues such as dignity, respect, voice and a decent living wage for janitors (Bronfenbrenner et al., 1998). In contrast to union organising is what can be termed a *servicing model* of unionism, emphasising the professional services a union can offer its members, such as advice on **legal aspects** of employment and other support. A key difference between the *servicing* and *organising* approaches is that the former is union officer-led, while organising relies on local activists to shape the union agenda (Fairbrother & Yates, 2003). Finally, commentators have also examined the potential value for unions from a more co-operative or *partnership* strategy (Coats, 2005; Guest & Peccei, 2001). Partnership (Haynes & Allen, 2000) can be defined by three features:

1 an emphasis on consultative structures
2 the involvement of employees and unions in formulating management plans
3 a respect by the parties for each other's interests.

Some of Britain's largest unions now consult with management alongside other non-union employee representatives in a spirit of partnership and mutual gains – something that would have been unthinkable a decade ago (Ackers et al., 2005).

However, whether these strategies are likely to reverse the decline in union membership is of course an altogether different question, and the jury is still out. One criticism is that the different strategies can be so diverse that they send contradictory messages to potential members and employers. In Britain and the USA for example, several unions have embraced what can be termed a mutual gains approach (partnership), while simultaneously endorsing a policy of union *organising* (Heery et al., 2000; Osterman et al., 2001). This has also been criticised in countries like Australia and Britain as being too centralised and controlled by national union leaders rather than determined by grass-roots activists (Cooper, 2000; Heery et al., 2000). There are further criticisms surrounding partnership as a viable union renewal strategy. Kelly (2005) has shown that wage levels tend to be lower and job losses higher among partnership than in non-partnership companies in the same sector. In addition to this, it has been argued that unions may become too dependent upon management under partnership arrangements, and therefore lose their capacity to resist unpalatable management plans because employee relations are based on co-operative dimensions (Kelly, 1998).

It is clear that these potential revitalisation strategies have not reversed the decline in union membership. Nonetheless, it is quite feasible that these responses may have altered the 'form and character' of trade unionism in a number of countries (Fairbrother & Yates, 2003). According to the British Trades Union Congress (TUC), *partnership* is unlikely to work when employees face a 'bad employer' (Hyman, 2001: 111). However in situations of intense globalisation, then *partnership* may be capable of finding solutions that are beneficial to workers, unions and employers (Heery et al., 2004: 19). Similarly, when encountering a hostile or anti-union employer, then the idea of a more assertive *organising* approach can be much more attractive to employees (Johnson & Jarley, 2004). Moreover, it appears that the *servicing model* of unionism is overly dependent upon full-time union officers, or what Fletcher and Hurd (1998) describe as 'stale unionism' that is desperately in need of revision and modernisation.

In summary, trade unions are an important actor in the regulation of **employment relations**. Their origins can be traced to the industrial revolution in Britain, although in some other countries various trade union bodies have followed a more political and ideological path. Nonetheless, trade unions function in four broad areas: *economic regulation, job regulation, power and legitimacy*, and *wider political and social change*. In almost all countries across the globe, trade union density has witnessed significant decline, for a variety of reasons. In response to this some trade unions have sought to adapt through a range of potential renewal strategies, three of which include *organising unionism*, a *servicing union model*, and *partnership* with employers. While it is evident that these revitalisation strategies have not reversed the decline in union membership, it is possible that they have begun to alter the form and character of trade unionism in certain situations: a union character that is more responsive to workers' needs.

TD

See also: **collective bargaining; conflict management; dispute settlement; employment relations; employee involvement and participation; frames of reference; grievance and disciplinary procedures; health and safety; labour markets; legal aspects; valuing work**

Suggested further reading
Ackers et al. (2005): A research-based chapter that reviews the changing dynamics of partnership in union and non-union settings.
Coats (2005): Provides a very articulate argument about the challenges and possible future strategies for unions.
Gall (ed.) (2009): Provides chapters on different union organisation campaigns and responses in different countries.
Metcalf (2005): A provocative pamphlet that raises some interesting and debatable ideas about unions' strengths and weaknesses in trade union organisation.

TRAINING AND DEVELOPMENT

Training and development (T&D) is a key area of HRM that can have a significant impact on a business. T&D has tactical links with HRP and performance management, and is a key instrument in the implementation of HRM. The field of employee development (ED) has become big business. For example, some surveys indicate that anywhere from 80 to 90 per cent of all organisations offer employees some form of formalised training or management **development** on an ongoing basis. Other statistical reports have shown that management may spend as much as 1 per cent of the company's payroll on T&D or **leadership development** (LD) activities.

Differences in terms

The terms 'training' and 'development' are often used interchangeably to refer to HRD initiatives, though each term can reflect unique requirements and objectives. It may be worth clarifying these terms used in HRD. Without clear objectives and expectations, it would be difficult to design an appropriate HRD programme (see Table 15).

Table 15 Training, education, development and learning

	Training	Education	Development	Learning
Programme content	Know-ledge and skills	Intellectual capability and conceptual understanding	Person's growth and competencies development	Knowledge transfer and sharing across organisation
Timing horizon	Present job	Future job	Future job/ career	Lifelong
Programme focus	Job	Individual	Organisational concerns	Organisational concerns
Typical format	On-the-job, off-the-job skill training	Instructor-led training courses or seminars	Coaching, mentoring	Organisational learning initiatives, KM

Training

The term 'training' often refers to the acquisition of knowledge and skills as a result of the teaching of vocational or practical skills and knowledge that relate to specific useful competencies. Training is a narrow HRD concept that involves specific planned instructional activities (such as training on specific equipment operating procedures) or skill training (such as task-related training, work familiarisation programmes). It is associated with 'learning related to the present job' (Nadler, 1984: 18). There is generally an agreement on what the training is about, and the supervisor usually has a plan to use the skill of the trained employee once the training is completed. Such training can generally be categorised as on-the-job and off-the-job training.

- *On-the-job training* takes place in a normal working situation, using the actual tools, equipment, documents or materials that trainees will use when fully trained. It has a reputation as the most effective for vocational work (Rowley, 2003).
- *Off-the-job training* takes place away from normal work situations – implying that the employee does not count as a directly productive worker while such training takes place. It has the advantage of allowing employees to get away from work and concentrate more thoroughly on the training itself (Rowley, 2003).

Education

On the other hand, education is the 'learning to prepare the individual for a different but identified job' (Nadler, 1984: 19). The distinction made is in regard to timing: training is for the present and education is for the future. In addition, it seems that education encompasses more content areas than training because education tends to develop intellectual capability and conceptual understanding.

Development

Some use the term 'ED' to roughly refer to an integrated set of planned programmes, provided over a period of time and delivered through a range of approaches, including off-the-job and on-the-job training programmes, educational programmes and seminars, self-study materials and mentoring programmes, among others. Instead, a development programme differs from training and education programmes in some aspects. First of all, development is more focused on the person's growth but not related to a specific present or future job (Nadler, 1984). Second, ED programmes tend to have a longer time period than training activities and the goal is more general, such as career development and professional competencies development. Another example is a management development programme which concerns itself not with the physical performance of tasks, but with the development of management knowledge (e.g. decision-making) and organisational skills (e.g. strategy formulation), resulting in improved management practice.

Learning

Learning in the organisational context is the development of capacity to transfer knowledge across the organisation, the sharing of expertise and information, as well as the emphasis on continuous adaptation. The focus of learning can include behaviour, cognitions, affect, or any combination of the three. Learning outcomes can be skill-based, cognitive, or affective.

Other than the differences in the content and duration of the programmes, training, education and development programmes are also different in terms of programme focus. Nadler (1984) suggests training be focal on the job, education be thought of with reference to the individual, and development be reserved for organisational concerns. Along with the changing business world, more diverse corporate structures and increasing job complexity, many large corporations have turned away from simple on-the-job training to more formalised education formats, and eventually to management development programmes.

Coaching and mentoring

Management development is concerned with encouraging managers to improve their skills. Particular emphasis is often given in such programmes to important aspects of general management, such as leadership, decision-making, communication, innovation and change. Coaching and mentoring programmes are one of the valuable management development tools. Through the programmes, an on-the-job relationship is established between an experienced leader and a less experienced individual on the same career track (Lee & Bruvold, 2003). Historically, both programmes were ones where high-potential employees and less-advantaged employees learned about organisational operations and were groomed for more responsibility. These programmes are gaining popularity. The movement of some large organisations away from narrow hierarchies to much flatter structures implies that many managers have found themselves with much larger jobs to cope with, and hence with much larger decisions to make. In some organisations, an individual may report to several project team leaders on a variety of projects over the course of a year. These organisations have often found that it makes sense to use project leaders as temporary coaches, focusing on current needs for skills and knowledge and to have permanent 'home managers' as mentors, focusing on longer-term development issues (Hunt & Weintraub, 2007).

Coaching emphasises the responsibilities of managers for developing employees. Coaching is defined as relationship-facilitated, on-the-job learning, with a goal of promoting an individual's ability to do the work associated with that individual's current or future work roles (Sims, 2006). Coaching combines observations with suggestions and addresses the individual's ability to enact a particular work role. Typically, coaching takes the form of a coaching session which may last for an hour or more and the coach advises and guides trainees in solving managerial problems, identifying their development needs and formulating the appropriate action steps (Kram, 1988). A learning organisation makes effective and regular use of coaching as a means of promoting both individual development and **organisational learning**. One advantage for coaching is that trainees get practical experience and see the results of their decisions. The idea behind coaching is to allow the trainees to develop their own approaches to management with the counsel of a more experienced manager. That is why managers and others who are not expert in counselling *per se* can often be highly effective at coaching around specific work-related issues. However, there is a danger that the coach will neglect training responsibilities or pass on inappropriate **management styles**. Hence, the coach's expertise and experience are critical with this method. Effective coaching requires patience and good communication skills. Furthermore, coaching requires relationship time. Ongoing relationships provide opportunities for individuals to get to know one another's strengths and weaknesses. Ongoing relationships also provide opportunities for trust to develop.

A similar development method, management mentoring, is a scheme in which experienced managers aid individuals in the earlier stage of their careers. Such a relationship provides an environment for conveying technical knowledge, interpersonal skills and organisation competencies from a more experienced mentor to a designated less experienced mentee. Mentoring functions can be divided into two broad categories: career functions and psychological functions (Sims, 2006). *Career functions* are those aspects of relationship that enhance career advancement. They include sponsorship, exposure and visibility, protection, or some challenging assignments. *Psychological functions* are those aspects that enhance the mentee's sense of competence, identity and effectiveness in a professional role. They include role modelling, acceptance and confirmation, counselling and friendship. The advantage of a management mentoring scheme is in having a mentor who provides continuing and customised support for individuals. It can be set up for those individuals who are taking on new responsibilities or who need specific support to handle difficult assignments. Nevertheless, mentoring is not without its problems. Young minority managers frequently report difficulty in finding mentors. Furthermore, mentors who are dissatisfied with their jobs and those who teach a narrow or distorted view of events may not help a young manager's development. Therefore, the ideal relationship would involve a degree of organisational distance between the mentor and the mentee, to increase confidentiality and objectivity as well as to free the dialogue from personal baggage.

Some organisations avoid formal coaching and mentoring programmes because successful programmes often involve assigning a right mix of coach and trainee, and mentor and mentee. Instead, some organisations use sponsor programmes that have experienced leaders show less experienced individuals the way to develop their work roles. Other companies employ external mentors and coaches, often consultants or well-known university professors, to provide advice and support senior executives on critical issues.

Other types of development programmes

Popular development programmes include work shadowing and secondment. Work shadowing involves placing a new or inexperienced person for a while with someone who performs well. This creates the opportunity for observation and learning on the job. The company makes a choice in setting up work shadowing and selecting the staff member who will be shadowed, not just for their expertise, but also for the willingness to help a less experienced person. Secondment has the advantage of broadening an employee's experience and vision by putting them in touch with practice in other parts of the organisation or outside the organisation. Longer secondments sometimes lead to change in career plans. Very few people now have a linear **career development** path where it is possible to see what lies ahead. The reality for most people is that they need both to maximise the potential for learning in the job they have now and constantly be alert to opportunities to move by degrees into new roles.

IP & CR

See also: **career development; cultural and emotional intelligence; development; international HRM; knowledge management; leadership development; management styles; organisational learning; teams**

Suggested further reading
Krempl & Pace (2001): Explains how to design, build and assess a training organisation that is spread across multiple locations. Provides a system development model, a questionnaire to review various locations and several suggestions to ensure plans can be executed within organisations.
Rowley & Warner (2008): Discusses a range of organisational settings, including multi-nationals and international joint ventures: HR, HRM, international HRM, strategic HRM, as well as human capital.
Swanson & Holton (2001): Provides a review of different theories that have contributed to the development of HRD.

VALUING WORK

Perhaps the earliest philosophy of valuing work is the Biblical injunction: 'The labourer is worthy of his hire'. Like most statements concerning work value, there is little help in determining what any individual job or person is worth. The current version is expressed through exchange theory, which notes inputs equals outcomes. The worker brings certain things to the job (or meets certain job requirements) and in exchange receives some set of outcomes, the most notable of which are rewards such as pay, but also include self-esteem and other intrinsic outcomes.

Theory

In fact, there is no inherent value in any work. Most inquiry into work value comes from economics and explanations of wage differentials range from labour theory of value to marginal revenue product theory, to supply demand theory, and to human capital theory. While each of these theories provides some understanding of why one person might earn more than another, none provide explicit guidelines for valuing work or workers. The ultimate goal of a rewards system is to provide an exact rewards package for each employee, and no theory provides the answer to the question 'What should person X receive for the work s/he contributes to this organisation?'

Practice

Traditional systems of work valuation practice have been process-focused and aim at providing an internal hierarchy of job value based on the unique value of each job to the organisation based on one form or another of job evaluation. More recently, some organisations have been less interested in internal value hierarchies and have instead focused on rates set by **labour markets** for various types of work. As work has changed to become more flexible and less easily definable (e.g. 'knowledge work') some organisations have moved away from valuing work and have instead valued the worker through such approaches as skill-based, credential-based, and competency-based pay systems. These emerging practices are discussed below.

Work as 'job'

Job evaluation (at its best) is a process designed to produce an internal hierarchy of job value based on an organisation's unique strategy, culture and values. There are several forms of job evaluation but the most common is the point factor system or one of its variants.

The first issue to be resolved is whether a single job evaluation or **assessment** system should be used for all jobs in the organisation. Few organisations include executives in the job evaluation system used for the bulk of jobs; **executive rewards** tend to be set on the basis of negotiations, or have a job evaluation system applying to executives alone. Other groups excluded from the job evaluation system (or have unique systems) include any group with unique terms and conditions: sales jobs, **collective bargaining** units, and certain professional groups such as actuaries and nurses, who may not be included in the primary job evaluation system. At one time, every major occupational family had its own job evaluation system (if any) but **discrimination** and administrative concerns have resulted in most organisations using a single system for the majority of workers.

Example: point factor systems

The point factor system begins with a consideration of what aspects of work are thought to add value to the organisation. In most organisations, for example, the education or **training and development** required to perform a job effectively is generally thought to be a key value component. Presumably, the more education or training required for a worker to perform a particular job, the more valuable the job is to the organisation, all other things being equal.

Most point factor systems use between seven and 10 factors. Some typical factors include education required, experience required, supervision received, supervisory responsibilities, creativity/innovation required, responsibility for budget/equipment, and working conditions. Other point factor variants such as the Hay System use fewer factors. Whatever the number of factors used, the requirement is that they capture all aspects of all work for the jobs that are calculated to add value to the organisation.

After the factors are chosen, they must be weighted. This is usually calculated in line with the organisation's strategy. For a high-tech organisation, education might well be the most important factor; it would likely be considered relatively less important in a retail sales organisation. Some arbitrary number of points (perhaps 2000) is allocated across factors reflecting their relative value to the organisation. Scales must then be developed for each factor. A scale consists of the scale title, a short definition of the scale subject, and between five and seven scale level definitions. The following experience scale provides an illustration of this technique:

Experience required

This factor measures the time normally required, on related work *and* on-the-job training in the job being evaluated, for an individual to attain satisfactory performance standards under normal supervision. In evaluating this factor it is important that only the experience which is in addition to the education or apprenticeship (including experience in lieu thereof) required be considered and that any time actually spent beyond that necessary to attain satisfactory performance be disregarded.

40 points	1st degree	up to and including 3 months
130 points	2nd degree	over 3 months, up to and including 12 months
220 points	3rd degree	over 1 year, up to and including 3 years
310 points	4th degree	over 3 years, up to and including 5 years
400 points	5th degree	over 5 years.

Points are then assigned to the scale so that it is an equal-interval scale. The experience factor in the above example is worth 400 points, so the fifth degree is worth 400 points. The first degree is worth 40 points, and an equal interval of 90 points is maintained.

When all the factor scales are completed, all jobs are evaluated. This is done by a job evaluation committee composed of job-knowledgeable employees and usually chaired by a compensation/rewards specialist. The committee proceeds on the basis of **job planning** descriptions written by incumbents and supervisors. When questions arise that the committee members cannot answer, it is usual to query the supervisor and/or incumbent for additional information.

When each job has been evaluated, a job hierarchy can be made, e.g. by constructing a rank ordering of jobs on the basis of total evaluation points received, from high to low. This hierarchy forms the basis of the salary structure for employees covered by the ranking process. The resultant hierarchy is divided into salary grades and the grades are priced using market rates for jobs in each grade. Jobs may be moved from one grade to another based on market rates, reporting relationships, career paths and other situations. However, the focus is on valuing work based on internal organisational values. More details of these processes can be found at www.worldatwork.com.

Market valuation

This internally focused approach can be contrasted with a more externally oriented evaluation of jobs or work. For, and as can be seen above, job evaluation is a time-consuming and expensive process and, when results differ from market rates, the market rate frequently takes precedence. This has led some companies to start with **labour market** values in the valuing of work.

In pure market pricing the organisation gets market rates for as many of its jobs as possible. Proponents of market pricing argue that market pricing results in a much more efficient use of salary dollars, since salary dollars are allocated in a way that optimises competitiveness across all jobs; no one is overpaid or underpaid except by design.

There are many association, third-party, and self-developed and commercial surveys available. Nonetheless, market rates will not be available for all jobs in a typical organisation. An organisation devoting significant resources to acquiring market data might still get rates for 90 per cent of its jobs, though these jobs are likely to include 95 per cent or more of its employees. Even when market rates are acquired, they may be based on such a small number of organisations/incumbents or on such an unrepresentative sample that the organisation has doubts as to the reliability of the data. Thus, even the pure market-pricing organisation needs to find a way to estimate market rates when market rates are not available.

Market-pricing organisations do this through statistical analysis, primarily through multiple regression techniques. Job data are collected for all jobs, usually from human resource **information systems** (HRIS). The kinds of data chosen are similar to those used in job evaluation, but no scaling or evaluation is required. Data used might include average budget associated with a job, the average number of direct reports to incumbents of the job, average incumbent education, experience, etc. These data become the independent variables in the regression analysis, and wage data are regressed on them. The resulting model can be used to provide the best point estimate of the wage for any job for which a market rate is not available. The model can also be used to evaluate the rates for jobs where the market data are found to be unreliable.

Market pricing organisations can choose to use a normal salary structure based on the model or use actual (or estimated) market rates for each job. Market pricing is becoming more popular with organisations, and especially since more employees do salary searches on public websites such as www.salary.com, and then demand to know why they are paid less than 'the going rate'. Without market rates, such complaints are hard to answer.

Valuing the person

Critics of market pricing note that survey data are suspect in many cases, and that by taking the market rate as the standard for each job the organisation is not taking account of differential values of work in their own situation that result from specific strategic, cultural or environmental considerations. Thus, a number of critics of job evaluation and market pricing emphasise how it is employees that add value, not jobs. These critics argue that organisations should base pay not on job value but on person value. The rationale for this approach is that work is becoming more ambiguous in its definition. As a consequence, employees need to be broadly trained and be able to apply their knowledge skills and abilities to many different and evolving tasks.

The first pay system to reflect this approach is skill-based pay. Skill-based pay is typically used in blue-collar work sites. A work process is divided into major tasks, and these are ranked in terms of how difficult these are to learn. Bundles of similar-difficulty tasks (typically three to five) are specified. An employee begins work doing only the tasks in the lowest level bundle, and so receives an entry-level rate of pay. As the employee masters these lower level skills s/he begins training on the second level bundle. When these are mastered, the employee receives an increase. With each additional bundle mastered, the employee receives an increase in pay.

The employee is still expected to do all tasks that need doing. Even the employees at the highest level in the skill hierarchy are expected to do any tasks that need doing, regardless of level. Proponents of skill-based pay argue that cross-training and requirement to do what needs to be done rather than some set of specific assigned tasks makes scheduling easier and reduces the impact of turnover and absenteeism. They also cite higher motivation levels and lower absenteeism and turnover. Critics note that wage sets in skill-based pay systems are higher than in traditional systems, that cross-training both reduces productivity during training and results in an employee population that may be over-trained in terms of actual work demand. Transitions to new production processes may create serious pay adjustment problems. Readers are guided to the suggested further reading section (below) for more insight into these debates.

Variations of skill-based pay systems include credential-based pay and competency-based pay. For example, teachers in the United States get one pay rate when they have a BA or BEd. After completing a fifth year, they get an increased rate. A Masters degree gets them a still higher rate, and a PhD or EdD results in a still higher rate, even though they may still be teaching in the same classroom. Actuaries typically get an increase for each part of the actuarial examination they pass.

Competency-based pay has been discussed more than implemented. It is really a skill-based pay system for so-called white-collar workers. Acquiring or increasing competencies valued by the organisation would result in salary increases. Critics note that competencies tend to be very similar to traits, and like traits, difficult to change: they argue that using competencies/traits as a basis for developing **compensation strategies** is inappropriate.

CF

See also: **compensation strategies; contracts of employment; executive rewards; information systems; job planning; labour markets; motivation and rewards; performance and rewards**

Suggested further reading
Armstrong & Baron (1995): Offers a British perspective on job evaluation.
Armstrong et al. (2003): Comparable worth and equal pay advocates argue that an accurate job evaluation system can counteract traditional wage discrimination. This book describes how such systems should work.
Fried & Davis (2004): Offers the professional association's perspective on market pricing techniques.
Ledford (2008): A WorldatWork journal that outlines factors likely to influence the long-term effectiveness of skill-based pay.
Treiman (1979): This report covers the problems of job evaluation systems, including reliability, validity and bias. It also includes typical scales from many different job evaluation systems.
WorldatWork (2006): Covers traditional job evaluation systems.
Wright et al. (2001): Presents a broader view of the value of the individual in the firm from a resource-based view perspective.

BIBLIOGRAPHY

ACAS (2003) *Managing Attendance and Employee Turnover*, London: Advisory, Conciliation and Arbitration Service.

ACAS (2006) *Recruitment and Induction*, London: Advisory, Conciliation and Arbitration Service.

Ackers, P. (1994) 'Back to Basics: Industrial Relations and the Enterprise Culture', *Employee Relations*, 16(8): 32–47.

Ackers, P. (1999) 'On Paternalism: Seven Observations on the Uses and Abuses of the Concept in Industrial Relations, Past and Present', *Historical Studies in Industrial Relations*, 5 (Spring): 173–93.

Ackers, P. (2001) 'Paternalism, Participation and Partnership: Rethinking the Employment Relationship, *Human Relations*, 54(3): 375–86.

Ackers, P. (2002) 'Reframing Industrial Relations: The Case for Neo-Pluralism', *Industrial Relations Journal*, 33(1): 2–19.

Ackers, P. (2004) 'Haunted by History: Industrial Relations Faces the Future', *Organization Studies*, 25(9): 1623–9.

Ackers, P. (2005) 'Theorizing the Employment Relationships: Materialists and Institutionalists', *British Journal of Industrial Relations*, 43(3), September: 537–43.

Ackers, P. (2007) 'Collective Bargaining as Industrial Democracy: Hugh Clegg and the Political Foundations of British Industrial Relations Pluralism', *British Journal of Industrial Relations*, 45 (1 March): 77–101.

Ackers, P. (2009) 'Employment Ethics', in T. Redman and A. Wilkinson, *Contemporary HRM*, 3rd edition, London: Pearson.

Ackers, P. and Black, J. (1991) 'Paternalism: An Organisation Culture in Transition', in M. Cross and G. Payne (eds) *Work and the Enterprise Culture*, London: Falmer/BSA.

Ackers, P. and Payne, J. (1998) 'British Trade Unions and Social Partnership: Rhetoric, Reality and Strategy', *The International Journal of Human Resource Management*, 34(4), December: 473–95.

Ackers, P. and Wilkinson, A. J. (eds) (2003) *Understanding Work and Employment: Industrial Relations in Transition*, Oxford: Oxford University Press.

Ackers, P. and Wilkinson, A. J. (2005) 'British Industrial Relations Paradigm: A Critical Outline History and Prognosis', *The Journal of Industrial Relations*, 47(4), December: 443–56.

Ackers, P. and Wilkinson, A. (2008) 'Industrial Relations and the Social Sciences', in in P. Blyton, N. Bacon, J. Fiorito and E. Heery (eds) *The Sage Handbook of Industrial Relations*, London: Sage: 53–68.

Ackers, P., Smith, C. and Smith, P. (1996) 'Against All Odds? British Trade unions in the New Workplace', in P. Ackers, C. Smith and P. Smith (eds) *The New Workplace and Trade Unionism: Critical Perspectives on Work and Organisation*, London: Routledge.

Ackers, P., Marchington, M., Wilkinson, A. and Dundon, T. (2005) 'Partnership and Voice, with or without Trade Unions: Changing UK Management Approaches to Organisational Participation', in M. Stuart and M. Martinez Lucio (eds) *Partnership and Modernisation in Employment Relations*, London: Routledge.

Ackroyd, S. and Thompson, P. (2003) *Organisational Misbehaviour*, London: Sage.

Adams, J. S. (1963) 'Towards an Understanding of Inequity', *Journal of Abnormal and Social Psychology*, 67(5): 422–36.

Adams, R., Bessant, J. and Phelps, R. (2006) 'Innovation Management Measurement: A Review', *International Journal of Management Reviews*, 8(1): 21–47.

Adler, N. J. and Bartholomew, S. (1992) 'Managing Globally Competent Manager', *The Executive*, 6(3): 52–65.

Adler, N. J. and Ghadar, F. (1990) 'Strategic Human Resource Management: A Global Perspective', in R. Pieper (ed.) *Human Resource Management in International Comparison*, Berlin: De Gruyter: 235–60.

Adler, P. S. (2003) 'Making the HRM Outsourcing Decision', *MIT Sloan Management Review*, 45: 53–60.

Aguinis, H. (2007) *Performance Management*, Upper Saddle River, NJ: Pearson/Prentice Hall.

Aikin, O. (2001) *Drawing up Employment Contracts: Developing Practice*, 3rd edition, London: Chartered Institute of Personnel and Development.

Albert, R. S. (1983) *Genius and Eminence: The Social Psychology of Creativity and Exceptional Achievement*, London: Elsevier.

Alderfer, C. and Smith, K. (1982) 'Studying Intergroup Relations Embedded in Organizations', *Administrative Science Quarterly*, 27: 35–64.

Angel, I. (2000) 'E-learning', CIPD conference proceedings, Harrogate, October.

Applebaum, E., Bailey, T., Berg, P. and Kalleberg, A. (2000) *Manufacturing Competitive Advantage: The Effects of High-Performance Work Systems on Plant Performance and Company Outcomes*, Ithaca, NY: Cornell University Press.

Argyris, C. (1960) *Understanding Organizational Behaviour*, Homewood, IL: Doresy.

Argyris, C. and Schön, D. (1978) *Organizational Learning: A Theory of Action Perspective*, Reading, MA: Addison-Wesley.

Armstrong, G. (1987) 'Human Resource Management: A Case of the Emperor's New Clothes', *Personnel Management*, August: 30–5.

Armstrong, M. (2006) *A Handbook of Human Resource Management Practice*, London: Kogan Page.

Armstrong, M. and Baron, A. (1995) *The Job Evaluation Handbook*, London: Chartered Institute of Personnel and Development.

Armstrong, M. and Baron, A. (1998) 'Out of the Tick Box', *People Management*, 4(15): 38–9.

Armstrong, M. and Brown, D. (2006) *Strategic Reward: Making It Happen*, London: Kogan Page.

Armstrong, M. and Murlis, H. (2004) *Reward Management: A Handbook of Remuneration Strategy and Practice*, 5th edition, London: Kogan Page.

Armstrong, S. and Mitchell, B. (2008) *The Essential HR Handbook: A Quick and Handy Resource for Any Manager or HR Professional*, Franklin Lake, NJ: The Career Press (see www.careerpress.com).

Armstrong, M., Cummins, A., Hastings, S. and Wood, W. (2003) *Job Evaluation: A Guide to Achieving Equal Pay*, London: Kogan Page.

Arthur, J. (1994) 'Effects of Human Resource Systems on Manufacturing Performance and Turnover', *Academy of Management Journal*, 37(3): 670–87.

Arthur, M. B. and Rousseau, D. M. (eds) (1996) *The Boundaryless Career: A New Employment Principles for a New Organizational Era*, Oxford: Oxford University Press.

Ashkenas, R., Ulrich, D., Jick, T. and Kerr, S. (1995) *The Boundaryless Organization*, San Francisco, CA: Jossey-Bass.

Audretsch, D. and Thurik, R. (2000) 'Diversity, Innovation and Entrepreneurship', paper presented at Indiana University's School of Public and Environmental Affairs conference 'Workplace Diversity: A Research Perspective on Policy and Practice', Brussels, 13–15 June.

Avruch, K. (2004) 'Culture as Context, Culture as Communication: Considerations for Humanitarian Negotiators', *Harvard Negotiation Law Review*, 9: 391–407.

Babcock, P. (2004) 'Slicing off Pieces of HRM', *HR Magazine*, 47: 10–12.

Bach, S. and Winchester, D. (2003) 'Industrial Relations in the Public Sector', in P. Edwards (ed.) *Industrial Relations: Theory and Practice*, 2nd edition, Oxford: Blackwell.

Bacon, N. (2003) 'Human Resource Management and Industrial Relations', in P. Ackers and A. Wilkinson (eds) *Understanding Work and Employment: Industrial Relations in Transition*, Oxford: Oxford University Press.

Bacon, N. (2008) 'Management Strategy and Industrial Relations', in P. Blyton, N. Bacon, J. Fiorito and E. Heery (eds) *The Sage Handbook of Industrial Relations*, London: Sage.

Bacon, N. (2009) 'Industrial Relations', chapter 8, in T. Redman and A. Wilkinson, *Contemporary HRM*, 3rd edition, London: Pearson.

Baldamus, W. (1961) *Efficiency and Effort*, London: Tavistock.

Balogun, J. and Hope Hailey, V. (1999) *Exploring Strategic Change*, Hemel Hempstead: Prentice Hall.

Balsam, S. (2007) *Executive Compensation: An Introduction to Practice and Theory*, Scottsdale, AZ: WorldatWork Press.

Bar-On, R. (2000) 'Emotional and Social Intelligence: Insights from the Emotional Quotient', in R. Bar-On and J. D. Parker (eds) *The Handbook of Emotional Intelligence: Theory, Development, Assessment and Application at Home, School, and in the Workplace*, San Francisco, CA: Jossey-Bass: 363–88.

Barbazette, J. (2006) *Training Needs Assessment: Methods, Tools and Techniques*, New York: John Wiley and Son.

Barber, A. E. (1998) *Recruiting Employees: Individual and Organizational Perspectives*, Thousand Oaks, CA: Sage.

Bartholomew, D. J., Forbes, A. F. and McClean, S. I. (1991) *Statistical Techniques for Manpower Planning*, Chichester: John Wiley.

Bartlett, C. A. and Ghoshal, S. (1989) *Managing across Boundaries: The Transnational Solution*, Boston, MA: Harvard Business School Press.

Bartlett, C. A. and Ghoshal, S. (1992) 'What Is a Global Manager?', *Harvard Business Review*, 70(5): 124–32.

Barton, G. M. (2006) *Recognition at Work: Crafting a Value-Added Rewards Program*, Scottsdale, AZ: WorldatWork.

Bateson, G. (1972) *Steps to an Ecology of Mind*, New York: Ballantine.

Batt, R. (1999) 'Work Organisation, Technology and Performance in Customer Service and Sales', *Industrial and Labor Relations Review*, 52: 539–64.

BBC (2006) http://news.bbc.co.uk/2/hi/business/5056992.stm, 26 June.

Bean, R. (1994) *Comparative Industrial Relations: An Introduction to Cross-national Perspectives*, London: Routledge.

Beardwell, I. and Holden, L. (2001) *Human Resource Management: A Contemporary Approach*, Harlow, UK: Pearson Education.

Beaumont, P. (1993) *HRM: Key Concepts and Skills*, London: Sage.

Bebchuk, L. and Fried, J. F. (2004) *Pay without Performance: The Unfilled Promise of Executive Compensation*, Cambridge, MA: Harvard University Press.

Bechet, T, P. (2008) *Strategic Staffing: A Comprehensive System for Effective Workforce Planning*, New York: American Management Association.

Becker, B. and Gerhart, B. (1996) 'The Impact of Human Resource Management on Organisational Performance: Progress and Prospects', *Academy Journal of Management*, 39(4): 779–801.

Becker, B., Huselid, M. and Ulrich, D. (2001) *The HR Scorecard: Linking People, Strategy and Performance*, Boston, MA: Harvard University Press.

Beer, M., Spector, B., Lawrence, P., Quinn Mils, D. and Walton, R. (1984) *Managing Human Assets*, New York: Free Press.

Belbin, R. M. (1993) *Team Roles at Work*, Oxford: Butterworth-Heinemann.

Benefits and Compensation Glossary, 11th edition (2005) Brookfield, WI: International Foundation of Employee Benefit Plans.

Bennis, W. (1991) Foreword in D. Jamieson and J. O'Mara (eds) *Manag-

ing Workforce 2000: Gaining the Diversity Advantage, San Francisco, CA: Jossey-Bass.

Berg, P. (1999) 'The Effects of High Performance Work Practices on Job Satisfaction in the United States Steel Industry', *Relations Industrial Industrial Relations*, 54: 111–35.

Berry, J. W., Segall, M. H. and Hagiticibasi, C. (eds) *Handbook of Cross-cultural Psychology: Volume 3: Social Behaviour and Applications*, 2nd edition, Needham Heights, MA: Allyn and Bacon.

Birkinshaw, J. M. and Morrison, A. J. (1995) 'Configuration of Strategy and Structure in Subsidiaries of Multinational Corporations', *Journal of Business Studies*, 4: 729–53.

Bjorkman, I. and Xiucheng, F. (2002) 'HRM and the Performance of Western Firms in China', *International Journal of Human Resource Management*, 13(6): 853–64.

Bjorndal McAdams, J. A. and Ison, L. K. (2006) *Mastering Market Data*, Scottsdale, AZ: WorldatWork.

Black, J. S. and Mendenhall, M. E. (1990) 'Cross-cultural Training Effectiveness: A Review and a Theoretical Framework for Future Research', *Academy of Management Review*, 15(1): 113–36.

Black, F. and Scholes, M. S. (1973) 'The Pricing of Options and Corporate Liabilities', *Journal of Political Economy*, 81 (3): 637–54.

Blanchflower, D.G, Saleheen, J. and Shadforth, C. (2007) *The Impact of Recent Migration from Eastern Europe on the UK Economy*, London: Bank of England.

Blyton, P. and Turnbull, P. (2004) *The Dynamics of Employee Relations*, 3rd edition, Basingstoke: Palgrave Macmillan.

Blyton, P., Bacon, N., Fiorito, J. and Heery, E. (eds) (2008) *The Sage Handbook of Industrial Relations*, London: Sage.

Boselie, P., Paauwe, J. and Jansen, P. (2001) 'Human Resource Management and Performance: Lessons from the Netherlands', *International Journal of Human Resource Management*, 12(7): 1107–25.

Bott, D. (2003) 'Employment Relations Procedures', in B. Towers (ed.) *The Handbook of Employment Relations, Law and Practice*, 4th edition, London: Kogan.

Bovbjerg, B. D. and Dicken, J. E. (2007) *Employer-Sponsored Health and Retirement Benefits: Effort to Control Employer Costs and the Implications for Workers*, Washington, DC: US General Accountability Office.

Bowey, A. M. (1974) *A Guide to Manpower Planning*, London: Macmillan.

Boxall, P. (1995) 'Building the Theory of Comparative HRM', *Human Resource Management Journal*, 5(5): 5–18.

Boxall, P. and Purcell, J. (2003) *Strategy and Human Resource Management*, Basingstoke: Palgrave Macmillan.

Boyd, C. (2003) *Human Resource Management and Occupational Health and Safety*, London: Routledge.

Bratton, J. and Gold, J. (2007) *Human Resource Management: Theory and Practice*, Palgrave Macmillan.

Braverman, H. (1974) *Labour and Monopoly Capitalism*, New York: Basic.

Brenner, L. (1996) 'The Disappearing HRM Department', *CFO*, 12 (March): 61–3.

Brian, B. and Gerhart, B. (1996) 'The Impact of Human Resource Management on Organisational Performance: Progress and Prospects', *Academy of Management Journal*, 39 (August): 779–801.

Brewster, C., Mayrhofer, W. and Morley, M. (2004) *Human Resource Management in Europe: Evidence of Convergence?* London: Elsevier.

Brewster, C., Sparrow, P. and Harris, H. (2005) 'Towards a New Model of Globalizing HRM', *International Journal of Human Resource Management*, 16(6): 949–70.

Brewster, C., Tregaskis, O., Hegewisch, A. and Mayne, L. (1996) Comparative Research in Human Resource Management: A Review and an Example, *International Journal of Human Resource Management*, 7(3): 585–604.

Brief, A. P. (ed.). (2008) *Diversity at Work*, Cambridge: Cambridge University Press.

Briscoe, D. R., Schuler, R. S. and Claus, L. (2009) *International Human Resource Management: Policies and Practices for Multinational Enterprises*, London: Routledge.

Brislin, R. and Horvath, A. M. (1997) 'Cross-cultural Training and Multicultural Education', in K. Bronfenbrenner, S. Friedman, R. Hurd, R. Oswald and R. Seeber (eds) (1998) *Organizing to Win: New Research on Union Strategies*, Ithaca, NY: Cornell University Press.

Brockman, K. and Brockman, J. (1996) *How Things Are: A Science Toolkit for the Mind*, London: Phoenix.

Brodie, D. (2005) *The Employment Contract: Legal Principles, Drafting and Interpretation*, Oxford: Oxford University Press.

Bronfenbrenner, K., Friedman, S., Hurd, R., Oswald, R. and Seeber, R. (eds) (1998) *Organizing to Win: New Research on Union Strategies*, Cornell University Press, Ithaca.

Brooking, A. (1996) *Introduction to Intellectual Capital*, Cambridge: The Knowledge Broker.

Brown, W. A. (1972) 'A Consideration of Custom and Practice', *British Journal of Industrial Relations*, 10(1): 42–61.

Brown, W., Marginson, P. and Walsh, J. (2003) 'The Management of Pay as the Influence of Collective Bargaining Diminishes', in P. Edwards (ed.) *Industrial Relations: Theory and Practice in Britain*, 2nd edition, Oxford: Blackwell.

Bruce, C. J. and Cerby-Hall, J. (1991) *Rethinking Labour-Management Relations*, London: Routledge.

Brungardt, G. (1996) 'The Making of Leaders: A Review of the Research in Leadership Development and Education', *Journal of Leadership Studies*, 3(3): 81–95.

Bryman, A. (2004) *The Disneyisation of Society*, London: Sage.

Budd, J. W. (2004) *Employment with a Human Face: Balancing Efficiency, Equity and Voice*, London: ILR Press.

Budd, J. and Bhave, D. (2008) 'Values, Ideologies, and Frames of Reference in Industrial Relations', in P. Blyton, N. Bacon, J. Fiorito and E. Heery (eds) *The Sage Handbook of Industrial Relations*, London: Sage.

Budhwar, P. S. and Bhatnagar, J. (eds) (2009) *The Changing Face of People Management in India*, London: Routledge.

Budhwar, P. S. and Sparrow, P. R. (2002) 'An Integrative Framework for Understanding Cross National Human Resource Management Principles', *Human Resource Management Review*, 10(7): 1–28.

Burke, J. and Cooper, C. (eds) (2008) *The Peak Performing Organization*, London: Routledge.

Burns, C. and Conchie, S. M. (2007) 'Trust and the Psychological Contract for Health and Safety', paper presented at the fourth EIASM workshop of trust within and between organizations, October, Amsterdam, The Netherlands.

Burroughs, K. (2006) 'Socialist Realism', *Financial Times 'How to Spend It'* magazine, August: 31.

Butterfield, K. D., Trevino, L. K. and Ball, G. A. (1996) 'Punishment from the Manager's Perspective: A Grounded Investigation and Inductive Model', *Academy of Management Journal*, 39: 1479–512.

Cameron, J. and Pierce, W. D. (2002) *Rewards and Intrinsic Motivation: Resolving the Controversy*, Westport, CT: Bergin and Garvey.

Cameron, S. (1987) 'Trade unions and Productivity: Theory and Evidence', *Industrial Relations Journal*, 18(3): 170–6.

Canter, D. and Donald, I. (1990) 'Accident by Intention', paper presented at the annual conference of the British Association for the Advancement of Science, Swansea, UK.

Cappelli, P. (2008) 'Talent Management for the Twenty-first Century', *Harvard Business Review*, 86(3), March: 74, 76–81.

Cappelli, P. (2008a) *Talent on Demand: Managing Talent in an Age of Uncertainty*, Cambridge, MA: Harvard Business School.

Cascio, W. F. (2000) 'Managing a Virtual Workplace', *The Academy of Management Executive*, 14(3): 81–90.

Cassel, C. (1999) 'A Fatal Attraction? Strategic HRM and the Business Case for Women's Progression at Work', *Personnel Review*, 25(5): 51–66.

CEBC (2004) *Driving Performance and Retention through Employee Engagement*, London: The Corporate Executive Board Company.

Chamberlain, N. W. and Kuhn, J. W. (1966) *Collective Bargaining*, New York: McGraw-Hill.

Chawla, S. and Renesch, J. E. (ed.) (2006) *Learning Organizations: Developing Cultures for Tomorrow's Workplace*, London: Taylor and Francis.

Chen, C. J. (2004) 'The Effects of Knowledge Attribute, Alliance Characteristics, and Absorptive Capacity on Knowledge Transfer Performance', *R&D Management*, 34(3): 311–21.

Chen, G. M. and Starosta, W. J. (1996) 'Intercultural Communication Competence: A Synthesis', in B. R. Burleson and A. W. Kunkel (eds) *Communication Yearbook*, Thousand Oaks, CA: Sage Publications 19: 353–83.

Child, J. (2000) 'Theorising about Organisation Cross-nationally', in J. L. Cheng and R. B. Perterson (eds) *Advances in International Comparative Management*, 13, Stanford, CA: JAI Press.

Child, J. and Kieser, A. (1979) 'Organisation and Managerial Roles in British and West German Companies: An Examination of the Culture-free Thesis', in C. J. Lammers and D. J. Hichson (eds) *Organisations Alike and Unlike: International and Inter-institutional Studies*, London: Routledge, 251–71.

Chingos, P. T. (ed.) (2002) *Paying for Performance: A Guide to Compensation Management*, New York: John Wiley and Son.

Ciarrochi, J., Forgas, J.P. and Mayer, J. D. (2006) *Emotional Intelligence in Everyday Life: A Scientific Inquiry*, New York: Psychology Press.

CIPD (2002) *Employment Law: Survey Report*, London: Chartered Institute of Personnel and Development.

CIPD (2005) *Tackling Age Discrimination in the Workplace: Creating a New Age for All*, London: Chartered Institute of Personnel and Development.

CIPD (2006) *Managing Diversity: Measuring Success*, London: Chartered Institute of Personnel and Development.

CIPD (2006a) *Recruitment, Retention and Turnover: Annual Survey Report 2006*, London: Chartered Institute of Personnel and Development.

CIPD (2006b) *Recruitment and Retention*, London: Chartered Institute of Personnel and Development.

CIPD (2007) *Employee Turnover and Retention*, London: Chartered Institute of Personnel and Development.

CIPD (2008) *Retention Factsheet*, London: Chartered Institute of Personnel and Development.

CIPD (2008a) *Recruitment, Retention and Turnover: Survey Report*, London: Chartered Institute of Personnel and Development.

Chiu, L. H. (1972) 'A Cross-cultural Comparison of Cognitive Styles in Chinese and American Children', *International Journal of Psychology*, 7(4): 235–42.

Clark, E. and Geppert, M. (2002) 'Management Learning and Knowledge Transfer in Transforming Societies: Approaches, Issues and Future Directions', *Human Resource Development International*, 5(3): 263–77.

Clarke, S. and Cooper, C. (2004) *Managing the Risk of Workplace Stress: Health and Safety Hazards*, London: Routledge.

Clarke, T. and Rollo, C. (2001) 'Corporate Initiative in Knowledge Management', *Education and Training*, 43(4/5): 206–14.

Clay, H. (1929) *The Problem of Industrial Relations and Other Lectures*, London: Gill and Macmillan.

Clegg, H. (1979) 'Pluralism in Industrial Relations', *British Journal of Industrial Relations*, 13(3): 309–16.

Coats, D. (2005) *Raising Lazarus: The Future of Organized Labour*, Fabian Society pamphlet no. 618, London.

Cohen, W. M. and Levinthal, D. A. (1990) 'Absorptive Capacity: A New Perspective on Learning and Innovation', *Administrative Science Quarterly*, 35(1): 128–52.

Cohn, S. (1993) *When Strikes Make Sense – and Why: Lessons from Third Republic French Coal Miners*, New York, Plenum Press.

Cokins, G. (2009) *Performance Management: Integrating Strategy Execution, Methodology, Risk, and Analytics*, New York: Wiley.

Collett, P. and Cook, T. (2000) 'A Survey on Managing Diversity in the UK, an Economic and Social Research Council funded project (ESRC H52427500996)', Department of Experimental Psychology, University of Oxford, untitled document: http://users.ox.ac.uk/~hert0159/diversity/mngdiv.

Collins, H. M. (2001) 'Tacit, Knowledge, Trust and the Q of Sapphire', *Social Studies of Science*, 31(1): 71–85.

Collins, J. and Porras, J. I. (2002) *Built to Last*, London: HarperCollins.

Colvin, A. J. S. (2003) Institutional Pressures, Human Resource Strategies, and the Rise of Nonunion Dispute Resolution Procedures', *Industrial and Labor Relations Review*, 56: 375–92.

Colvin, A. J. S. (2004) The Relationship between Employee Involvement and Workplace Dispute Resolution', *Relations Industrielles*, 59(4): 681–704.

Conchie, S. M., Donald, I. J. and Taylor, P. J. (2006) 'Trust: Missing Piece(s) in the Safety Puzzle', *Risk Analysis*, 26: 1097–104.

Conger, J. A. and Riggio, R. E. (eds) (2007) *The Practice of Leadership: Developing the Next Generation of Leaders*, San Francisco, CA: Jossey-Bass.

Contu, A. and Willmott, H. (2003) 'Re-embedding Situatedness: The Importance of Power Relations in Learning Theory', *Organization Science*, 14(3): 283–96.

Conway, N. and Briner, R. B. (2007) *Understanding Psychological Contracts at Work: A Critical Evaluation of Theory and Research*, Oxford: Oxford University Press.

Cooke, B. (2004) 'HR/Benefits Outsourcing: Updating the Conventional Thinking', *Employee Benefit Plan Review*, 58: 18–21.

Cooper, C. and Rousseau, D. (eds) (1998) *Trends in Organizational Behaviour*, New York: John Wiley and Son.

Cooper, M. and White, B. (1995) 'Organisational Behaviour', in S. Tyson (ed.) *Strategic Prospects for HRM*, Institute of Personnel and Development.

Cooper, R. (2000) 'Getting Organised: A White Collar Union Responds to Membership Decline', *Journal of Industrial Relations*, 43(4): 422–37.

Copeland, L. (1988) 'Valuing Diversity', Part 2, 'Pioneers and Champions of Change', *Personnel*, July: 44–9.

Costigan, R. D., Iter, S. S., Insinga, R. C., Kranas, G., Berman, J. J. and Kureshov, V. A. (2005) 'An Examination of the Relationship of a Western Performance-Management Process to Key Workplace Behaviours in Transition Economies', *Canadian Journal of Administrative Science*, 22(3): 255–67.

Cowie, J. (2004) *Improving Staff Retention: Study 765*, London: Incomes Data Services.

Cox, S. J. and Cox, T. R. (1991) 'The Structure of Employee Attitudes to Safety: A European Example', *Work and Stress*, 5: 93–106.

Coyle-Shapiro, J. and Kessler, I. (2000) 'Consequences of the Psychological Contract for the Employment Relationship: A Large Scale Survey, *Journal of Management Studies*, 37: 903–30.

Craggs, R. A. (2002) *Entering Global Markets: An Approach to Designing HR Programs and Policies*, Scottsdale, AZ: WorldatWork.

Csíkszentmihályi, M., Rathunde, K. and Whalen, S. (1993) *Talented Teenagers: The Roots of Success and Failure*, Cambridge: Cambridge University Press.

Cullinane, N. and Dundon, T. (2006) 'The Psychological Contract: A Critical Review', *International Journal of Management Reviews*, 8(2): 113–29.

Cutler, J. (2005) *Cross-cultural Communication Trainer's Manual: Volume One: Designing Cross-cultural Training*, Aldershot: Ashgate Publishing.

Daniels, K. and Macdonald, L. (2005) *Equality, Diversity and Discrimination: A Student Text*, London: Chartered Institute of Personnel and Development.

Davenport, T. O. (1999) *Human Capital*, San Francisco, CA: Jossey Bass.

Davis, P. and Freedland, M. (eds) (1983) *Kahn-Freund's Labour and the Law*, London: Stevens.

Davis, S. H. (2005) 'How to Reduce Executive Failure through Induction', *People Management*, 11(9) May: 40–1.

Day, D. V. (2000) 'Leadership Development: A Review in Context', *Leadership Quarterly*, 11(4): 581–614.

de Cieri, H. and Dowling, P. J. (1999) 'Strategic Human Resource Management in Multinational Enterprises: Theoretical and Empirical Developments', in P. M. Wright, L. D. Dyer, J. W. Boudreau and G. T. Milkovich (eds) *Strategic Human Resource Management in the Twenty First Century*, Greenwich, CT: JAI Press: 305–27.

de Long, T. and Vijayaraghavan, V. (2003) 'Let's Hear It for B Players', *Harvard Business Review*, June: 96–102.

Dearlove, D. (2003) 'Outside is the In Place for Human Resources', *Times*, 30 October, UK.

Delancy, J. and Huselid, M. (1996) 'The Impact of Human Resource Management Practices on Perceptions of Organisational Performance', *Academy of Management Journal*, 39(4): 802–35.

Delery, J. E. and Doty, H. D. (1996) 'Modes of Theorizing in Strategic Human Resource Management: Tests of Universalistic, Contingency and Configurational Performance Predictions', *Academy of Management Journal*, 39: 802–35.

Delua, J. M. and McDowell, R. N. (1992) 'Managing Diversity: A Strategic "Grass-roots" Approach', in S. E. Jackson (ed.) *Diversity in the Workplace: Human Resources Initiatives, Society for Industrial and Organisational Psychology*, New York, NY: The Professional Practice series, Guildford Press.

D'Netto, B. and Sohal, A. S. (1999) 'Human Resource Practices and Workforce Diversity: An Empirical Assessment', *International Journal of Manpower*, 20(8): 530–47.

Derouin, R. E., Fritzsche, B. A. and Salas, E. (2004) 'Optimizing

E-learning: Research-based Guidelines for Learner-controlled Training', *Human Resource Management*, 43(2/3): 147–62.

DeSanctis, G. and Monge, P. (1998) 'Communication Processes for Virtual Organizations', *Journal of Computer-Medicated Communications*, 3(4): 1–12.

Dickens, L. (1994a) 'The Business Case for Women's Equality: Is the Carrot Better than the Stick?', *Employment Relations*, 16(8).

Dickens, L. (1994b) 'Wasted Opportunities? Equal Opportunity in Employment', in K. Sission (ed.) *Personnel Management in Britain*, Oxford: Blackwell.

Dickens, L. and Hall, M. (2003) 'Labour Law and Industrial Relations: A New Settlement', in L. Dickens (1994a) 'The Business Case for Women's Equality: Is the Carrot Better than the Stick?', *Employment Relations*, 16(8): 8–22.

Dolan, S., Belout, A. and Balkin, D. B. (2000) 'Downsizing without Downgrading: Learning how Firms Manage Their Survivors, *International Journal of Manpower*, 21(1): 34–47.

Domberger, S. (1998) *The Contracting Organisation: A Strategic Guide to Outsourcing*, Oxford: Oxford University Press.

Donald, I. (1995) 'Psychological Insights into Managerial Responsibility for Public and Employee Safety', in R. Bull and D. Carson (eds) *Handbook of Psychology in Legal Contexts*, Chichester: Wiley: 625–42.

Donald, I. and Canter, D. (1993) 'Psychological Factors and the Accident Plateau', *Health and Safety Information Bulletin*, 215: 5–8.

Donald, I. and Canter, D. (1994) 'Employee attitudes and safety in the Chemical Industry', *Journal of Loss Prevention in the Process Industries*, 17: 203–8.

Dowling, P. J. (1988) 'International and Domestic Personnel/Human Resource Management: Similarities and Differences', in R. S. Schuler, S. A. Youngblood and V. L. Huber (eds) *Readings in Personnel and Human Resource Management*, 3rd edition, St Paul, MN: West Publishing.

Dowling, P. J., Welch, D. and Schuler, R. S. (1999) *International Human Resource Management: Managing People in a Multinational Context*, 3rd edition, London: South Western College Publishing.

Duarte, D. L. and Snyder, N. T. (1999) *Mastering Virtual Teams: Strategies, Tools and Techniques that Succeed*, San Francisco, CA: Jossey-Bass.

Dulebohn, J. H., Molloy, J. C., Pichler, S. M. and Murray, B. (2009) 'Employee Benefits: Literature Review and Emerging Issues', *Human Resource Management Review*, 19(2): 86–103.

Duggan, M. H. and Jurgens, J. C. (2006) *Career Development Techniques: A Complete Guide for Human Service Professionals*, Reading, MA: Addison-Wesley.

Dundon, T. (2002) 'Policies and Procedures', in T. Redman and A. Wilkinson (eds) *The Informed Student Guide to Human Resource Management*, London: Thomson Learning.

Dundon, T. and Eva, D. (1998) 'Trade Unions and Bargaining for Skills', *Employee Relations*, 20(1): 57–72.

Dundon, T. and Gollan, P. (2007) 'Re-conceptualising Non-union Voice', *International Journal of Human Resource Management*, 18 (7): 1182–98.

Dundon, T. and Rollinson, D. (2004) *Employment Relations in Non-union Firms*, London: Routledge.

Dundon, T. and Wilkinson, A. (2003) 'Employment Relations in Small and Medium Sized Enterprises', in B. Towers (ed.) *Handbook of Employment Relations and Employment Law*, London: Kogan Press.

Dundon, T. and Wilkinson, A. (2009) 'Employee Participation', in T. Redman and A. Wilkinson (eds) *Contemporary Human Resource Management*, 3rd edition, London: Financial Times/Prentice Hall.

Dundon, T., Wilkinson, A., Marchington, M. and Ackers, P. (2004) 'The Meaning and Purpose of Employee Voice', *International Journal of Human Resource Management*, 15(6): 1149–70.

Dunphy, D. and Stace, D. (1993) 'The Strategic Management of Corporate Change', *Human Relations*, 46(8): 905–18.

Dye, R. and Sibony, O. (2007) 'How to Improve Strategic Planning', *McKinsey Quarterly*, 3: 40–8.

Earley, P. C. (2003) 'Redefining Interactions across Cultures and Organizations: Moving Forward with Cultural Intelligence', *Research in Organizational Behaviour*, 24(1): 271–99.

Earley, P. C. and Ang, S. (2003) *Cultural Intelligence: Individual Interactions across Cultures*, Stanford, CA: Stanford University Press.

Easterby-Smith, M., Araujo, L. and Burgoyne, J. G. (eds) (1999) *Organization Learning and the Learning Organization: Developments in Theory and Practice*, London: Sage Publications.

EBRI (2009) *Leave Benefits: Fundamentals of Employee Benefits Programs*, Washington, DC: Employee Benefit Research Institute, chapter 31.

Edenborough. R. (2002) *Effective Interviewing*, Edinburgh: Kogan Page.

Edwards, P. (1995) 'The Employment Relationship', in P. Edwards (ed.) *Industrial Relations: Theory and Practice in Great Britain*, Oxford: Blackwell.

Edwards, P. (ed.) (2003) *Industrial Relations: Theory and Practice in Britain*, 2nd edition, Oxford: Blackwell.

Edwards, P. K., Ferner, A. and Sission, K. (1996) 'The Conditions for International Human Resource Management: Two Case Studies', *International Journal of Human Resource Management*, 7(1): 20–40.

Elkouri, F. and Elkouri, E. (1997) *How Arbitration Works*, New York: BNA Books.

Ellig, B. R. (2007) *The Complete Guide to Executive Compensation*, revised and expanded edition, New York: McGraw-Hill.

Ellis, S. and Sonnerfield, J. A. (1995) 'Diverse Approaches to Managing Diversity', *Human Resource Management*, 33(1).

Elvira, M. E. and Davila, A. (eds) (2005) *Managing Human Resources in Latin America*, London: Routledge.

Erez, M. and Earley, P. C. (1993) *Culture, Self-identity, and Work*, New York: Oxford University Press.

Erikson, E. H. (1968) *Identity, Youth and Crisis*, New York: Norton.

Evans, P., Pucik, V. and Barsoux, J. L. (2002) *The Global Challenge: Frameworks for International Human Resource Management*, London: McGraw-Hill.

Evans, S. and M. Hudson (1993) 'Standardised Packages Individually Wrapped? A Study of the Introduction and Operation of Personal Contracts in the Port Transport and Electricity Supply Industry', *Warwick Papers in Industrial Relations*, no. 44, University of Warwick, July.

Fairbrother, P. and Yates, C. (eds) (2003) *Trade Unions in Renewal: A Comparative Study*, London: Routledge.

Farrell, W. (2007) 'A World of Differences: Train and Maintain Your Global Workforce', *Chief Learning Officer*, 6(7): 22–5.

Fay, C. H. and Tare, M. (2007) 'Market Pricing Concerns, *WorldatWork Journal*, 16(2): 61–9.

Fields, D., Chan, A., Aktar, S. and Blum, T. (2006) 'Human Resource Management Strategies under Uncertainty', *Cross Cultural Management: An International Journal*, 13(2): 171–86.

Finn, W. (1999) 'The Ins and Outs of Human Resources', *Director*, 53: 66–7.

Fitz-enz, J. (2000) *The ROI of Human Capital*, New York: Amacom.

Flanders, A. (1968) 'Collective Bargaining: A Theoretical Analysis', *British Journal of Industrial Relations*, 6(1): 1–26.

Flanders, A. (1970) *Management and Unions*, London: Faber and Faber.

Flanders, A. (1974) *Management and Unions*, London: Faber.

Flavell, J. H. (1987) 'Speculations about the Nature and Development of Metacognition', in F. E. Weinert and R. H. Kluwe (eds) *Metacognition, Motivation, and Understanding*, Hillsdale, NJ: Lawrence Erlbaum: 21–9.

Fletcher, B. and Hurd, R. (1998) 'Beyond the Organizing Model: The Transformation Process in Local Unions', in K. Bronfenbrenner, S. Friedman, R. Hurd, R. Oswald and R. Seeber (eds) *Organizing to Win: New Research on Union Strategies*, Ithaca, NY: Cornell University Press.

Fletcher, C. (2007) *Appraisal, Feedback and Development*, London: Routledge.

Fletcher, C. and Perry, E. L. (2001) 'Performance Appraisal and Feedback: A Consideration of National Culture and a Review of Contemporary Research and Future Trends', in N. Anderson, D. S. Ones, H. K. Sinangil and C. Wiswesvaran (eds) *Handbook of Industrial, Work and Organizational Psychology*, 1: 127–44, Thousand Oaks, CA: Sage Publications.

Flin, R., Burns, C., Mearns, K., Yule, S. and Robertson, E. M. (2006) 'Measuring Safety Climate in Health Care', *Quality and Safety in Health Care*, 15: 109–15.

Flynn, N. (2007) *Public Sector Management*, London: Sage.

Folger, R. and Cropanzano, R. (1998) *Organizational Justice and Human Resource Management*, Thousand Oaks, CA: Sage.

Fombrun, C. J., Tichy, N. M. and Devanna, M. A. (1984) *Strategic Human Resource Management*, New York: Wiley.

Forsaith, J. and Townsend, N. (2000) *Health and Safety Administration Handbook*, London: Chartered Institute of Personnel and Development.

Fowler, A. (1996) *Employee Induction: A Good Start*, London: IPM/CIPD.

Fox, A. (1966) 'Industrial Sociology and Industrial Relations', Royal Commission on Trade Unions and Employers Associations, research paper 3, HMSO, London.

Fox, A. (1974) *Beyond Contract: Work, Power and Trust Relations*, London: Faber and Faber.

Fox, A. (1985) *Man Mismanagement*, London: Hutchinson.

Fried, N. E. and Davis, J. H. (2004) *Developing Statistical Job-Evaluation Models*, Scottsdale, AZ: WorldatWork.

Fundamentals of Employee Benefit Programs (2009) 6th edition, Washington, DC: Employee Benefit Research Organization.

Gainey, T. W., Klaas, B. S. and Moore, D. (2002) 'Outsourcing the Training Function: Results from the Field', *Human Resource Planning*, 25: 18–21.

Gall, G. (2004) 'British Employer Resistance to Trade Union Recognition', *Human Resource Management Journal*, 14(2): 36–53.

Gall, G. (ed.) (2009) *Union Revitalisation in Advanced Economies: Assessing the Contribution of Union Organising*, London: Palgrave Macmillan.

Garvin, D. (1993) 'Building a Learning Organization', *Harvard Business Review*, 71(4): 78–91.

Gennard, J. and Judge, G. (2005) *Employee Relations*, 4th edition, London: Chartered Institute of Personnel and Development.

Gerhart, B. and Rynes, S. L. (2003) *Compensation: Theory, Evidence, and Strategic Implications*, Thousand Oaks, CA: Sage.

Gheraridi, S. (2000) 'Practice-based Theoretizing on Learning and Knowing in Organizations', *Organization*, 7(2): 211–23.

Gibson, C. B. and Cohen, S. G. (eds) (2003) *Virtual Teams that Work: Creating Conditions for Virtual Team Effectiveness*, San Francisco, CA: Jossey-Bass.

Giddens, A. (2006) *Sociology*, Cambridge: Polity.

Giddens, A. (2009) *Sociology*, Oxford: Blackwell.

Giles, C. (2009) 'Flexible Workers Reduce Need to Get on Their Bike', *Financial Times*, 10 June: 3.

Gilley, J. W. and Eggland, S. A. (1989) *Principles of Human Resources Development*, Reading, MA: Addison-Wesley.

Gladwell, M. (2002) 'The Talent Myth: Are Smart People Overrated?', *The New Yorker*, 22 July, available at www.gladwell.com/2002/2002_07_22_a_talent.htm.

Glendon, I. A., Clarke, S. and McKenna, E. F. (2006) *Human Safety and Risk Management*, London: Taylor and Francis.

Goetschy, J. and Jobert, A. (2004) 'Employment relations in France', in G. Bamber, R. Lansbury and N. Wailes (eds) *International and Comparative Employment Relations: Globalisation and the Developed Market Economies*, 4th edition, London: Sage.

Goldstein, I. L., Macey, W. H. and Prien, E. P. (2001) 'Needs Assessment Approaching for Training Development', in H. Meltzer and W. R. Nord (eds) *Making Organizations More Humane and Productive: A Handbook for Practitioners*, New York: Wiley-Interscience.

Goleman, D. (1995) *Emotional Intelligence*, New York: Bantam Books.

Gollan, P. and Wilkinson, A. (2007) 'Implications of the EU Information and Consultation Directive and the Regulations in the UK: Prospects for the Future of Employee Representation', *International Journal of Human Resource Management*, 18(7): 1145–58.

Gomez, R., Gunderson, M. and Lucak, A. (2002) 'Mandatory Retirement: A Constraint in Transitions to Retirement', *Employee Relations*, 24(8): 736–47.

Gomez-Mejia, L. and Werner, S. (eds) (2008) *Global Compensation: Foundations and Perspectives*, New York: Routledge.

Goodman, A. (1995) *Basic Skills for the New Arbitrator*, New York: Solomon.

Goodrich, C. L. (1975) *The Frontier of Control*, London: Pluto Press.

Gostick, A. and Elton, C. (2007) *The Carrot Principle: How the Best Managers Use Recognition to Engage Their People, Retain Talent and Accelerate Performance*, New York: Free Press.

Greenberg, J. (2006) 'Losing Sleep over Organizational Injustice: Attenuating Insomniac Reactions to Underpayment Inequity with Supervisory Training in Interactional Injustice', *Journal of Applied Psychology*, 91: 58–69.

Greer, C., Youngblood, S. and Gray, D. (1999) 'Human Resource Management Outsourcing: The Make or Buy Decision', *Academy of Management Executive*, 13(3): 85–96.

Graham, M. D., Roth, T. A. and Dugan, D. (2008) *Effective Executive Compensation: Creating a Total Rewards Strategy*, New York: American Management Association.

Granrose, C. S. and Portwood, J. D. (1987) 'Matching Individual Career Plans and Organizational Career Management', *Academy of Management Journal*, 30(4): 699–720.

Grubman, E. L. (1998) *The Talent Solution*, New York: McGraw-Hill.

Guest, D. (1992) 'Right Enough to be Dangerously Wrong: An Analysis of the "In Search of Excellence Phenomenon"', in G. Salaman et al. (eds) *Human Resource Strategies*, London: Sage: 5–19.

Guest, D. (1997) 'Human Resource Management and Performance: A Review and Research Agenda', *International Journal of Human Resource Management*, 3(8): 263–76.

Guest, D. (1998) 'Is the Psychological Contract Worth Taking Seriously?', *Journal of Organizational Behaviour*, 19: 649–64.

Guest, D. (2001) 'Human Resource Management: When Research Confronts Theory', *International Journal of Human Resource Management*, 12(7): 1092–106.

Guest, D. (2004) 'The Psychology of the Employment Relationship: An Analysis Based on the Psychological Contract', *Applied Psychology*, 53: 541–55.

Guest, D. and Conway, N. (1998) 'Fairness at Work and the Psychological

Contract: Issues in People Management', London: Institute of Personnel and Development.

Guest, D. and Conway, N. (2002) 'Communicating the Psychological Contract: An Employee Perspective', *Human Resource Management Journal*, 12: 22–39.

Guest, D. and Peccei, R. (2001) 'Partnership at Work: Mutuality and the Balance of Advantage', *British Journal of Industrial Relations*, 39(2): 207–36.

Guest, D., Michie, J., Sheehan, N. and Conway, N. (2000a) *Employment Relations, HRM and Business Performance: An Analysis of the 1998 Workplace Employee Relations Survey*, London: Chartered Institute of Personnel and Development.

Guest, D., Michie, J., Sheehan, M., Conway, N. and Metochi, M. (2000b) *Effective People Management: Initial Findings of the Future of Work Study*, London: CIPD.

Gueutal, H. G. and Stone, D. L. (eds) (2005) *The Brave New World of e-HR: Human Resources Management in the Digital Age*, San Francisco, CA: Jossey-Bass.

Guldenmund, F. W. (2000) 'The Nature of Safety Culture: A Review of Theory and Research', *Safety Science*, 34: 215–57.

Gupta, K. (1999) *A Practical Guide to Needs Assessment*, San Francisco, CA: Jossey-Bass.

Gupta, N. and Shaw, J. D. (1998) 'Let the Evidence Speak: Financial Incentives Are Effective', *Compensation and Benefits Review*, March/April: 27–32.

Hall, K. (2009) 'Japan: No Model for Executive Compensation', *Business Week*, Executive Suite, 12 February.

Hall, L. and Torrington, D. (1998) *The Human Resource Function: The Dynamics of Change and Development*, London: Financial Times-Pitman Publishing.

Hamblin, A. C. (1974) *Evaluation and Control of Training*, Maidenhead, UK: McGraw-Hill.

Hamel, G. and Parahalad, C. K. (1985) 'Do You Really Have a Global Strategy?', *Harvard Business Review*, July–August: 139–48.

Hammer, M. and Champy, J. A. (1993) *Reengineering the Corporation: A Manifesto for Business Revolution*, New York: Harper Business Books.

Hammond, D. (2002) 'Firms Resist HRM Outsourcing', *People Management*, 13(8) June: 7.

Harris, H., Brewster, C. and Sparrow, P. (2003) *International Human Resource Management*, London: Chartered Institute of Personnel and Development.

Harry, W. and Jackson, K. (2007) 'Global Wave: A Critique of Western HRM Theory', *Management Revue*, 18: 472–82.

Harzing, A-W. and Ruysseveldt, J. V. (eds) (2004) *International Human Resource and Staffing*, London: Sage Publications Ltd.

Hay, D. (2004) *Managing the Impact of Recognition*, Scottsdale, AZ: WorldatWork.

Haynes, P. and Allen, M. (2000) 'Partnership as Union Strategy: A Preliminary Evaluation', *Employee Relations*, 23(2): 164–87.

Heery, E., Healy, G. and Taylor, P. (2004) 'Representation at Work: Themes and Issues', in G. Healy, E. Heery, P. Taylor and W. Brown (eds) *The Future of Worker Representation*, Basingstoke: Palgrave Macmillan.

Heery, E., Simms, M., Simpson, D., Delbridge, V and Salmon, J. (2000) 'Organising Unionism Comes to the UK', *Employee Relations*, 22(1): 38–57.

Heller, F., Pusic, E., Strauss, G. and Wilpert, B. (1998) *Organisational Participation: Myth and Reality*, Oxford: Oxford University Press.

Heller, K. A., Mönks, F. J. and Subotnik, R. (eds) (2000) *International Handbook of Giftedness and Talent*, London: Pergamon.

Hendry, C. (1994) *Human Resource Strategies for International Growth*, London: Routledge.

Heneerz, U. (1996) *Transnational Connections*, London: Routledge.

Heneman, R. L. (1992) *Merit Pay: Linking Pay Increases to Performance Ratings*, Reading, MA: Addison-Wesley.

Heneman, R. L. (2002) *Strategic Reward Management: Design, Implementation and Evaluation*, Greenwich, CT: Information Age Publishing.

Hernez-Broome, G. and Hughes, R. J. (2004) 'Leadership Development, Past, Present, and Future', *Human Resource Planning*, 27(1): 24–32.

Herod, R. (2009a) *Expatriate Compensation Strategies: Applying Alternative Approaches*, Alexandria, VA: Society for Human Resource Management.

Herod, R. (2009b) *Expatriate Compensation: The Balance Sheet Approach*, Alexandria, VA: Society for Human Resource Management.

Herzberg, F. W. (1968) 'One More Time: How Do You Motivate Employees?', *Harvard Business Review*, January–February: 109–20.

Herzberg, F. W. (2008) *One More Time: How Do You Motivate Employees?*, Boston, MA: Harvard Business Press.

Herzberg, F. W., Mausner, B. and Snyderman, B. (1957) *The Motivation to Work*, New York: Wiley.

Hicks-Clarke, D. and Iles, P. (2000) 'Climate for Diversity and Its Effects of Career and Organisational Attitudes and Perceptions', *Personnel Review*, 29(3): 324–45.

Hodgkinson, M. (2000) 'The Role of Higher Education Institutions in Facilitating Organization Learning with HRD Managers', *Human Resource Development International*, 3(3): 361–75.

Hofmann, D. A., Morgeson, F. P. and Gerras, S. J. (2003) 'Climate as a Moderator of the Relationship between Leader–Member Exchange and Content Specific Citizenship: Safety Climate as an Examplar', *Journal of Applied Psychology*, 88: 170–8.

Hofstede, G. (1984) *Culture's Consequences: International Differences in Work-Related Values*, abridged edition, London: SAGE.

Hofstede, G. (1991) *Culture and Organizations: Software of the Mind*, London: McGraw Hill.

Hofstede, G. (1993) 'Cultural Constraints in Management Theories', *Academy of Management Executive*, 7: 81–94.

Hofstede, G. (2003) *Culture's Consequences: Comparing Values, Behaviours, Institutions, and Organizations across Nations*, Thousand Oaks, CA: Sage Publications.

Hollinshead, G., Nicholls, P. and Tailby, S. (2003) *Employee Relations*, Harlow: Prentice-Hall/Financial Times.

Hollway, W. (1991) *Work Psychology and Organization Behaviour: Managing the Individual at Work*, London: Sage.

Holt Larsen, H. and Mayrhofer, W. (eds) (2006) *Managing Human Resources in Europe*, London: Routledge.

Honeyball, S. (1989) 'Employment Law and the Primacy of Contract', *Industrial Law Journal*, 18(2): 97–108.

Hooker, J. (2003) *Working across Culture*, Stanford, CA: Stanford University Press.

Hu, Y.-S. (1992) 'Global or Stateless Corporations Are National Firms with International Operations', *California Management Review*, 34(2): 107–26.

Hundley, S. P., Jacobs, F. and Drizin, M. (2007) *Workforce Engagement*, Scottsdale, AZ: WorldatWork.

Hunt, J. M. and Weintraub, J. R. (2007) *The Coaching Organization*, Thousand Oaks, CA: Sage Publications.

Huselid, M. A. (1995) 'The Impact of Human Resource Management Practices on Turnover, Productivity and Corporate Financial Performance', *Academy of Management Journal*, 38(3): 635–72.

Huselid, M. A. (1995) 'The Impact of Human Resource Management: An Agenda for the 1990s', *International Journal of Human Resource Management*, 1: 17–43.

Huselid, M. A. and Bechker, B. (1996) 'Methodological Issues in Cross-Sectional and Panel Estimates of the Human Resource-Firm Performance Link', *Industrial Relations*, 35(3): 400–22.

Huselid, M. A., Jackson, S. E. and Schuler, R. S. (1997) 'Technical and Strategic Human Resource Management Effectiveness as Determinants of Firm Performance', *Academy of Management Journal*, 40(1): 171–88.

Hyman, R. (1975) *Industrial Relations: A Marxist Introduction*, London: Macmillan.

Hyman, R. (2001) *Understanding European Trade Unionism: Between Market, Class and Society*, London: Sage.

Hyman, R. (2003) 'The Historical Evolution of British Industrial Relations', in P. Edwards (ed.) *Industrial Relations: Theory and Practice in Britain*, 2nd edition, Blackwell, Oxford.

Ichniowski, C., Kochan, T., Levin, D., Olson, C. and Strauss, G. (1996) 'What Works at Work: Overview and Assessment', *Industrial Relations*, 35(3): 299–333.

IHRIM (International Human Resource Information Management) Go-To-Guides, The Advanced Management Series, three volumes: 2001, 2002, 2003, Burlington, MA: IHRIM.

ILO (1980) *Conciliation and Arbitration Procedures in Labour Disputes*, Geneva: ILO.

Incomes Data Services (2005) *Assessment Centres*, IDS study no. 800, June, London: IDS.

Incomes Data Services (2006) *Online Recruitment*, IDS study no. 819, April, London: IDS.

Incomes Data Services (2008) *Improving Staff Retention*, HR study no. 863, London: IDS.

Ivancevich, J. M. (1969) 'Selection of American Managers for Overseas Assignments', *Personnel Journal*, 18(3): 189–200.

Jackson, K. and Tomioka, M. (2003) *The Changing face of Japanese Management* London: Routledge.

Jackson, K. and Debroux, P. (2009) *Innovation in Japan: Emerging Patterns, Enduring Myths*, London: Routledge.

Jackson, M. (1982) *Trade Unions*, London: Longman.

Jackson, S. W. and Schuler, R. S. (1995) 'Understanding Human Resource Management in the Context of Organisations and Their Environments', *Annual Review of Psychology*, 46: 237–64.

Jacoby, S. M. (1997) *Modern Manors: Welfare Capitalism since the New Deal*, Princeton, NJ: Princeton University Press (reviewed by the author in *Historical Studies in Industrial Relations*, 8, Autumn 1999: 188–94).

Jankowicz, A. D. (2000) *Business Research Projects*, London: Thomson Learning.

Jensen, D., McMullen, T. and Stark, M. (2007) *The Manager's Guide to Rewards: What You Need to Know to Get the Best for – and from – Your Employees*, New York: Amacom.

Jensen, M. C. and Murphy, K. J. (2007) *CEO Pay and What to Do About It: Restoring Integrity to Executive Compensation and Capital-Market Relations*, Cambridge, MA: Harvard University Press.

Johnson, N. and Jarley, P. (2004) 'Justice and Union Participation: An Extension and Test of Mobilisation Theory', *British Journal of Industrial Relations*, 42(3): 543–62.

Kahn-Freund, O. (1967) 'A Note on Status and Contract in British Labour Law', *Modern Law Review*, 30: 635–44.

Kahn-Freund, O. (1977) *Labour and the Law*, London: Stevens.

Kandola, B. and Fullerton, J. (1994) *Managing the Mosaic: Diversity in Action*, London: Institute of Personnel and Development.

Kanfer, R, Chen, G. and Pritchard, R. D. (eds) (2008) *Work Motivation: Past, Present, and Future*, New York: Routledge.

Kang, H. R., Yang, H. D. and Rowley, C. (2006) 'Factors in Team Effectiveness: Cognitive and Demographic Similarities of Software Development Team Members', *Human Relations*, 59(12): 1681–710.

Kaplan, R. S. and Norton, D. P. (1996) *The Balanced Scorecard: Translating Strategy into Action*, Cambridge, MA: Harvard Business School Press.

Katz, D. and Kahn, R. L. (1978) *The Social Psychology of Organizations*, 2nd edition, New York: John Wiley and Son.

Katzenback, J. R. and Smith, D. K. (2003) *The Wisdom of Teams: Creating the High-performance Organization*, Maidenhead, UK: McGraw-Hill.

Kaufman, B. (2004) *The Global Evolution of Industrial Relations: Events, Ideas and the IIRA*, Geneva: ILO.

Kavanagh, M. J. and Thite, M. (eds) (2008) *Human Resources Information Systems: Basics, Applications and Directions*, Thousand Oaks, CA: Sage Publications.

Kelly, J. (1996) 'Union Militancy and Social Partnership', in P. Ackers, C. Smith and P. Smith (eds) *The New Workplace and Trade Unionism*, London: Routledge.

Kelly, J. (1998) *Rethinking Industrial Relations: Mobilisation, Collectivism and Long Waves*, London: Routledge.

Kelly, J. (2005) 'Social Partnership Agreements in Britain', in M. Stuart and M. Martinez Lucio (eds) *Partnership and Modernisation in Employment Relations*, London: Routledge.

Kennerly, J. A. (1994) *Arbitration Cases in Industrial Relations*, London: Pitman.

Kerr, C., Dunlop, J. T., Harbison, F. H. and Myers, C. A. (1962) *Industrialism and Industrial Man: The Problems of Labour and Management in Economic Growth*, London: Heinemann Education.

Kersley, B., Alpin, C., Forth, J., Bryson, A., Bewley, H., Dix, J. and Oxenbridge, S. (2006) *Inside the Workplace: Findings from the 2004 Workplace Employment Relations Survey*, London: Routledge.

Kessler, I. and Purcell, J. (1995) 'Individualism and Collectivism in Theory and Practice: Management Style and the Design of a System', in P. Edwards (ed.) *Industrial Relations: Theory and Practice in Britain*, Oxford: Blackwell.

Kheet, T. and Lurie, W. (1999) *The Keys to Conflict Resolution*, New York: Four Walls.

Kilburg, R. R. (1996) 'Toward a Conceptual Understanding and Definition of Executive Coaching', *Consulting Psychology Journal: Practice and Research*, 48(2): 134–44.

Kim, D. H. (1993) 'The Link between Individual and Organizational Learning', *Sloan Management Review*, 35(1): 37–50.

Kirkpatrick, I. and Hoque, K. (2005) 'The Decentralisation of Employment Relations in the British Public Sector', *Industrial Relations Journal*, 36(1): 100–21.

Kirton, G. and Greene, A.-M. (2005) *The Dynamics of Managing Diversity: A Critical Approach*, Oxford: Elsevier Butterworth-Heinemann.

Klaas, B. (2009) 'Grievance and Discipline', in A. Wilkinson, N. Bacon, T. Redman and S. Snell (eds) *Handbook of Human Resource Management*, London: Sage.

Kline, J. (2005) *Ethics for International Business: Decision-making in a Global Political Economy*, London: Routledge.

Knowles, M. S. (1990) *The Adult Learner: A Neglected Species*, 4th edition, Houston, TX: Gulf.

Kochan, T. and Barocci, T. (1985) *Human Resource Management and Industrial Relations*, Boston, MA: Little Brown.

Kohn, A. (1993) 'Why Incentive Plans Cannot Work', *Harvard Business Review*, September–October: 54–63.

Kram, K. (1988) *Mentoring at Work*, New York: University Press of America.

Krempl, S. F. and Pace, W. R. (2001) *Training Across Multiple Locations: Developing a System that Works*, San Francisco, CA: Berrett-Koehler.

Kwon, R. (2009) 'Taiwan's Workers Opt for More Qualifications', *Financial Times*, 2 April.

Laabs, J. (1998) 'The Dark Side of Outsourcing', *Workforce*, 77, September: 17–18.

Lam, S. S. and Schaubroeck, J. (1998) 'Integrating HR Planning and Organizational Strategy', *Human Resource Management Journal*, 8(3): 5–19.

Lane, C. (1995) *Industry and Society in Europe: Stability and Change in Britain, Germany and France*, Aldershot: Edward Elgar.

Latham, G. P. (2007) *Work Motivation: Theory, Research, and Practice*, Thousand Oaks, CA: Sage Publications.

Latham, G. P. and Pinder, C. C. (2005) 'Work Motivation: Theory and Research at the Dawn of the Twenty-First Century', *Annual Review of Psychology*, 56(1): 485–516.

Laurent, A. (1986) 'The Cross-Cultural Puzzle of International Human Resource Management', *Human Resource Management*, 25(1): 91–102.

Lawler, I., Edward, E. and Mohrman, S. A. (2003) 'HRM as a Strategic Partner: What Does It Take to Make It Happen?', *Human Resource Planning*, 26(3): 15–29.

Ledford, G. E. (2008) 'Factors Affecting the Long-Term Success of Skill-Based Pay', WorldatWork Journal 17(1): 6–17.

Lee, C. H. and Bruvold, N. T. (2003) 'Creating Value for Employees: Investment in Employee Development', *International Journal of Human Resource Management*, 14(6): 981–1000.

Lee, T. and Harrison, K. (2000) 'Assessing Safety Culture in Nuclear Power Stations', *Safety Science*: 34: 61–97.

Legge, K. (1995) *Human Resource Management: Rhetorics and Realties*, London: Macmillan.

Lever, S. (1997) 'An Analysis of Managerial Motivations behind Outsourcing Practices in Human Resources', *Human Resource Planning*, 20: 37–47.

Levinson, H., Price, C. R., Munden, K. J. and Solley, C. M. (1962) *Men, Management and Mental Health*, Cambridge, MA: Harvard University Press.

Levitt, T. (1983) 'The Globalisation of Markets', *Harvard Business Review*, 3: 92–102.

Lewis, D. and Sargeant, M. (2004) *Essentials of Employment Law*, 8th edition, London: CIPD Publishing.

Lewis. P., Thornhill, A. and Saunders, M. (2003) *Employee Relations: Understanding the Employment Relationship*, Harlow: Financial Times/Prentice Hall.

Liu, P. L. and Tsai, C. H. (2007) 'The Influence of Innovation Management on New Product Development Performance in Taiwan's Hi-Tech Industries', *Research Journal of Business Management*, 1(1): 20–9.

Liff, S. (1993) 'From Equality to Diversity: Organisations, Gender and Power', Warwick Papers in Industrial Relations, 48 (December).

Lilly, J. D., Gray, D. A. and Virick, M. (2005) 'Outsourcing the Human Resource Function: Environmental and Organisational Characteristics that Affect HR Performance', *Journal of Business Strategies*, 22(1): 55–73.

Lipman, F. D. and Hall, S. E. (2008) *Executive Compensation: Best Practices*, New York: Wiley.

Litvin, D. (1997) 'The Discourse of Diversity: From Biology to Management', *Organisation*, 4(2): 187–209.

Locke, E. A. and Associates (1999) *The Essence of Leadership*, New York: Lexington.

Locke, E. A. and Latham, G. P. (1984) *Goal-Setting: A Theory that Works*, Englewood Cliffs, NJ: Prentice Hall.

Locke, E. A. and Latham, G. P. (1990) *A Theory of Goal Setting and Task Performance*, Englewood Cliffs, NJ: Prentice Hall.

Logan, J. (2001) 'Is Statutory Recognition Bad News for British Unions? Evidence from the History of North American Industrial Relations', *Historical Studies in Industrial Relations*, 11 (Spring): 63–108.

Lowry, P. (1990) *Employment Disputes and the Third Party*, London: Macmillan.

Mabey, C. and Salaman, G. (1995) *Strategic Human Resource Management*, Oxford: Blackwell.

Mabey, C., Skinner, D. and Clark, T. (1998) *Experiencing Human Resource Management*, London: Sage.

McAdams, J. L. (1996) *The Reward Plan Advantage*, San Francisco, CA: Jossey-Bass.

MacAfee, M. (2007) 'How to Conduct Exit Interviews', *People Management*, 13(14), 12 July: 42–3.

McCall, M. R. Jr. and Hollenbeck, G. P. (2002) *Developing Global Executives: The Lessons of International Experience*, Boston, MA: Harvard Business School Press.

McCauley, C. D., Moxley, R. S. and van Velsor, E. (eds) (1998) *Handbook of Leadership Development*, San Francisco, CA: Jossey-Bass.

McDougall, M. (1996) 'Equal Opportunities Versus Managing Diversity, Another Challenge for Public Sector Management?', *International Journal of Public Sector Management*, 9(5): 62–72.

MacDuffie, J. (1995) 'Human Resource Bundles and Manufacturing Performance: Organisational Logic and Flexible Production Systems in the World Auto Industry', *Industrial and Labour Relations Review*, 48(2): 197–221.

McElwain, J. E. (1991) 'Succession Plans Designed to Manage Change', *HR Magazine*, 36(2): 67–71.

McFadzean, E. (2002) 'Developing and Supporting Creative Problem Solving Teams: Part 2 – Facilitator Competencies', *Management Decision*, 40(6): 537–51.

McGregor, D. (2005) *The Human Side of Enterprise: Annotated Guide*, New York: McGraw-Hill.

McInerney, C. R. and Day, R. E. (eds) (2007) *Rethinking Knowledge Management*, Berlin: Springer.

McKenna, E. (2000) *Business Psychology and Organisational Behaviour: A Student's Handbook*, Hove, East Sussex: Psychology Press.

McLoughlin, I. and Gourlay, S. (1994) *Enterprise without Unions: Industrial Relations in the Non-Union Firm*, Buckingham: Open University Press.

McMahon, J. R. and Hand, J. S. (2006) *Designing and Conducting a Salary Survey*, Scottsdale, AZ: WorldatWork.

Manas, T. M. and Graham, M. D. (2003) *Creating a Total Rewards Strategy: A Toolkit for Designing Business-Based Plans*, New York: American Management Association.

Marchington, M. (2005) 'Employee Involvement: Patterns and Explanations', in B. Harley, G. Hyman and P. Thompson (eds) *Participation and Democracy at Work: Essays in Honour of Harvie Ramsay*, London: Palgrave.

Marchington, M. and Grugulis, I. (2000) 'Best Practice Human Resource Management: Perfect Opportunity or Dangerous Illusion?', *International Journal of Human Resource Management*, 11(4): 905–25.

Marchington, M. and Wilkinson, A. (2002) *People Management and Development: Human Resource Management at Work*, London: Chartered Institute of Personnel and Development.

Marchington, M. and Wilkinson, A. (2005) 'Direct Participation', in S. Bach (ed.) *Personnel Management*, 4th edition, Oxford: Blackwell.

Marchington, M. and Wilkinson, A. (2008) *Human Resource Management at Work: People Management and Development*, London: Chartered Institute of Personnel and Development.

Marchington, M., Wilkinson, A. J., Ackers, P. and Dundon, T. (2001) *Management Choice and Employee Voice*, London: Chartered Institute of Personnel and Development.

Marchington, M., Wilkinson, A., Goodman, J. and Ackers, P. (1992) 'New Developments in Employee Involvement', Employment Department Research Paper, series no. 2.

Margerison, C. and Leary, M. (1975) *Industrial Conflict: The Mediator's Role*, Bradford: MCB Books.

Marinaccio, L. (1994) 'Outsourcing: A Strategic Tool for Managing Human Resources', *Employee Benefit Journal*, 19 March: 39–42.

Markey, R., Gollan, P., Hodgkinson, A., Chouraqui, A. and Veersmas, U. (2001) *Models of Employee Participation in a Changing Global Environment: Diversity and Interaction*, Aldershot: Ashgate.

Markowich, M. M. (2007) *Employee Benefits Basics*, Scottsdale, AZ: WorldatWork.

Marlow, S. (2002) 'Regulating Labour Management in Small Firms', *Human Resource Management Journal*, 12(3): 1–25.

Marquardt, M. (2002) *Building the Learning Organization: Mastering the 5 Elements for Corporate Learning*, New York: Davies-Black Publishing.

Marquardt, M. J. and Kearsley, G. (1999) *Technology-Based Learning: Maximizing Human Performance and Corporate Success*, Boca Raton, FL: St Lucie Press.

Martocchio, J. (2006) *Employee Benefits: A Primer for Human Resource Professionals*, 2nd edition, New York: McGraw-Hill.

Maslow, A. H. (1954) *Motivation and Personality*, New York: Harper and Row.

Maslow, A. H. (1987) *Motivation and Personality*, 3rd edition, New York: Harper and Row.

Mayer, J. D. and Salovey, P. (1997) 'What is Emotional Intelligence?', in P. Salovey and D. Sluyter (eds) *Emotional Development and Emotional Intelligence: Implications for Educators*, New York: Basic Books: 3–31.

Mayo, A. (1999) 'Making Human Capital Meaningful', *Knowledge Management Review*, January/February: 26–9.

Mayo, A. (2001) *The Human Value of The Enterprise: Valuing People as Assets*, London: Nicholas Brealy.

Mead, R. and Andrews, T. G. (2009) *International Management: Culture and Beyond*, Chichester: John Wiley.

Mearns, K., Flin, R., Gordon, R. and Fleming, M. (1997) *Organisational and Human Factors in Offshore Safety*, OTH 543 report, Suffolk: HSE Books.

Mearns, K., Flin, R., Gordon, R. and Fleming, M. (1998) 'Measuring safety climate on offshore installations', *Work and Stress*, 12: 238–54.

Mendenhall, M. and Oddou, G. (1985) 'The Dimensions of Expatriate Acculturation', *Academy of Management Review*, 10: 39–47.

Metcalf, D. (2005) *British Unions: Resurgence or Perdition?*, Provocation Series, vol. 1, no. 1, London: The Work Foundation.

Meyers, P. S. (1996) *Knowledge Management and Organization Design*, Oxford: Butterworth-Heinemann.

Michaels; E., Handfield-Jones, H. and Axelrod, B. (2001) *The War for Talent*, Cambridge, MA: Harvard Business School Press.

Miles, R. and Snow, C. (1978) *Organizational Strategy, Structure and Process*, New York: McGraw-Hill.

Milkman, R. (ed.) (2000) *Organising Immigrants*, Ithaca, NY: IRL Press.

Milkovich, G. T. and Wigdor, A. K. (1991) *Pay for Performance: Evaluating Performance Appraisal and Merit Pay*, Washington, DC: National Academy Press.

Miller, D. (1996) 'Equality Management: Towards a Materialist Approach', *Gender, Work and Organisation*, 3(4): 202–14.

Millmore, M., Lewis, P., Saunders, M., Thornhill, A. and Morrow, T. (2007) *Strategic Human Resource Management: Contemporary Issues*, Harlow, UK: Prentice Hall.

Millward, N., Bryson, A. and Forth, J. (2000) *All Change at Work: British Employment Relations 1980–1998, as Portrayed by the Workplace Industrial Relations Survey Series*, London: Routledge.

Minor, F. J. (1986) 'Computer Applications in Career Development Planning', in D. T. Hall and Associates (eds) *Career Development in Organizations*, San Francisco, CA: Jossey-Bass: 205–6.

Mládková, L. (2007) 'Management of Tacit Knowledge in Organization', *Economics and Management*, 803–8.

Mohrman, S. A. (1998) 'The Contexts for Geographically Dispersed Teams and Networks', in C. Cooper and D. Rousseau (eds) *Trends in Organizational Behaviour*, New York: John Wiley and Son: 63–80.

Monger, J. (2004) 'International Comparisons of Labour Disputes in 2002', *Labour Markey Trends*, 112(4): 145–53.

Morgan, G. (1986) *Images of Organization*, London: Sage.

Morrison, E. W. and Robinson, S. (1997) 'When Employees Feel Betrayed: A Model of How Psychological Contract Violation Develops', *Academy of Management Review*, 22: 226–56.

Mullins, L. (2006) *Management and Organisational Behaviour*, Harlow, UK: Prentice Hall/Financial Times.

Mumby, D. (2005) 'Theorising Resistance in Organizational Studies: A Dialectical Approach', *Management Communication Quarterly*, 19(1): 19–44.

Murphy, S. E. and Riggio, R. E. (eds) (2003) *The Future of Leadership Development*, Mahwah, NJ: Lawrence Erlbaum Associates.

Murphy, T. E. (2010) *Benefits and Beyond: A Comprehensive and Strategic Approach to Retirement, Health Care, and More*, Los Angeles, CA: Sage.

Murray, P. and Blackman, D. (2006) 'Managing Innovation through Social Architecture, Learning, and Competencies: A New Conceptual Approach', *Knowledge and Process Management*, 13(3): 132–43.

Nadler, L. (1984) 'Human Resource Development', in L. Nadler (ed.) *The Handbook of Human Resource Development*, New York: John Wiley and Son: 1–47.

Neal, A. and Griffin, M. A. (2006) 'A Longitudinal Study of the Relationships among Safety Climate, Safety Motivation, Safety Behavior, and Accidents at the Individual and Group Levels', *Journal of Applied Psychology*, 91: 946–53.

Negrelli, S. and Sheldon, P. (2004) 'Employment Relations in Italy', in G. Bamber, R. Lansbury and N. Wailes (eds) *International and Comparative Employment Relations: Globalisation and the Developed Market Economies*, 4th edition, London: Sage.

Noes, R. A. (2008) *Employee Training and Development*, New York: McGraw-Hill/Irwin.

Nolan, P. (1983) 'The Labour Market', in G. Bain (ed.) *Industrial Relations in Britain*, Oxford: Blackwell.

Nolan, P. and Marginson, P. (1988) 'Skating on Thin Ice?: David Metcalf on Trade unions and Productivity', *Warwick Papers on Industrial Relations*, no. 22, University of Warwick, Coventry.

Nolan, P. and O'Donnell, K. (2003) 'Industrial Relations, HRM and Performance', in P. Edwards (ed.) *Industrial Relations: Theory and Practice*, 2nd edition, Oxford: Blackwell.

Nonaka, I. and Takeuchi, J. (1995) *The Knowledge-creating Company*, New York: Oxford University Press.

Nonaka, I., Umemoto, K. and Senoo, D. (1996) 'From Information Processing to Knowledge Creation: A Paradigm Shift in Business Management', *Technology in Society*, 18(1): 203–18.

Nozick, R. (1974) *Anarchy, State and Utopia*, New York: Basic Books.

O'Connor, T. (1997) 'Using Learning Styles to Adapt Technology for

Higher Education', retrieved March 25, 2008, from http://iod.unh.edu/ EE/articles/learning-styles.html.

Ohmae, K. (2009) *The Next Global Stage: Challenges and Opportunities in Our Borderless World*, Philadelphia, PA: Wharton School Publishing.

Osterman, P., T. Kochan, R. M. Locke and M. J. Piore (2001) *Working in America: A Blueprint for the New Labour Market*, Cambridge, MA: MIT Press.

O'Sullivan, S. L. (1999) 'The Distinction between Stable and Dynamic Cross-cultural Competencies: Implications for Expatriate Trainability', *Journal of International Business Studies*, 30(4): 709–25.

Paauwe, J. and Boselie, P. (2005) '"Best Practice . . . in Spite of Perform-ance": Just a Matter of Imitation?' *International Journal of Human Resource Management*, 16(6): 987–1003.

Pauleen, D. J. (2007) *Cross-cultural Perspectives on Knowledge Management*, Westport, CT: Libraries Unlimited.

Parus, B. (2002) *Market Pricing: Methods to the Madness*, Scottsdale, AZ: WorldatWork.

Patterson, M., West, M., Lawthom, R. and Nickell, S. (1997) *The Impact of People Management Practices on Business Performance*, London: Institute of Personnel and Development.

Pedler, M., Burgoync, J. and Boydell, T. (1997) *The Learning Company: A Strategy for Sustainable Development*, 2nd edition, London: McGraw Hill.

Pelling, H. (1987) *A History of British Trade Unionism*, 4th edition, Har-mondsworth: Pelican.

People Management (2005) 'How to Select an Agency', *People Management*, 20 June: 22.

People Management (2007) 'Guide to Recruitment Marketing', *People Management*, 28 June: 18.

Perkins, S. J. (2006) *International Reward and Recognition*, London: Chartered Institute of Personnel and Development.

Personnel Today (2006) 26 September: 7.

Peterson, B. (2004) *Cultural Intelligence: A Guide to Working with People from Other Cultures*, Yarmouth, MA: Intercultural Press.

Pfeffer, J. (1992) *Managing with Power: Politics and Influence in Organisations*, Boston, MA: Harvard Business School Press.

Pfeffer, J. (1994) 'Competitive Advantage through People: Unleashing the Power of the Work Force', Harvard Business School, Boston, MA.

Pfeffer, J. (1998) *The Human Equation: Building Profits by Putting People First*, Boston, MA: Harvard Business School Press.

Pickard, J. (1998) Externally Yours, *People Management*, 23 July: 34–7.

Pieper, R. (1990) *Human Resource Management: An International Comparison*, Berlin: De Gruyter.

Piore, M. J. and Sabel, C. F. (1984) *The Second Industrial Divide: Possibilities for Prosperity*, New York: Basic Books.

Polet, R. and Nomden, K. (1997) 'Improving the Management of European Regional Development Policy', *European Planning Studies*, 5(6): 777–93.

Poole, M., Landsbury, R. and Wailes, N. (2001) 'A Comparative Analysis of Developments in Industrial Democracy', *Industrial Relations*, 40(3): 490–525.

Porter, L. W., Bigley, G. A. and Steers, R. M. (eds) (2003) *Motivation and Work Behavior*, New York: McGraw-Hill.

Porter, M. (1985) *Competitive Advantage: Creating and Sustaining Superior Performance*, New York: Free Press.

Porter, M. E. (1986) 'Changing Patterns of International Competition', *California Management Review*, 28(2): 29–40.

Porter, M. E. (1990) *The Competitive Advantage of Nations*, London: Macmillan.

Prahalad, C. K. and Doz, Y. (1987) *The Multinational Mission: Balancing Local Demands and Global Vision*, New York: The Free Press.

Provis, C. (1996) 'Unitarism, Pluralism, Interests and Values', *British Journal of Industrial Relations*, 34(4): December: 473–95.

Purcell, J. (1987) 'Mapping Management Styles in Employee Relations', *Journal of Management Studies*, 24(5): 533–48.

Purcell, J. (1999) 'Best Practice and Best Fit: Chimera or Cul-de-sac?', *Human Resource Management Journal*, 9(3): 26–41.

Purcell, J. and Ahlstrand, B. (1993) *Strategy and Style in Employee Relations*, Oxford: Oxford University Press.

Purcell, J. and Sisson, K. (1983) 'Strategies and Practice in the Management of Industrial Relations', in G. Bain (ed.) *Industrial Relations in Britain*, Oxford: Basil Blackwell.

Purcell, J., Kinnie, N., Swart, J., Rayton, B. and Hutchinson, S. (2008) *People Management and Performance*, London: Routledge.

Quinn, J. B. (1999) 'Strategic Outsourcing: Leveraging Knowledge Capabilities', *Sloan Management Review*, 40 (Summer): 39–42.

Ramlall, S. (2004) 'A Review of Employee Motivation Theories and Their Implications for Employee Retention within Organizations', *Journal of American Academy of Business*, Oxford no. 5 1/2: 52–63.

Rankin, N. (2008) 'Labour Turnover Rates and Costs in the UK in 2007', *IRS Employment Review*, Oxford, 894, 4 April: 6 pp.

Rapport, N. and Overing, J. (2000) *Social and Cultural Anthropology: The Key Concepts*, London: Routledge.

Reardon, R. C., Peterson, G. W., Sampson, J. P. and Lenz, J. G. (2005) *Career Development and Planning: A Comprehensive Approach*, London: Thomson Custom.

Reda, J. F., Reifler, S. and Thatcher, L. G. (2008) *Compensation Committee Handbook*, 3rd edition, New York: John Wiley and Son.

Redman, T. and Wilkinson, A. (2006) *Contemporary Human Resource Management*, London: Financial Times/Prentice Hall.

Renwick, D. and Gennard, D. (2001) 'Grievance and Discipline', in T. Redman and A. Wilkinson (eds) *Contemporary Human Resource Management*, London: Financial Times/Prentice Hall.

Renzl, B., Matzler, K. and Hinterhuber, H. (eds) (2006) *The Future of Knowledge Management*, New York: Palgrave Macmillan.

Revans, R. (1980) *Action Learning: New Techniques for Action Learning*, London: Blond and Briggs.

Reynolds, C. (1999) *2000 Guide to Global Compensation and Benefits*, San Diego, CA: Harcourt Professional Publishing.

Reynolds, C. (2006a) *Compensating Globally Mobile Employees*, Scottsdale, AZ: WorldatWork.

Reynolds, C. (2006b) *Compensating North American Expatriates*, Scottsdale, AZ: WorldatWork.

Roberts, G. (2005) *Recruitment and Selection*, Maidenhead: Chartered Institute of Personnel and Development.

Roehling, M. V. (1997) 'The Origins and Early Development of the Psychological Contract Construct', *Journal of Management History*, 3: 204–17.

Rollinson, D. (2002) 'Grievance', in T. Redman and A. Wilkinson (eds) *The Informed Student Guide to Human Resource Management*, London: Thomson Learning.

Rollinson, D. and Dundon, T. (2007) *Understanding Employment Relations*, London: McGraw Hill.

Rosenbloom, J. S. (ed.) (2005) *The Handbook of Employee Benefits: Design, Funding and Administration*, 6th edition, New York: McGraw Hill.

Rosenzweig, P. and Nohria, N. (1994) 'Influences of Human Resource Management Practices in Multinational Firms', *Journal of Business Studies*, 20(2): 229–52.

Rousseau, D. (1989) 'Psychological and Implicit Contracts in Organizations', *Employee Responsibilities and Rights Journal*, 2: 121–39.

Rousseau, D. (1995) *Psychological Contracts in Organisations: Understanding the Written and Unwritten Agreements*, London: Sage.

Rousseau, D. (2010) 'The Individual–Organizational Relationship: The Psychological Contract', in S. Zedeckm (ed.) *The American Psychological Association Handbook of Industrial and Organizational Psychology*, USA: American Psychological Association (APA), USA.

Rousseau, D. and Tijoriwala, S. (1998) 'Assessing Psychological Contracts: Issues, Alternatives and Measures', *Journal of Organisational Behaviour*, 19: 679–96.

Rowley, C. (2001a) 'Alan Fox', in M. Witzel (ed.) *Biographical Dictionary of Management*, Bristol: Thoemmes Press: 325–7.

Rowley, C. (2001b) 'Hugh Clegg', in M. Witzel (ed.) *Biographical Dictionary of Management*, Bristol: Thoemmes Press: 168–70.

Rowley, C. (2002a) 'Conciliation', in T. Redman and A. Wilkinson (eds) *The Informed Student Guide to HRM*, London: Thomson Learning: 39.

Rowley, C. (2002b) 'Mediation', in T. Redman and A. Wilkinson (eds) *The Informed Student Guide to HRM*, London: Thomson Learning: 157.

Rowley, C. (2002c) 'Allan Flanders', in M. Warner (ed.) *The International Encyclopedia of Business and Management*, London: Thomson Learning: 2036–41.

Rowley, C. (2003) *The Management of People: HRM in Context*, London: Spiro Press.

Rowley, C. and Benson, J. (2002) 'Convergence and Divergence in Asian HRM', *California Management Review*, 42(2): 90–109.

Rowley, C. and Cooke, F. (eds) (2010) *The Changing Face of Management in China*, London: Routledge.

Rowley, C. and Harry, W. (2010) *Managing People Globally: An Asian Perspective*, Oxford: Chandos.

Rowley, C. and Poon, H. F. (2008) 'HRM Best Practices and Transfers to the Asia Pacific Region', in C. Wankel (ed.) *21st Century Management: A Reference Handbook*, Thousand Oaks, CA: Sage Publications: 209–20.

Rowley, C. and Warner, M. (2004) 'HR Development in the Asia Pacific Region', *Journal of World Business*, 39(4): 308–10.

Rowley, C. and Warner, M. (2007a) 'Globalizing International HRM', *International Journal of Human Resource Management*, 18(5): 703–16.

Rowley, C and Warner, M. (eds) (2007b) *Management in South-East Asia: Business Culture, Enterprises and Human Resources*, London: Routledge.

Rowley, C. and Warner, M. (eds) (2008) *Globalising International Human Resource Management*, London: Routledge.

Rowley, C. and Yang, H. (2008) 'Performance Management in South Korea', in A. Varma, P. Budhwar and A. DeNisi (eds) *Performance Management Systems around the Globe*, London: Routledge: 316–40.

Rowley, C., Benson, J. and Warner, M. (2004) 'Towards an Asian Model of Human Resource Management? A Comparative Analysis of China, Japan and South Korea', *International Journal of Human Resource Management*, 15(4): 917–33.

Rowley, C. (with Yukongdi, V. and Wei, Q.) (2010) 'Managing Diversity: Women Managers in Asia', in M. Ozbilgin and J. Syed (eds) *Managing Gender Diversity in Asia*, London and New York: Edward Elgar: 345–93.

Roy, D. (1980) 'Repression and Incorporation: Fear Stuff, Sweet Stuff, and Evil Stuff: Management's Defences against Unionisation in the South', in T. Nichols (ed.) *Capital and Labour: A Marxist Primer*, Glasgow: Fontana.

Rubery, J., Earnshaw, J. and Marchington, M. (2004) 'Blurring the Boundaries to the Employment Relationship: From Single to Multi-Employer Relationships', in M. Marchington, D. Grimshaw, J. Rubery and H. Willmott (eds) *Fragmenting Work: Blurring Organisational Boundaries and Disordering Hierarchies*, Oxford: Oxford University Press.

Ryan, S., Wailes, N. and Bamber, G. (2004) 'Globalisation, Employment and Labour: Comparative Statistics', in G. Bamber, R. Lansbury and N. Wailes (eds) *International and Comparative Employment Relations: Globalisation and the Developed Market Economies*, 4th edition, London: Sage.

Rynes, S. L. and Milkovich, G. T. (1986) 'Wage Surveys: Dispelling Some Myths about the Market Wage' *Personnel Psychology*, 39(1): 71–90.

Sako, M. (1998) 'The Nature and Impact of Employee "Voice" in the European Car Components Industry', *Human Resource Management Journal*, 9(1): 5–13.

Salamon, M. (2000) *Industrial Relations: Theory and Practice*, Harlow: Pearson Education.

Saunders, M., Thornhill, A. and Lewis, P. (2007) *Research Methods for Business Students*, London: Financial Times/Prentice-Hall.

Schein, E. H. (1978) *Career Dynamics: Matching Individual and Organisational Needs*, Reading, MA: Addison-Wesley.

Schein, E. H. (1996) 'Career Anchors Revisited: Implications for Career Development in the 21st Century', *Academy of Management Executive*, 10(4): 80–8.

Schuler, P., Sowling, P. and de Cieri, H. (1993) 'An Integrative Framework of Strategic International Human Resource Management', *Journal of Management*, 19(2): 419–59.

Schultz, T. W. (1961) 'Investment in Human Capital', *American Economic Review*, 51 (March): 1–17.

Scullion, H. (1995) 'International Human Resource Management', in J. Storey (ed.) *Human Resource Management: A Critical Text*, London: Routledge.

Scullion, H. (2010) 'International Human Resource Management', in J. Storey (ed.) *Human Resource Management: A Critical Text*, 2nd edition, London: International Thompson Business Press.

Scullion, H. and Collings, D. S. (eds) (2006) *Global Staffing*, London: Routledge.

Scullion, H. and Collings, D. S. (2006) 'International Talent Management', in H. Scullion and D. S. Collings (eds) *Global Staffing*, London: Routledge: 87–116.

Seltz, S. P. and Heneman, R. L. (2004) *Linking Pay to Performance*, Scottsdale, AZ: WorldatWork.

Senge, P. (2006) *Fifth Discipline: The Art and Practice of the Learning Organization*, London: Doubleday.

Sera, K. (1992) 'Corporate Globalisation: A New Trend', *Academy of Management Executive*, 6(1): 89–96.

Sheridan, J. (1992) 'Organizational Culture and Employee Retention' *Academy of Management Journal*, 35(5): 1036–56.

Sims, R. S. (2006) *Human Resource Development: Today and Tomorrow*, Greenwich, CT: Information Age Publishing.

Sisson, K. and Storey, J. (2000) *The Realities of Human Resource Management*, Buckingham: Open University Press.

Sisson, K. and Marginson, P. (2003) 'Management: Systems, Structure and Strategy', in P. Edwards (ed.) *Industrial Relations: Theory and Practice in Britain*, 2nd edition, Oxford Blackwell.

Siu, O. (2001) 'A Study of Safety Climate, Work Stress and Safety Performance among Construction Workers in Hong Kong: A Facet Approach', *Proceeding of Facet Theory: Integrating Theory Construction with Data Analysis*, 15–18 July, Prague, Czech Republic.

Skinner, B. F. (1953) *Science and Human Behavior*, New York: Macmillan.

Smith, C. and Meiskins, P. (1995) 'System, Society and Dominance Effects in Cross-national Organisational Analysis', *Work, Employment and Society*, 2: 241–67.

Sparrow, P., Brewster, C. and Harris, H. (2004) *Globalizing Human Resource Management*, London: Routledge.

Spencer, L., McCelland, D. and Spencer, S. (1994) *Competency Assessment Methods*, Boston, MA: Hay/McBer.

Spreitzer, G. M., McCall Jr., M. W. and Mahoney, J. D. (1997) 'Early Identification of International Executive Potential', *Journal of Applied Psychology*, 82(1): 6–29.

Stogdill, P. M. (1948) 'Personal Factors Associated with Leadership', *Journal of Psychology*, 25(1): 35–71.

Storey, J. (1989) 'From Personnel Management to Human Resource Management', in J. Storey (ed.) *New Perspectives on Human Resource Management*, London: Routledge.

Storey, J. (ed.) (1989) *New Perspectives on Human Resource Management* London: Routledge.

Storey, J. and Bacon, N. (1993) 'Individualism and Collectivism: into the 1990s', *International Journal of Human Resource Management*, 4: 665–84.

Stumpf, S. A. and London, M. (1981) 'Management Promotions: Individual and Organizational Factors Influencing the Decision Process', *Academy of Management Review*, 6(4): 539–49.

Stringer, D. (1995) 'The Role of Women in Workplace Diversity Consulting', *Journal of Organisational Change Management*, 8(1): 44–51.

Swanson, R. A. and Holton III, E. F. (2001) *Foundations of Human Resource Development*, San Francisco, CA: Berrett-Koehler.

Takeuchi, N., Wakabayashi, M. and Chen, Z. (2003) 'The Strategic HRM Configuration for Competitive Advantage: Evidence from Japanese Firms in China and Taiwan', *Asia Pacific Journal of Management*, 20(4): 447–80.

Tan, J. S., Earley, P. C. and Ang, S. (2006) *CQ: Developing Cultural Intelligence at Work*, Stanford, CA: Stanford University Press.

Taylor, E. (1994) 'A Learning Model for Becoming Interculturally Competent', *International Journal of Intercultural Relations*, 18(3): 389–408.

Taylor, S. (1998) *Employee Resourcing*, London: Chartered Institute of Personnel and Development.

Taylor, S. (2002) *People Resourcing*, London: Chartered Institute of Personnel and Development.

Taylor, S. (2002a) *The Employee Retention Handbook: Developing Practice*, London: Chartered Institute of Personnel and Development.

Taylor, S. (2006) 'Are You Keeping Your Employees Happy?', *The HR Director*, 28 (September): 8–13.

Taylor, S. (2008) *People Resourcing*, London: Chartered Institute of Personnel and Development.

Tekleab, A. and Taylor, S. (2003) 'Aren't There Two Parties in the Employment Relationship? Antecedents and Consequences of Organization-Employee Agreement on Contract Obligations and Violations', *Journal of Organizational Behavior*, 24: 585–608.

Terry, M. (1977) 'The Inevitable Growth of Informality', *British Journal of Industrial Relations*, 15(1): 75–90.

Thomas, H. C. (2003) 'How to Design Induction Programmes', *People Management*, 9(9) May: 42–3.

Thomas, R. R. (1990) 'From Affirmative Action to Affirming Diversity', *Harvard Business Review*, March–April.

Thorndike, E. L. (1920) 'Intelligence and Its Uses', *Harper's Magazine*, 140(1): 227–35.

Thornhill, A., Lewis, P., Millmore, M. and Saunders, M. (2000) *Managing Change: A Human Resource Strategy Approach*, London: Financial Times/ Prentice Hall.

Tjosvold, D. and Leung, K. (2003) *Cross-cultural Management: Foundations and Future*, Hampshire, UK: Ashgate Publishing.

Toplis, J., Dulewicz, V. and Fletcher, C. (2004) *Psychological Testing*, Maidenhead: Chartered Institute of Personnel and Development.

Torbiorn, I. (1982) 'Living Abroad: Personal Adjustment and Personnel Policy in the Overseas Setting', New York: Wiley.

Torrington, D., Hall, L. and Taylor, S. (2009) *Fundamentals of Human Resource Management*, Harlow: Pearson.

Torrington, D., Taylor, S. and Hall, L. (2008) *Human Resource Management*, London: Prentice Hall.

Toynbee, P. (2001) 'Who's Afraid of Global Culture', in W. Hutton and A. Giddens (eds) *On The Edge: Living the Global Capitalism*, London: Jonathan Cape: 191–212.

Traxler, F. (2003) 'Bargaining (De)centralisation, Macroeconomic Performance and Control over the Employment Relationship', *British Journal of Industrial Relations*, 41(1): 1–28.

Traxler, F., Blanske, S. and B. Kittel (2001) *National Labour Relations in Industrialized Countries: A Comparative Study of Institutions, Change and Performance*, Oxford: Oxford University Press.

Treiman, D. J. (1979) *Job Evaluation: An Analytic Review*, Washington: National Academy of Sciences.

Tuckman, B. (1965) 'Development Sequence in Small Groups', *Psychological Bulletin*, 63(4): 384–99.

Tuckman, B. W. and Jensen, M. C. (1977) 'Stages of Small-group Development Revisited', *Group and Organization Studies*, 2(4): 419–70.

Tung, R. (1981) 'Selection and Training of Personnel for Overseas Assignments', *Columbia Journal of World Business*, 23: 129–43.

Tung, R. (1995) 'Managing Cross-national and Intro-national Diversity', *Human Resource Management*, 32(4): 461–77.

Tung, R. L. (1984) 'Strategic Management of Human Resources in the Multinational Enterprise', *Human Resource Management*, 23(2): 129–43.

Turner, N., Chmiel, N. and Walls, M. (2005) 'Railing for Safety: Job Demands, Job Control, and Safety Citizenship Role Definition', *Journal of Occupational Health Psychology*, 10: 504–12.

Turner, P. (2002) 'How to Do HR Forecasting and Planning', *People Management*, 8(6) March: 48–9.

Tyson, S. and Fell, A. (1986) *Evaluating the Personnel Function*, London: Hutchinson.

Ulrich, D. (1996) *Human Resource Champions*, Boston, MA: Harvard Business School Press.

Ulrich, D. (1998) 'A New Mandate for Human Resources', *Harvard Business Review*, January–February: 124–34.

van Dam, N. (2003) 'Educating a Global Workforce', *Chief Learning Officer*, 2(6): 17.

van der Heijden, K. (1996) *Scenarios: The Art of Strategic Conversation*, Chichester: John Wiley.

van der Heijden, K., Bradfield, R., Burt. G. and Cairns, G. (2002) *The Sixth Sense*, Chichester: John Wiley.

van der Spek, R. and Spijkervet, A. (1997) 'A Knowledge Management: Dealing Intelligently with Knowledge', *Knowledge Management and its Integrative Elements*, Boca Raton, FL: CRC Press.

Varma, A., Budhwar, P. and DeNisi, A. (eds) (2008) *Performance Management Systems*, London: Routledge.

Vroom, V. H. (1964) *Work and Motivation*, New York: Wiley.

Wakabayashi, M. and Graen, G. (1989) 'Human Resource Development of Japanese Managers: Leadership and Career Investment', *Research in Personnel and Human Resource Management*, supplement 1, Greenwich, CT: JAI Press: 235–56.

Walker, A. J. (ed.) (2001) *Web-Based Human Resources: The Technologies and Trends That Are Transforming HR*, New York: McGraw Hill.

Walker, R. E. and Foley, J. M. (1973) 'Social Intelligence: Its History and Measurement', *Psychology Reports*, 33: 839–64.

Wallace, J. and O'Sullivan, M. (2006) 'Contemporary Strike Trends since 1980: Peering through the Wrong End of a Telescope', in *Global Industrial Relations*, M. Morley, P. Gunnigle and D. Collings (eds) London: Routledge.

Walton, R. (1985) 'From Control to Commitment in the Workplace', *Harvard Business Review*, 63, March–April: 76–84.

Wanous, J. P. (1992) *Organizational Entry: Recruitment, Selection, Orientation and Socialisation of Newcomers*, Reading, MA: Addison-Wesley.

Waters, M. (1995) *Globalisation*, London: Routledge.

Watkins, K. E. and Marsick, V. J. (1993) *Sculpting the Learning Organization*, San Francisco, CA, Jossey-Bass.

Webb, S. and Webb, B. (1897) *Industrial Democracy*, London: Longman.

Weber, M. (1947) *The Theory of Social and Economic Organization*, translated by A. M. Henderson and Talcott Parsons, London: Collier Macmillan Publishers.

Weber, M. (2001) *The Protestant Ethic and the Spirit of Capitalism*, London: Routledge.

Wedderburn, K. W. (Lord) (1986) *The Worker and the Law*, 3rd edition, Penguin, Harmondsworth.

Werner, J. M. and DeSimone, R. L. (2006) *Human Resource Development*, 4th edition, Mason, OH: Thomson/South Western.

Wheeler, H. N., Klaas, B. S. and Mahony, D. M. (2004) *Workplace Justice without Unions*, Kalamazoo, MI: Upjohn Institute.

Whiddet, S. and Hollyforde, S. (2003) *The Competencies Handbook*, London: Institute of Personnel and Development.

White, G. and Druker, J. (eds) (2000) *Reward Management: A Critical Text*, London: Routledge.

Whitley, R. (1992) 'The Comparative Analysis of Business Systems', in R. Whitley (ed.) *European Business Systems: Firms and Markets in Their National Contexts*, Oxford: Oxford University Press.

Whitley, R. (1999) *Divergent Capitalism: The Social Structuring and Change of Business System*, Oxford: Oxford University Press.

Williams, K. Y. and O'Reilly, C. A. (1998) 'Demography and Diversity in Organisations: A Review of 40 Years of Research', in B. M. Staw and L. L. Cummings (eds) *Research in Organisational Behaviour*, Greenwich, CT: JAI Press: 77–140.

Wilkinson, A. (1998) 'Empowerment: Theory and Practice', *Personnel Review*, 27(1): 40–56.

Wilkinson, A. (2002) 'Empowerment', in M. Poole and M. Warner (eds) *International Encyclopaedia of Business and Management Handbook of Human Resource Management*, London: ITB Press: 501–17.

Wilkinson, A. and Dundon, T. (2010) 'Direct Participation', in A. Wilkinson, P. Gollan, M. Marchington and D. Lewin (eds) *Oxford Handbook of Organisational Participation*, Oxford: Oxford University Press.

Wilkinson, A., Dundon, T., Marchington, M. and Ackers, P. (2004) 'Changing Patterns of Employee Voice: Case Studies from the UK and Republic of Ireland', *The Journal of Industrial Relations*, 46(3): 297–321.

Winterscheid, B. C. (1980) 'A Career Development System Coordinates Training Efforts', *Personnel Administrator*, August: 28–32.

Wise, L. R. and Tschirhart, M. (2000) 'Examining Empirical Evidence on Diversity Effects: How Useful Is Diversity Research for Public Sector Managers?' *Public Administration Review*, 60(5): 386–94.

Wolff, C. (2007) 'Arriva; Dramatic Results on Diversity', *Equal Opportunities Review*, 160: 5–11.

Wood, S. (1995) The Four Pillars of HRM: Are They Connected? *Human Resource Management Journal*, 5(5): 49–59.

Wood, S. (1999a) 'Getting the Measure of the Transformed High-Performance Organisation', *British Journal of Industrial Relations*, 37: 391–418.

Wood, S. (1999b) 'Human Resource Management and Performance', *International Journal of Management Review*, 1(4): 367–413.

Wood, S. and Albanses, M. (1995) 'Can We Speak of a High Commitment Management on the Shop Floor?', *Journal of Management Studies*, 32(2): 215–47.

Wood, S. and de Menezes, L. (1998) 'High Commitment Management in the UK: Evidence from the Workplace Industrial Relations Survey and Employers' Manpower and Skills Survey', *Human Relations*, 51(4): 485–515.

Wood, S. and Wall, T. D. (2007) 'Work Enrichment and Employee Voice in Human Resource Management-performance Studies', *International Journal of Human Resource Management*, 18(7): 1335–72.

Woodall, J., Gourlay, S. and Short, D. (2000) 'Trends in Outsourcing HRD in the UK: The Implications for Strategic HRD', working paper.

Woolf, H. (ed.) (1990) *Webster's New World Dictionary of the American Language*, New York: John Wiley and Son.

WorldatWork (2006) *Survey Handbook and Directory: A Guide to Finding and Using Salary Surveys*, Scottsdale, AZ.

WorldatWork (2007) *Job Evaluation: Methods to the Process*, Scottsdale, AZ.

Wrench, J. (2002) 'A Critical Analysis of Critiques of Diversity Management', paper presented at the 7th International Metropolis conference 'Togetherness in Difference': Citizenship and Belonging, Oslo, 9–13 September 2002.

Wright, P., Dunford, B. and Snell, S. (2001) 'Human Resources and the Resource-Based View of the Firm', *Journal of Management*, 27: 701–21.

Yip, G. S. (1995) *Total Global Strategy*, Englewood Cliffs, NJ: Prentice Hall.

Yoo, Y., Rowley, C. and Lee, J. N. (2008) *Trends in Mobile Technology and Business in the Asia-Pacific Region*, Oxford: Chandos Publishing.

Youndt, M., Snell, S., Dean, J. and Lepak, D. (1996) 'Human Resource Management, Manufacturing Strategy and Firm Performance', *Academy of Management Journal*, 39(4): 836–66.

Young, S. and Hamill, J. (1992) *Europe and the Multinationals*, London: Edward Elgar.

Zakaria, N. (2000) 'The Effects of Cross-cultural Training on the Acculturation Process of the Global Workforce', *International Journal of Manpower*, 21(6): 492–511.

Zhu, Y., Rowley, C. and Warner, M. (2007) 'HRM with Asian Characteristics', *International Journal of Human Resource Management*, 18(5): 745–68.

Zhu, Y., Rowley, C. and Warner, M. (2009) 'HRM in Asia', in H. Bidgoli (ed.) *The Handbook of Technology Management*, Hoboken, NJ: Wiley.

Zingheim, P. K. and Schuster, J. R. (2000) *Pay People Right! Breakthrough Reward Strategies to Create Great Companies*, San Francisco, CA: Jossey-Bass.

Zohar, D. (1980) 'Safety Climate in Industrial Organizations: Theoretical and Applied Implications', *Journal of Applied Psychology*, 65: 96–102.

RESOURCES

Journals

Readers should refer to the many journals specialising in discussions of HRM. Good business schools and libraries stock many or most of these. Many others are available and, of course, in languages other than English. Several other journals are listed in the *Suggested further reading* sections following each concept entry and in the Bibliography. From the perspective given by the place of publication for this book, our selective list of journals includes the following.

Asia Pacific Journal of Human Resources
Career Development International
British Journal of Industrial Relations
Education and Training
European Journal of Industrial Relations
European Journal of Work and Organizational Psychology
Employee Relations
Gender, Work and Organization
Human Resource Development International
Human Resources and Decision Sciences
Human Resource Development International
Human Resource Management
Human Resource Management Journal
Human Resource Management Review
International Journal of Human Resource Management
International Journal of Employment Studies
International Labor Review
International Journal of Manpower
International Journal of Selection and Assessment
International Journal of Training and Development
Industrial Relations

Industrial Relations Journal
Industrial Relations Review
International Journal of Manpower
International Journal of Selection and Assessment
International Journal of Training and Development
Journal of European Industrial Training
Journal of Industrial Relations
Journal of Labour Research
Journal of Management Development
Journal of Vocational Education and Training
Journal of Workplace Learning
New Technology, Work and Employment
Personnel Review
Sociologie de Travail
Training and Development Journal
Work, Employment and Society
Work and Occupations
Work and Stress

Readers might also check for HRM special issues offered by a range
of other journals as well and HRM-related articles in normal issues,
such as:

Asia Pacific Business Review
Asia Pacific Journal of Business Administration
Academy of Management Journal
Academy of Management Review
California Management Review
Capital and Class
Culture and Organization
Harvard Business Review
Human Relations
International Business Review
International Journal of Business Studies
International Journal of Management
International Journal of Public Administration
International Journal of Management Reviews
International Studies of Management and Organization
Journal of Business
Journal of Business Research
Journal of Change Management
Journal of General Management

Journal of International Business Studies
Journal of International Management
Journal of Management
Journal of Management Studies
Journal of World Business
Management International Review
Management Revue
Organization Studies
Public Management Review
Thunderbird International Business Review

There are also the range of publications and reports from organisations such as, in the UK, Industrial Relations Services (http://www.irsresearch.co.uk/) and, especially on rewards, Income Data Services (http://www.incomesdata.co.uk/).

Websites

As is the nature of the internet, weblinks and websites come and go. A number of the journals listed above offer electronic versions of their articles. A growing number of HRM communities now communicate exclusively online. It is impossible to be definitive in our recommendations. As a compromise, we list here – alphabetically and without comment – a narrow selection of websites recommended to us by the contributors to this book.

www.acas.org.uk – UK based (and partly government-funded) Advisory, Conciliation and Arbitration Service (ACAS).
www.berr.gov.uk – UK government's Department for Business, Innovation and Skills, also developing a remit for higher and professional/vocation education and training.
www.bps.org.uk – The British Psychological Society, offering research insights into the psychology of work and employment.
www.cipd.co.uk – UK-based Chartered Institute of Personnel and Development (CIPD), also a validating agency for HRM professionals.
www.ehrc.gov.uk – The Equality and Human Rights Commission (UK).
www.hrmguide.net – Global network of linked HRM resources connecting HRM researchers and practitioners across English-language-speaking regions such as Australia, Canada, the UK, the USA, New Zealand.

www.hrmthejournal.com – Association of discussion fora and publication networks for researchers and practitioners in HRM/international HRM.

http://www.hse.gov.uk/legislation/hswa.htm – The UK's Health and Safety Executive, giving information about the UK Health and Safety at Work Act (1974).

www.ilo.org – Geneva-based International Labour Organization (ILO), a tripartite agency of the United Nations.

http://osha.europa.eu/en/ – The European Association of Occupational Health and Safety.

www.peoplemanagement.co.uk – In-house journal of the CIPD: *People Management*.

www.shrm.org – US-based Society for Human Resource Management (SHRM), also a certificating agency for HRM professionals.

www.tuc.org.uk – London-based Trades Union Congress (TUC), umbrella organisation for UK-registered trade unions.

www.worldatwork.org – US-based community specialising in research into compensation and rewards at work.

www.wfpma.com – Globally connected World Federation of Personnel Management Associations (WFPMA), offering networked access to associations such as:

> Asia Pacific Federation of Human Resource Management (APFHRM)
>
> European Association for Personnel Management (EAPM)
>
> Interamerican Foundation of Personnel Administration (FIDAP)
>
> American Society for Personnel Administration (now SHRM – link listed above)
>
> North American Human Resource Management Association (NAHRMA)
>
> Canadian Council of HR Associations (CCHRA)
>
> AMEDIRH and COMARI of Mexico
>
> Institute of People Management (IPM) of South Africa
>
> African Federation of Human Resources Management Associations (AFHRMA)

Readers are invited to expand on this list by conducting searches using, as key words for example, the key concept entries listed and discussed in this book. Readers are also invited to send us feedback and suggest updates for the concepts discussed in this book.

INDEX